Advance Praise

'Visualization' and 'intelligence' are what set this book apart. *The Power of Data Storytelling* will make you think differently about the way you present arguments and the usage of data in those discussions.

Siddhartha Rastogi, *Managing Director, Ambit Capital*

'If history were taught in the form of stories, it would never be forgotten'. Kipling's quote holds equally true for data. Stories leave a powerful impact, which is not possible with data alone. Very often, teams struggle to connect the dots in understanding valuable insights behind data and have a hard time in making critical data-based decisions. This can be solved if loose-hanging valuable data gets a shape. This book tells us exactly how we can make data more meaningful with the power of data storytelling. A must-read for all corporate professionals.

Bhawna Agarwal, *CEO, Serial Entrepreneur; Advisor to VCs*

Sejal has impressively encapsulated the 'art and science of data storytelling'. This book is a handy guide for professionals across industries and experience levels to effectively communicate their views to their audience, who often have a very short attention span.

Jitendra Gohil, *CFA, Head of Equity Research at a leading multinational bank*

The simple yet powerful concepts discussed in this book will help put your thoughts and data in a compelling and impactful manner. Through this book, you will learn a structured approach to organize thoughts, data and analysis, which will change the way one communicates with data.

Nachiket Naik, *Managing Director, IREP Credit Capital*

A great storytelling on the concept and principles of data storytelling. An absolute must in the exponential and explosive, current and future world of the data big bang!

Dr Vikas V. Gupta, *CEO and Chief Investment Strategist,*
OmniScience Capital

Data presentations are less about data and more about the meaning behind the data. Sejal introduces simple and practically applicable writing and visualization nuances that help bring out the data insight to make your reports and presentations much more impactful. A beginner or an experienced professional will find something new to take away from this book.

Siddharth Ladsariya, *Angel Investor, Director,*
Everest Flavours Ltd; Founder,
Young Volunteer's Organization

THE P WER OF DATA

Storytelling

SEJAL VORA

Los Angeles | London | New Delhi
Singapore | Washington DC | Melbourne

First published in 2019 by

SAGE Publications India Pvt Ltd
B1/I-1 Mohan Cooperative Industrial Area
Mathura Road, New Delhi 110 044, India
www.sagepub.in

SAGE Publications Inc
2455 Teller Road
Thousand Oaks, California 91320, USA

SAGE Publications Ltd
1 Oliver's Yard, 55 City Road
London EC1Y 1SP, United Kingdom

SAGE Publications Asia-Pacific Pte Ltd
18 Cross Street #10-10/11/12
China Square Central
Singapore 048423

Published by Vivek Mehra for SAGE Publications India Pvt Ltd, typeset in 11/14 pts Amasis by Fidus Design Pvt Ltd, Chandigarh.

Library of Congress Cataloging-in-Publication Data
Name: Vora, Sejal, author.
Title: The power of data storytelling / Sejal Vora, Corporate Trainer.
Description: Thousand Oaks: SAGE Publications India Pvt Ltd, [2019]
Identifiers: LCCN 2018060841 | ISBN 9789353282905 (print (pb)) | ISBN 9789353282929 (web) | ISBN 9789353282912 (E pub 2.0)
Subjects: LCSH: Business presentations—Technological innovations. | Digital storytelling. | Information visualization.
Classification: LCC HF5718.22 V67 2019 | DDC 658.4/52—dc23
LC record available at https://lccn.loc.gov/2018060841

ISBN: 978-93-532-8290-5 (PB)

SAGE Team: Neha Pal, Mahira Chadha, Ankit Verma and Kanika Mathur

For

My father—I am, because of you

My brother—miss you dearly

My mother—my pillar of strength

Thank you for choosing a SAGE product!
If you have any comment, observation or feedback,
I would like to personally hear from you.

Please write to me at **contactceo@sagepub.in**

Vivek Mehra, Managing Director and CEO, SAGE India.

Bulk Sales

SAGE India offers special discounts
for purchase of books in bulk.
We also make available special imprints
and excerpts from our books on demand.

For orders and enquiries, write to us at

Marketing Department
SAGE Publications India Pvt Ltd
B1/I-1, Mohan Cooperative Industrial Area
Mathura Road, Post Bag 7
New Delhi 110044, India

E-mail us at **marketing@sagepub.in**

Subscribe to our mailing list
Write to **marketing@sagepub.in**

This book is also available as an e-book.

Contents

Preface

Numbers have an important story to tell.
They rely on you to give them a voice.

—Stephen Few

As an investment research analyst for a decade, every day came with a new set of data, bringing a new adventure along with it. To me it seemed like the numbers were luring me into their mesmerizing world to share some secrets which no one else knew. Digging through the data mesh to uncover interesting insights was particularly exciting, rewarding and satisfying. Every number had a story to tell, and it was upon me to find these stories and share them with the world!

After a decade in the corporate world, it was my time to take a tough decision and follow my passions, the first step to which was becoming a corporate trainer. But even as a corporate trainer, the wonderland of numbers kept luring me in, and it appeared as if the universe was compelling me to go on a certain track. The multiple interactions I had across a host of industries kept leading me to one main point—telling stories to make your messages impactful.

From the variety of data and research analysts whose core jobs entail data analysis and its presentation to the multiple reports and presentations prepared for the consumption of internal management teams and even financial market product's relationship managers and advisors, all of them had one thing in common.

They were all seeking to learn more about how to make their data communications impactful. But most of these people aren't even aware of the simple changes they can apply to make their messages stick.

Data storytelling is a fairly new concept, especially in India, and every time I start talking about it, the first question I get is 'What is a data story?' Storytelling per se is not new to humans, but applying its core elements to data is a new concept, and I believe that I have been leading a march to create awareness for this.

They say that you can only teach what you know best. Building and communicating stories from data is what I know best and that is what I teach through my training programmes. The enormous and excellent response received from these programmes made me realize how important data storytelling has become for businesses and how little people know about doing this. There was a clear gap that I was trying to fill. But there was still a need for solid reference material, and I was constantly being asked if there was a book to refer to!

Taking my cue, I set out on a journey to fulfil this need and introduce the world to the simple nuances that can change the way we communicate with data.

This book is a result of a clear need identified through various interactions during my corporate training programmes across organizational levels and from varied industries. *The Power of Data Storytelling* is meant for every person who wants to do a better job at presenting their data analysis and insights as also for organization leaders who would like to inculcate a data storytelling culture within their organizations.

At its core, this book makes you think differently about your daily data analysis and presentation tasks through new concepts and tools. This approach will considerably simplify the data storytelling process and make it much more efficient. Not only will you learn how to build strong stories, but you will also learn how minor changes to your writing and visualization activities can make all the difference on how the audience perceives a message.

As you start presenting data through stories, you will see a marked difference in the reactions received from your audience. In addition to leaving a strong impact on them, data stories significantly aid in adding credibility to you and your work. When the audience start receiving interesting information in a simplified manner, they start appreciating your efforts and are easily able to distinguish your work from the rest of the pack.

A constant feedback I receive from my training programmes is 'You made us think'. With this book, I aim to make you think differently about the way you communicate with data. It will give you a new direction and thought perspective through its easily applicable tools and concepts, which can help take your data storytelling journey to the next level.

Acknowledgements

Thank you to everyone who over the years has touched my life in one way or another. A special thank you to my family and friends who are my very reason for existence; Viktor Hjort, Tim Jagger and Imtiaz Sheffudin—my bosses from Morgan Stanley and Royal Bank of Scotland—from whom I learnt my biggest 'data lessons'; my editor Neha Pal, commissioning agent Manisha Mathews and the entire team at SAGE for their constant guidance and support through the publication of this book.

Introduction: We Are All Storytellers

We are all storytellers. We all live in a network of stories. There isn't a stronger connection between people than storytelling.

—Jimmy Neil Smith, Director of the International
Storytelling Center

Curtains drawn in, windows shut; sprawled across the bed, I visualize myself amidst clear blue waters swimming with the most exquisite marine life. My lips curve into a smile thinking of the wonderful experience it could be. A ray of light finds its way from a small gap within the curtains as I hear a familiar voice: 'Hi there, its 6 AM; the weather outside is…,' a wake-up alarm from my mobile's personal assistant preparing me for the day's weather conditions!

Eyes still shut, lying on bed, the only thing that moves is my hand—frantically trying to reach for the mobile, so I can snooze the alarm and get just five more minutes of my precious sleep! Slowly as I start moving, rubbing my eyes while still looking for an excuse that lets me go right back into bed, my hand picks the mobile and I straight away go to Instagram. Slowly my sleep goes away as the app draws me into 'stories'—showing what my friends were up to while I was asleep.

After the chaotic morning routine, as I finally manage to get dressed for work and reach the breakfast table, I open the newspaper and read 'stories' about one more fraud disclosed by a bank, a bandh announced by some political party and the rape of a teenage girl. Disappointed, as I am about to put the paper aside, my eye catches an amusing 'story' of a $400 million divorce settlement for yet another celebrity couple!

Coming out from the $400 million expensive settlement, I finally step out from my house to embark on my journey to office. Travelling to and from work is the only time I get to catch up with my loved ones and I always try to make the most of it! Today I am talking to my favourite girlfriend—the one who knows everything about everyone! She says, 'I heard Shweta was at the late night movies with Aarav. What's the "story" there?' And all I can do is let out an amused laugh!

As I swipe my ID card and enter the office premises, the cool air-conditioned breeze immediately calms my nerves after the long commute. A few smiling faces and greetings across the corridor, and I'm ready for work. For the past week, I've been working on an important presentation. I'm happy with the way it has shaped up, and I walk towards my boss' cabin and hand him the draft in antici-pation. He glances through the slides without a word, and then suddenly looks up and says, 'This is all good, but what's the "story" here?'

Feeling a little off after that feedback, I am in no mood of making little conversations or racking my brain with more work. The Pinterest app comes to my rescue. As I scroll down my 'storyboard', interesting 'stories' about decorating the home library catch my eye and keep me entertained through the lunch hour.

Finally back home, done with dinner and exchanging interesting 'stories' from everyone's day, I am back on my bed, eyes glued to the television. The show I'm watching today is a 'story' about a young girl who is convicted of murder and spends half her youth behind bars while the verdict on her appeal is still awaited!

Did this seem like a page out of your life?

Did you also identify with this daily routine?

STORIES ARE PAGES FROM OUR LIFE!

Stories are all around us, even in the most routine tasks and things we often take for granted—from the first fairy tale we hear as children to the religious story that comforts us in old age, from the dreams that wake us at dawn to the fictional stories that put us to sleep at night, the conversations we have at home or the different forms of communication at work. We are always surrounded by stories—either telling them or receiving them.

When introducing ourselves at a party or talking about ourselves in an interview, we are telling a story. When the children are trying to convince us to buy a latest video game or when we pitch an idea or a product to the boss or a client, we are both telling stories. When giving a friendly advice on a certain personal issue or while giving a professional opinion to make business decisions, we are still telling stories.

Storytelling is not something that 'we do', it is who 'we are'. It is not a conscious act like eating, walking or talking; it is just how our brain is hardwired to function. Consciously or unconsciously, it transforms every thought and every form of communication into a story narrative.

STORYTELLING IS TIMELESS

Storytelling is an ancient art, believed to have been in existence since the very early dawn of mankind and has evolved over time with the evolving human race. The earliest cave paintings, sculptures decorating historical monuments and the world's famous paintings are all an artistic display of 'stories'. Religious scriptures often relied on 'stories' to pass on their teachings, while in literature the word 'book' became synonymous with the word 'story'.

The advent of technology and media from the early twentieth century caused disruptions to traditional 'storytelling' formats.

The first big impact of storytelling on millions of lives was the introduction of movies, followed by television. These 'stories' have played an important part in our lives and to a certain extent even shaped our society. Further to this, the Internet gave us the power to tell our 'stories' frequently and with fewer words, from anywhere, and to reach anyone with Internet connection across the globe.

STORIES ARE SOCIAL CONNECTORS

The first visible impact of storytelling was seen in marketing and brand building where 'stories' played an essential role in connecting people to brands. The biggest social media businesses are flourishing on the basis of storytelling, where people are able to share the stories of their lives with each other through a common online platform. Today, as businesses realize the importance of data-driven decision-making, data analysis-led communications are becoming the biggest contender for a dose of storytelling.

According to some studies, an average person spends about two hours on social media every day,[1] which many of us might be quick to judge as a waste of time! But most of this time spent surfing through 'stories' posted by others serves as a basic human need—the need to connect with our fellow beings. In fact, much before Facebook turned into a highly valued business, it is believed to have been originated out of this basic human need—the need for college students to know and connect with fellow students. Mark Zuckerberg, a student at Harvard School, created a program called Facemash that would let students select the best-looking person from the photos that were available on the website. This site was later rechristened as Facebook, and is

---

[1] Evan Asano, 'How Much Time Do People Spend on Social Media' (2017). Available at: https://www.socialmediatoday.com/marketing/how-much-time-do-people-spend-social-media-infographic (accessed on 16 August 2018).

currently the world's number one social networking platform. Just as we have the basic needs for food and shelter, we also have a basic need to belong to a group and form relationships.

STORIES ARE HOW WE THINK AND TALK

You're never going to kill storytelling, because it's built into the human plan. We come with it.

—Margaret Atwood

A story is a linked set of events that some characters go through, forming a chain from the beginning to the end. They depict a clear theme leading to a specific conclusion or providing a certain message.

Humans think and talk in terms of this event chain link all day long! We begin at a point which leads to successive events, all interlinked with one another, leading us towards an end, a conclusion, a decision or a message. The people from our lives, including ourselves, are often the characters of our stories. The human brain is hardwired to storytelling. Knowingly or unknowingly, we are always a part of stories, either in our heads or in our conversations.

Inside each of us is a natural-born storyteller, waiting to be released.

—Robin Moore

Everyone has a storyteller within them and everyone has experiences that make interesting stories. The difference between what seems interesting and what doesn't is simply the way the story is told. Some people are natural storytellers; they know where to begin, where to add a pause, how to sequence the events and where and when to end. For others, storytelling is like any other skill, which can be learnt and developed with time and practice.

WHO IS THIS BOOK FOR?

Data storytelling has a versatile application across any area where data is used to present analysis or insights. It can find place in annual reports; investment analyst reports; presentations for management, finance and treasury departments; management information system (MIS) reporting and analysis; business performance summary; operational performance summary; revenue or cost analysis; compliance or audit results; management speeches and any other business or even student presentation. Wherever there is data and the need to communicate the meaning behind the data, there is scope for a data story.

Data analysts or any other professional analysing data as a part of their job regularly present the results of their analytical exercises to an internal or external audience. They do so in the form of complete presentations, one chart or email explanation, all of them effectively selling an idea, a message or a conclusion to an audience. Applying the art of storytelling to such data communications can significantly alter the impact you leave on an audience while adding credibility for yourself and differentiating you from peers.

Decision-makers are under constant pressure to make productive business decisions in a time-bound manner. But data-heavy presentations with bad charts make this task difficult as you end up analysing the presentations yourself, spending a bulk of your valuable time deciphering these conclusions. The issue gets worsened by the fact that it is not just one presentation but multiple such presentations you come across in a day!

As decision-makers, your life would become much easier if someone were to start presenting the full picture behind the numbers, that is, tell the story of how and why the numbers moved rather than simply dumping numbers at you. Inculcating the habit of data storytelling within an organization can save a lot of time and contribute positively to business by enabling effective and timely decision-making.

HOW TO USE THIS BOOK?

This book introduces you to a host of simple, practically applied tools and concepts that will facilitate your data-storytelling journey. The first step to tell a good story is to have one. Most people struggle to tell good stories because they haven't been able to find and build one from their data. Data analysis gives insights which need to be converted into story elements. This book first emphasizes on the need to build a strong story along with planning a story narrative.

Once you have built the story, it is time to start crafting one. Begin with developing an understanding of simple elements which can uplift your story before you begin writing and visualizing. At this stage, you will learn about various attributes and when to apply them in regular writing and data-visualization exercises to convert data into impactful stories. In addition to the variety of examples discussed throughout the book, I get into a detailed case study at the end, which shows practical application of each of the tools and concepts learnt throughout the book.

For the first read, I recommend reading the chapters in a chrono-logical order since it's full of concepts which build on previously learnt concepts. Thereafter, you can jump to the topic of your choice as a quick refresher or for guidance.

The following is a summary of the learnings you will develop in each of the chapters and how it will support your data-storytelling journey:

1. **Stories Bring Data to Life:** This book begins with answering a pertinent question: What role can a story play in the data world? This chapter discusses how the

abundance of data and the scientific impact of storytelling on human minds make stories an integral part of all data communications.

2. **The Essence of Data Storytelling:** If the story is fiction and the data is real, how can we merge these two? This chapter breaks some of the myths with respect to data storytelling by showing what a data story is made of. Developing this understanding is key to unlocking the value of the forthcoming chapters.

3. **Getting to the Core:** Data analytics by themselves do not give a story. The story wheel framework introduced in this chapter gives you a structured approach that helps find and build a good story from within your data. Once we have the story in our grasps, communicating the same becomes much simpler.

4. **Planning Is Everything:** If you have ever thought that 'I know what I need to convey, but it may not leave the impact I intended it to', then this chapter is your guide. The story arc and story map discussed in this chapter help you plan a strong narrative which ensures that the message always comes across as you intended it to. This stage is essential for detailed reports and presentations, however, it becomes optional for smaller data stories.

5. **The Quick Fix:** If planning is not your thing, or if you believe that the underlying data does not justify detailed planning requirements, then you can skip the earlier two chapters and use the story triangle from this chapter to meet basic planning needs. Jumping straight to crafting a story without any planning is not recommended under any situation, hence the quick fix.

6. **Making Good Stories Great:** It is always a little extra that makes all the difference. Incorporating a few simple audience-engaging and enabling elements into data storytelling can transform a good story into a great one.

Developing an understanding of these before the crafting stage ensures that you get it right the first time!

7. **Writer to Storyteller:** Writing about data and insights does not make it a story. A story structure needs to be weaved into the write-up. You will learn to leverage on the planning phase and transform from being a writer to a storyteller. The chapter also discusses writing essentials along with tips that make the story better.

8. **Use Visuals to Your Advantage:** Visuals are a very powerful tool to convey any message. It's time to move on from using visuals as a data-representation tool to using them as a storytelling tool. First step—right chart selection, a story then needs to be weaved into the chart, which when combined with visual aesthetics makes an impactful visual story.

9. **The Final Act:** In this chapter, I take you backstage to show how a data story is created step by step. The two case studies discussed in this chapter will help you understand how it all comes together. Thereafter, one needs to rely on ample practice to develop the data-storytelling skill.

By the end of this book, you will be equipped with tools and concepts which can be put to immediate use to transform your data into stories. Further, you will gain a completely new thought perspective to guide all your data communications. But like any other skill, data storytelling also needs time and practice to develop; hence, it is recommended to give yourself enough time and opportunities to practise the learnings from this book.

Stories Bring Data to Life

Stories have the ability to convert dry facts and figures into objects of desire, unleashing the true power of data.

Seventeen ingredients from everyday life get spruced up when mixed in a paper bowl to form a snack available in every Mumbai street. Tasteless white puffed rice forms the base of this dish, which gets converted into a colourful mélange of flavours. The first to go in are three diced veggies available in every home, flavoured with three types of chutneys that appeal to all taste buds, enhanced by a hearty sprinkle of four different spices. Three appetizing condiments topped with three crunchy colourful garnishes make this dish come to life in less than two minutes. Each morsel of this *bhel* tingles a spicy–tangy–sweet sensation, transporting us to the gastronomic equivalent of heaven.

* * * *

Most traditional Indian cultures frown upon alcohol consumption, four Indian states have a complete alcohol ban, number of dry days can go up to 30 in some states, and yet every week of 2017 witnessed the launch of a new beer brand on an average, with as many as 52 brands or variants introduced during the year.

Changing demographics and increasing affluence are shifting the tide in favour of alcohol consumption, driving up the beer market size to 460 billion, making it even bigger than the liquid milk and tea markets in India.[2]

Stories add an X factor to any dry piece of information, transforming them into objects of desire—topics that we want to know about can excite us and often leave a strong impression on us. Even ordinary, daily consumption items get converted into fascinating substances when weaved into the story thread. A quick hunger remedy provided by bhel or bonding over beer might be a regular part of our lives, which never got a second thought until now. My beer and bhel stories are likely to have created enough amusement to remind you of the 17 ingredients of bhel and the 52 new beer brands every time you order these, at least in the near future.

IT'S RAINING DATA!

Businesses today produce tons of data, and every competitor generates identical sets of data. Data storytelling enables us to use this data effectively by giving us the ability to interpret data and convey its meaning in an efficient, productive, actionable and timely manner, thereby also making one's data stand out from the rest.

In 2017, IBM, one of the world's leading manufacturers of computer hardware, middleware and software, reported that we create 2.5 quintillion bytes of data every day and that 90 per cent

---

[2] Sagar Malviya, 'Nearly 52 New Beer Brands and Their Variants Were Introduced Last Year: The Beer Cafe Data' (2018). Available at: https://economictimes.indiatimes.com/industry/cons-products/liquor/nearly-52-new-beer-brands-and-their-variants-were-introduced-last-year-the-beer-cafe-data/articleshow/62372415.cms (accessed on 25 January 2018).

of data in the world has been created in the last two years.[3] The last decade saw the rise of 'Big Data', the buzzword which became a part of all data analytics conversations. And while Big Data is not expected to lose its sheen, I do see a clear shift in trend from 'collecting and storing Big Data' to 'using Big Data'. Today, as corporates sit on huge data resources, generating management information system (MIS) reports which did not exist a few years back, the need to 'use' this data is only becoming bigger!

DATA STORYTELLING IS A SOUGHT-AFTER JOB SKILL

Data storytelling is not just the need of the hour but is also considered as a sought-after skill in the present scenario. Google's Chief Economist Dr Hal R. Varian had stated, 'The ability to take data—to be able to understand it, to process it, to extract value from it, to visualize it, to communicate it—that's going to be a hugely important skill in the next decades'.[4]

As per LinkedIn, data analysis is the second most in-demand job skill for 2018, having entered and maintained the top two positions since 2014 (top most in demand skill being Cloud and Distributed Computing).[5] With the increasing demand for data storytelling, it is not surprising that for the first time ever, data presentation entered LinkedIn's top skills list in 2017,

---

[3] Ralph Jacobson, '2.5 Quintillion Bytes of Data Created Every Day. How Does CPG & Retail Manage It?' (2013). Available at: https://www.ibm.com/blogs/insights-on-business/consumer-products/2-5-quintillion-bytes-of-data-created-every-day-how-does-cpg-retail-manage-it/ (accessed on 16 August 2018).

[4] McKinsey & Company, 'Hal Varian on How the Web Challenges Managers' (2009). Available at: https://www.mckinsey.com/industries/high-tech/our-insights/hal-varian-on-how-the-web-challenges-managers (accessed on 16 August 2018).

[5] Rachel Bowley, 'LinkedIn Data Reveals the Most Promising Jobs and In-Demand Skills of 2018' (2018). Available at: https://blog.linkedin.com/2018/january/11/linkedin-data-reveals-the-most-promising-jobs-and-in-demand-skills-2018 (accessed on 11 January 2018).

at the number eight position, and successively moved to number seven in 2018. In fact, as per a business newspaper, *The Economic Times*, the top skill required to retain your job in 2018 is to 'tell a data story'.[6]

THE SIGNIFICANCE OF DATA-DRIVEN DECISION-MAKING

The Financial Services Authority (FSA) report on the failure of the Royal Bank of Scotland (RBS) concluded that 'multiple poor decisions' were at the heart of its problems. Inadequate due diligence for the ABN AMRO acquisition was among the six major reasons why RBS needed a bailout. The lack of visibility on the significant risks involved in the transaction made it a gamble.

* * * *

For over 100 years, Kodak was synonymous with photographs, but one bad decision to stay away from the digital trend and its failure to foresee a shift in market trend due to this technological innovation led to its ultimate demise. By the time Kodak entered into the digital market, other competitors had already captured significant market share.

Businesses, big or small, across all industries, make a multitude of decisions on a daily basis that affect the bottom line and shape the future of their company. Decisions on strategies, customers and markets, operations and management are ideally based on data that the business has access to. Data, however, is only as good as the decisions it enables one to make. And with the data overload, it becomes harder and harder to separate the chaff from the grain to

---

[6] Devashish Chakravarty, 'Top 5 Skills That Are Required to Retain a Job in 2018' (2018). Available at: https://economictimes.indiatimes.com/wealth/earn/top-5-skills-that-are-required-to-retain-a-job-in-2018/articleshow/62094864.cms (accessed on 13 January 2018).

find the true meaning and insights which can support effective decision-making, thus compelling the need for data storytelling.

And while organizations worldwide use some form of data to guide them in their operational and financing decision-making, it is still not being done in the most efficient and effective way. I have often found that organizational decision-makers face two key challenges:

1. A host of the data being generated by business doesn't reach the decision-makers at all.
2. Most presentations only report data as it is. The insights, the meaning and story are often lacking.

When insights generated from data are fed into right channels, organizations can see a marked change in their performance across all spheres. But data by itself does not lead to decision-making. The data has to be sliced and diced to derive some meaning, which then needs to be communicated to decision-makers. To enable quick and efficient decisions, to set you apart from your competition, somebody needs to find and convey this meaning behind data.

The key competitive differentiator in today's data-driven world is the ability to use this data to make effective business decisions.

SCIENCE MAKES STORIES POWERFUL

Yes, you read it right—science makes stories powerful. While storytelling can be termed as an art, the reason behind the often awe-inspiring or mesmerizing reactions obtained by a story is actually quite scientific, as stated in Figure 1.1.

The power of a story is unleashed by its ability to fire up an activity within the human brain.

Figure 1.1 Scientific Impact of Storytelling

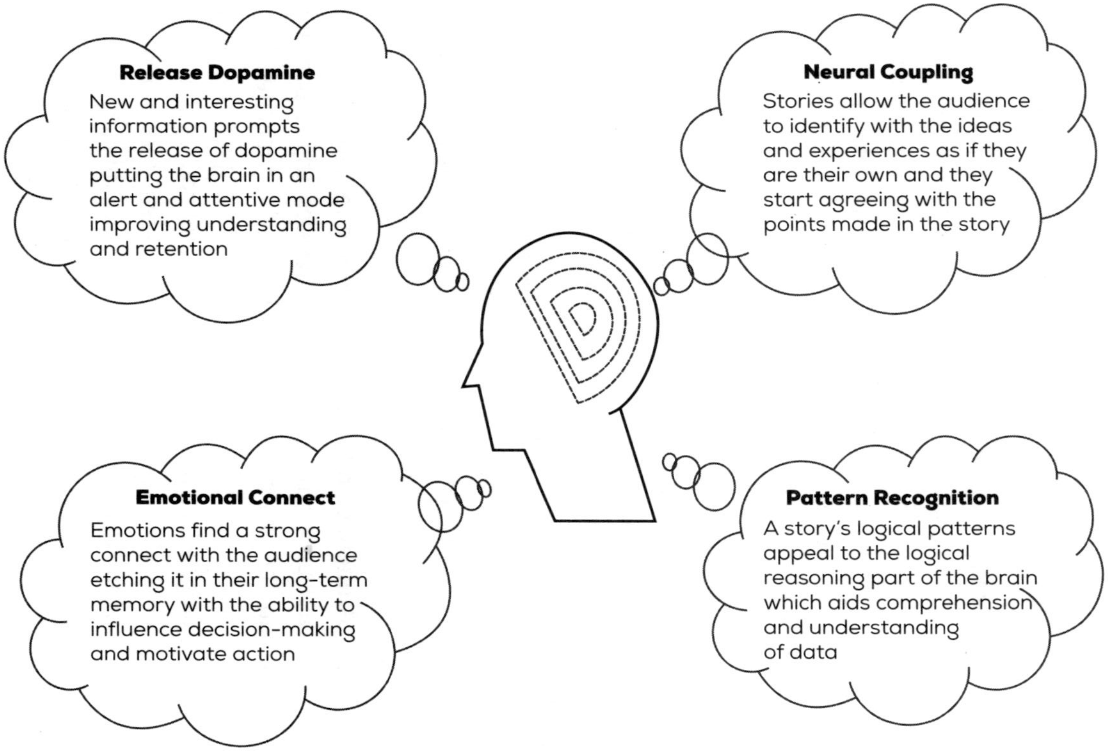

Release Dopamine
New and interesting information prompts the release of dopamine putting the brain in an alert and attentive mode improving understanding and retention

Neural Coupling
Stories allow the audience to identify with the ideas and experiences as if they are their own and they start agreeing with the points made in the story

Emotional Connect
Emotions find a strong connect with the audience etching it in their long-term memory with the ability to influence decision-making and motivate action

Pattern Recognition
A story's logical patterns appeal to the logical reasoning part of the brain which aids comprehension and understanding of data

Stories have the power to influence our brain's functioning and elicit desired responses. Given ahead are the four broad points that show what makes them the go-to tool for all forms of communication, especially when communicating with data:

1. **Grabs attention:** The first impact of a story is felt through a dopamine rush which impacts the brain's learning process and memory. Dopamine is a neurotransmitter—a chemical messenger, which passes information from one neuron to the next. A spike in dopamine released by the body is commonly associated with anticipatory desire and motivation. 'When dopamine levels rise, you subconsciously want more of the good feeling it gives you, so you're driven to concentrate on whatever you're doing to keep getting it', says Lucy Jo Palladino, a psychologist and the author of *Find Your Focus Zone.*[7]

   Dry facts and figures become interesting when moulded into a story, leading to a dopamine rush which grabs audience attention and enhances their learning mechanism.

2. **Audience buy-in:** Experiencing a story alters the audience's neurochemical processes which puts them in the storyteller's shoes. When the brain receives a story, its neurons fire in the same patterns as the storyteller's brain. Known as 'neural coupling', it creates coherence and alignment between the storyteller's brain and the audience. They start thinking from the storyteller's perspective and start agreeing with the points being made.

---

[7] CNN, 'Fuzzy Brain? Improve Your Attention Span' (2008). Available at: http://edition.cnn.com/2008/HEALTH/11/14/rs.increase.your.attention.span/ (accessed on 9 December 2008).

*Incorporating data storytelling helps overcome the big
challenge of getting an audience buy-in on complex
analytics and conclusions being presented.*

3. **Emotional connect:** Studies[8] have shown that our emotional state at the time of an event occurring can affect our ability to memorize its details, suggesting that emotionally charged situations can lead us to create longer-lasting memories of the event. Emotions also have a positive influence on recalling such memories as they lure us into reliving the same feelings. Data when converted into stories generates emotions (more on this is discussed in Chapter 6), which park such data events in the audience's long-term memory while also increasing their inclination towards a recommended decision or action.

*Emotions generated through a data story make an
impression on the audience, facilitating retention and
recall. The emotional connect also makes it easier to
persuade and motivate a desired action.*

4. **Pattern recognition:** A linked set of events that forms the basis of a story's narrative structure is conducive for human understanding and memory because it presents information in a logical structure which the human mind is most adapted to interpret. When any information is presented in front of us, our immediate response is to find patterns which can help us decode the information presented.

*When data gets enveloped in a story structure,
it starts depicting patterns the human mind can easily
catch, understand and remember.*

---

[8] Donald G. MacKay, Meredith Shafto, Jennifer K. Taylor, Diane E. Marian, Lise Abrams, and Jennifer R. Dyer, 'Relations between Emotion, Memory, and Attention' (2004). Available at: http://mackay.bol.ucla.edu/MacKay%20%282004%29%20-%20Emotion%2C%20memory%2C%20and%20attention.pdf (accessed on 13 November 2018).

BAD STORIES ARE EVERYWHERE

Your audience should not have to analyse the data themselves. Its meaning and conclusions should be intuitively visible at the first glance.

The treasury department of a corporate conglomerate showed me multiple presentations created by them on daily, weekly, monthly and quarterly bases, seeking my views on improving their quality and impact. Some of these even went directly to the chairman and his Board. All I could see, slide after slide, were data tables or charts which only reported the data without providing any significant insight into it, and compelling the audience to analyse and arrive at a particular conclusion. Unfortunately, this is the state of most data communication across organizations as shown in Figure 1.2.

Most people are used to making such charts on a regular basis and might wonder why I call them 'bad'. The answer lies in two broad points: missing story and bad visual aesthetics.

Here's what makes them bad:

1. Excessive information on all charts which makes it difficult to read patterns and understand the data.
2. The charts do not provide any clear insight or conclusion, requiring the audience to analyse these charts themselves.
3. Bad visual aesthetics: Wrong chart types, bad colour choices (yes—even on a grey scale), large gap width between bars and bad data labels are some repeated mistakes.

The aforementioned points summarize the most common charting issues, which you will learn to overcome through this book.

Figure 1.2 We Are Surrounded by Bad Charts

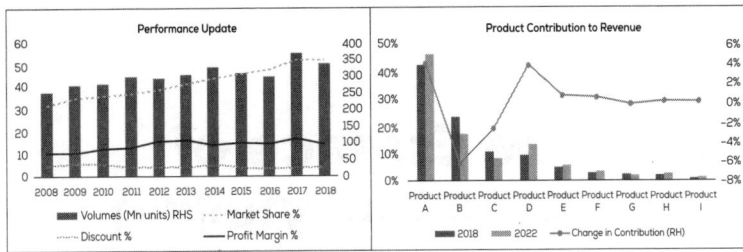

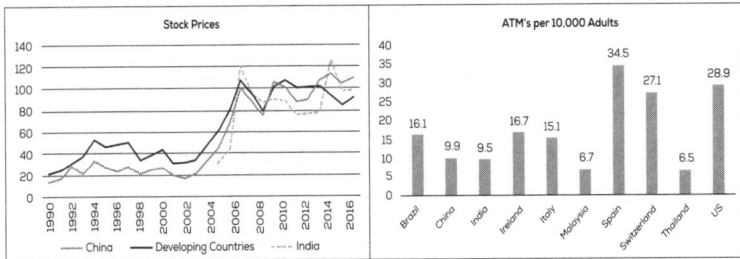

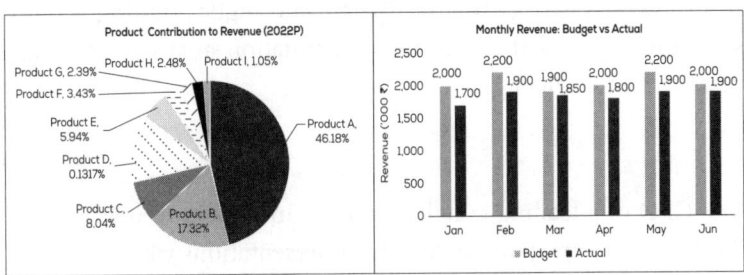

Note: The data has been generated for explanatory purposes only.

2 The Essence of Data Storytelling

I once met the equity research head at one of India's prominent investment banks who asked me to create a customized training programme for the company's equity relationship managers, which would enable them to convey the 'story behind the stock recommendations' to their clients. This investment bank is well known for its high-quality research reports, and he felt that somehow it wasn't getting translated into higher trading activity since the impact of the stock recommendation story was not being realized by the client.

* * * *

The CFO of a leading conglomerate in India said to me one day, 'Sejal, my guys prepare multitude of presentations which are used at different levels of the organization, some even at the Board level. And while they do a decent job, it's still a lot of data and its presentation needs to be improved'. I said, 'Sir, what they need is to stop reporting numbers and "start telling data stories" which provide an insight into the data while also finding a connect with their audience'.

* * * *

The credit risk department of a well-known MNC investment bank's KPO in India regularly writes internal rating notes for financial and non-financial corporates. I conducted an analytical writing training programme for this department, wherein the business's key requirement was for the analysts to be able to 'bring out the story behind the rating rationale in their writing'.

* * * *

Finance for non-finance is a widely conducted training programme across most corporates. Even for this basic programme, I had a client (a leading BPO) who told me that their non-finance managers should not only be able to understand the meaning of the often-used financial jargons but should also be able to understand and interpret the 'story behind these numbers'.

* * * *

As stated in the four examples mentioned above, across every business, industry and even professionals, I regularly come across instances that show that data storytelling is becoming the go-to tool for all forms of data articulation, presentation and communication. This influx of data storytelling stems primarily from the abundant data and the need to convert these into impactful messages which can enable business decision-making.

In my frequently conducted data visualization training programmes, I always begin by asking participants what do they understand when they hear the term 'data visualization'. And there is always at least one participant who comes up with the apt definition that data visualization is the process of 'converting data into a visual story'.

HOW STORIES TRANSFORM DATA

Purposeful storytelling isn't show business, it's good business.

—Peter Guber, Entrepreneur and Author

Figure 2.1 Data to Story Transformation

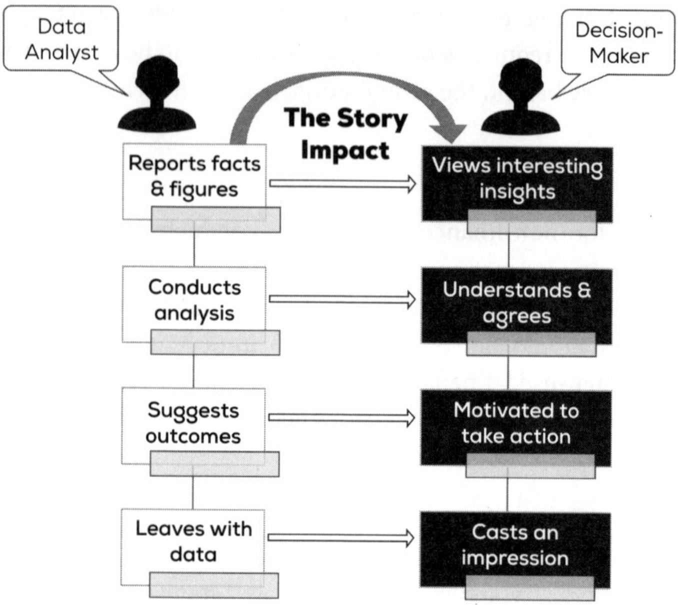

Stories were once considered as a prerogative of the marketing department, which used them as a tool to find an emotional connect with their audience and ignite brand loyalty. Stories today are incorporated in all forms of business communication to send across a clear message while also finding a strong connect with an audience—both internal and external. Figure 2.1 demonstrates the story impact which the data analyst makes on the decision-maker through his/her storytelling.

Four-Dimensional Impact of Data to Story Conversion

With the gaining significance of data communications, I believe that every business aspect that deals with data is in a dying need of a story to make the dry facts and figures more interesting, engaging and impactful. Let's understand the four-dimensional impact that the story makes, which data doesn't:

1. *Data is boring—stories make it interesting* by providing insights which are not visible at the fore. They don't just report data but also show why and how the data moved and what implications it led to.

2. *Data is complex—stories facilitate understanding* by presenting information in a structured, logically ordered format, which makes pattern recognition easier for the human brain.

3. *Data doesn't command action—stories do*: Through stories, audience can understand, appreciate and agree with the storyteller's point of view, and are thus motivated to take the suggested course of action.

4. *Data is forgotten—stories leave impressions* on the human mind, transporting them into the brain's long-term memory.

WHAT IS DATA STORYTELLING?

A number by itself means nothing. It makes sense only when it is relative to something.

A single number or a single piece of information by itself provides no pertinent information on which any conclusion or strong message can be built. A series of numbers by themselves in a table or chart also add no value. A number makes sense only when it is part of a sequence of events which lead to a conclusion. A data point gets transformed into a story when (also refer to Figure 2.2):

1. The data point in question is a result of events that occurred before.

2. The data point in question affects some future events that lead to a conclusion.

Figure 2.2 Data to Story Conversion

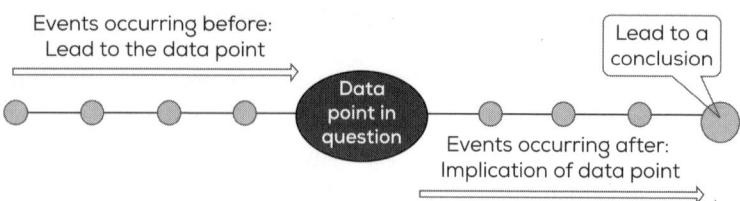

The essence of data storytelling lies in connecting the right dots within the data analysis so that its depth, meaning and significance can be absorbed by an audience who may not have the time or ability to interpret data and, hence, rely upon you to provide the requisite insights. When representing the exactly same information, even a small tweak to attain this logically linked set of events can change the understanding and impact of the message.

To this linked set of events, we add a beginning in the form of a context or background information about the topic at hand while weaving in the characters along with their requisite events. A data story identifies and draws audience's attention on the key events and characters, which form the core premise of the story, directly leading towards a conclusion.

> *A data story is complete only when the audience has a clear understanding of the key event, the theme that forms this linked set of events and the conclusion it leads to.*

Many people live with a misconception that data cannot be mixed with stories because they think that stories are fictional and use flowery language. Some also feel that stories always paint a rosy picture and have a high emotional quotient.

This misconception stems from a misunderstanding of a story's definition. The core elements of a story, as identified from its dictionary meaning, are simply the linked set of events, characters, beginning and ending. Table 2.1 shows how these core story elements get applied into a data story.

Table 2.1 Story Elements in a Data Story

Characteristics of a Story	Application in Data Storytelling
A story is based on the occurrence of certain events.	The events in a data story are the movement of an underlying set of numbers, the trend or relationship of numbers.
A story is a link of events.	Multiple data points come together to form the events of a data story. The order in which these data points are presented are essential in determining its overall understanding and impact.
A story is a full picture of the linked events.	Every angle of the data analysis is represented through a story. It shows why and how the numbers were arrived at.
The events are experienced by characters.	A data story's characters can be a company or department. The type of data, that is, revenue or profit, are also characters which go through events.
It has a beginning.	A data story's starting point is setting a context to the upcoming topic and providing necessary background information.
It has an ending.	A data story is created to achieve a specific business purpose. Every data story has a conclusion, which addresses this business purpose.

Any insight worth sharing is preferably best shared as a data story. Too often, data storytelling is interpreted as just data visualizing, but in my experience it extends to all channels used for communicating your insights. Visualization, oral presentation or written paragraphs or reports are all different forms of communicating with data which can be made more effective when done in the form of a story.

* * * *

When presenting simple regional revenue data, most people only report the stats of where and by how much the revenue moved across these regions. The story is formed when:

1. The audience can understand why/how these numbers moved and what was their impact.
2. The order and grouping of these numbers make the insights clear.

Table 2.2 and Figures 2.3–2.5 represent how simply realigning and grouping the right numbers together transform data into a data story and help bring out an impactful message.

Table 2.2 Regional Revenue Data Example

Regional Revenue ($ million)		
Region	**2016**	**2017**
China (CN)	53	55
Hong Kong (HK)	120	118
India (IN)	32	38
Indonesia (ID)	18	17
Malaysia (MY)	25	29
Singapore (GS)	95	92
Thailand (TH)	22	25
Total	375	383

Figure 2.3 What Most People Do?

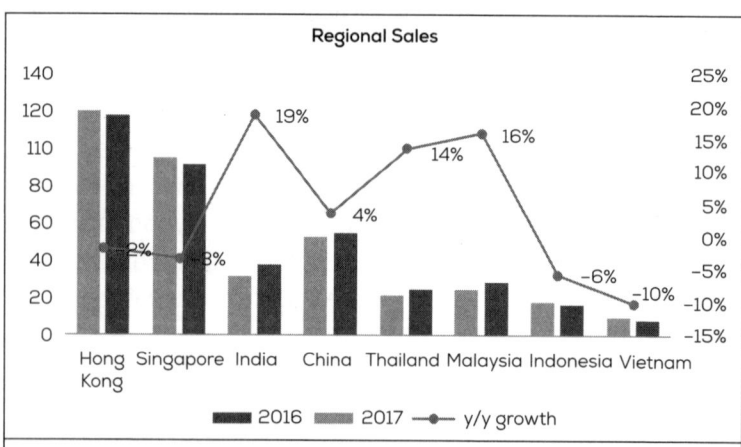

- Hong Kong contributed 31% to 2016 revenue and reported a drop in revenue by 2% at $118 million in 2017 versus $120 million in 2016.
- Singapore, the second biggest revenue contributor, also showed poor growth falling by 3% y/y to $92 million in 2017 from $95 million in 2016.
- India recorded highest revenue growth of 19% y/y to $38 million in 2017 from $32 million in 2016. Thailand and Malaysia also showed strong growth of 14% and 16% respectively. Together, their revenue contribution increased to 24% in 2017 from 21% in 2016.
- Revenues from Indonesia and Vietnam declined by 6% and 10% respectively, while China gained slightly by 4%, recording a revenue of $55 million in 2017 versus $53 million in 2016.

Figure 2.4 Data to Story Conversion for Regional Performance

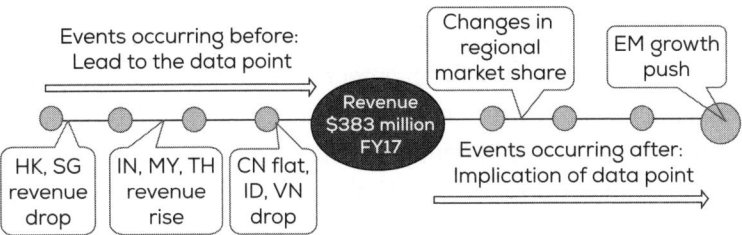

Figure 2.5 The Result When Data Storytelling Principles Are Applied

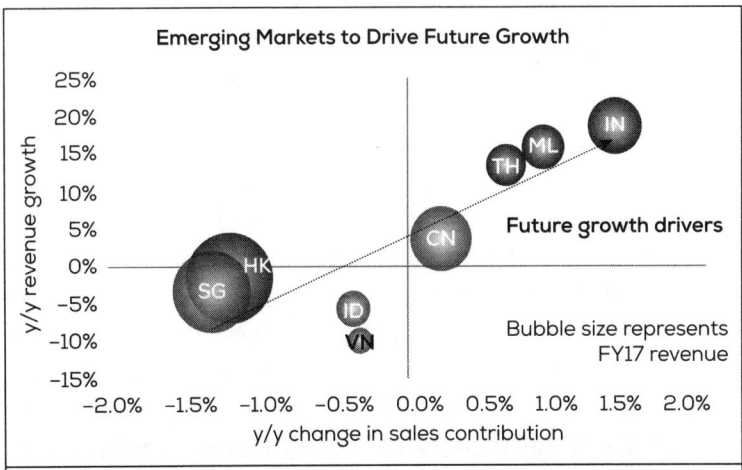

- Hong Kong and Singapore continued to dominate regional sales; however, losing some ground as 2017 revenue decline (2% and 3% respectively) reduced their overall revenue contribution to 54% in 2017 from 57% in 2016.

- Emerging markets like India, Malaysia and Thailand on the other hand recorded a revenue growth between 14% and 19%. This led to an increase in their revenue contribution to 24% in 2017 from 21% in 2016, while also making them future growth drivers for the company's revenue generation.

- China maintained its significance with a marginal 4% revenue growth, while Indonesia and Vietnam performed poorly on both absolute and relative grounds.

∗ ∗ ∗ ∗

A wholesaler of a certain in-demand perishable imported product purchases a daily shipment for resale to retailers within the country. They start accepting orders a week in advance; the selling price for this in-demand product is primarily determined by the inventory position. The business's aim is to maximize profit while clearing the perishable inventory. The business maintains a detailed record of every transaction in a single Excel sheet, which they wanted to use effectively to determine the daily selling price for each successive shipment on the basis of the order and inventory position. Converting this data into a chart (Figure 2.6) helped solve this daily dilemma.

Figure 2.6 captures the daily order and inventory positions for the upcoming seven working days to automatically adjust the price, with the base price specified as ₹1,000. On 1 July, the business gets a clear view of how much inventory needs to be sold for each day of the current rolling seven-day week and the target order price as on 1 July for delivery on these successive dates. On 2 July, the rolling seven-day week moves forward and the target order price changes with the changing order and inventory position. Excel functionality ensures that every day the charts refresh themselves and the current date, that is, the date of the report, gets dropped off while details of a successive seventh working day get added.

DATA STORYTELLING NEEDS PRACTICE

As data analysts, most of our time and effort are spent on uncovering the complicated trends and relationships within data. And unlike specific technical know-how, communication is not a core part of an analyst's job description; hence, it often gets overlooked. Moreover, some analysts live with a perception that storytelling just isn't important for their kind of job profile.

Figure 2.6 An Informative and Enabling Data Story

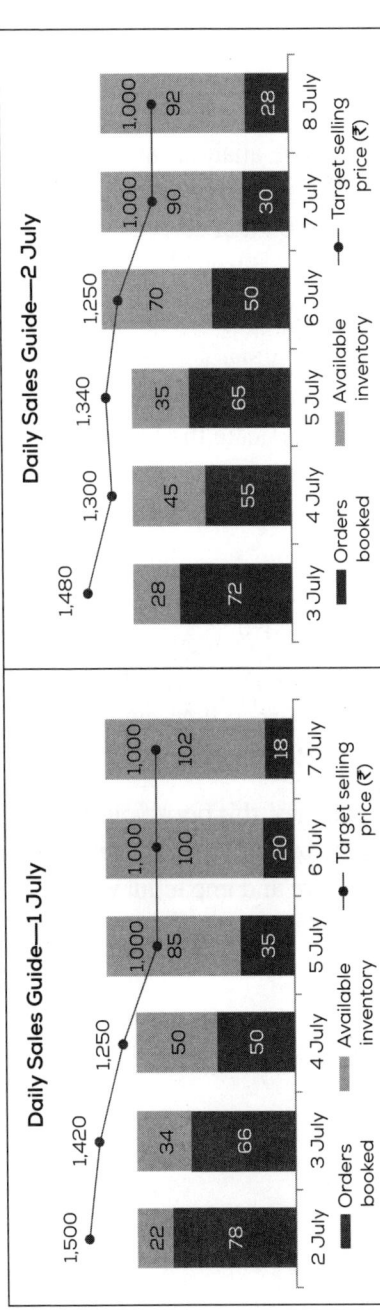

They might believe storytelling to be a less valuable investment of their time and they'd rather prefer to spend more time doing justice to their technical capabilities. Building a good story takes some time; hence, most analysts are reluctant to devote that much time even if it would make them more effective, while some also live with a perception that storytelling is only for fiction and not for facts.

Until very recently, storytelling did not find place in major school or college curriculums. While we were taught to read numbers and perform various calculations and analyses, nobody really taught us how to communicate the findings. And while we developed MS Office skills early on, a standard bar or line graph doesn't always tell a good story. All it does is represent the numbers in a visual format.

Data storytelling has only recently started gaining traction and is already becoming a key job requirement for most data-driven profiles. If you haven't given it a thought until now, it's time to start your data-storytelling journey right away to get an edge to your data- and analytics-related careers.

The upcoming chapters of this book will serve as a guide to help you find data stories, build the narrative and communicate the data story in an effective and impactful way.

(3) Getting to the Core

'Want to go for a movie?' This question itself sets us in an excitement mode, as watching films is an experience cherished by many. Inside the dark hall, cut off from the external world, we're lost in the mesmerizing foreign locales, the gripping action scenes or the dramatic story revolving around a few characters that keep us glued on for the next three hours. A tub of popcorn and soda in hands while our eyes are glued to the screen, it is an experience we want to keep coming back to.

But have you ever seen a Bollywood or Hollywood movie from the eyes of a director or a producer—the people who deliver this end product for you to devour?

Be it a 3-hour classic Bollywood family drama or even a 45-second ad film that plays in between, a considerable amount of time is spent on pre-production to achieve a high-quality end product. It is widely believed that when making any kind of a film, 60 per cent of the time is spent in pre-production, 10 per cent in production and 30 per cent in post-production.

The same story-planning concepts apply in our data story world with minor tweaks to fit the kind of work we do. Next time, think of yourself as a producer while getting down to the task. Data story pre-production including a structured planning process commands 40 per cent of our time, the actual writing or chart making, that is, production, needs another 40 per cent time, with editing and checking in the form of post-production commanding the balance 20 per cent time.

Take a moment and think that how much time you end up spending at each stage.

The moment an Excel sheet pops up in front of us, we have this urge to start analysing data while simultaneously writing and charting without once considering 'why we are undertaking the exercise' or 'what message we want to convey'. The only way to tell a good story is to first have a good story within our grasp. Using a structured planning process can help build a good story much more efficiently.

> *The only way to tell a good story is to first build a good story.*

STORYTELLING IS LIKE DRIVING A CAR!

Like all other teenagers, my twin brother and I were quite excited to get behind the wheel and start driving. On attaining the legal driving age, our father was only too happy to help us get the requisite licenses. It seems that driving skills came more easily to my brother, who started driving independently from the very first week. I, on the other hand, had to undergo a full month of driving lessons, followed by months of practice, a minor accident and multiple car scratches to match up to his level of skills and confidence! Today, with years of practice behind me, I pride myself on being an excellent driver who can navigate through the busiest streets of Mumbai or highways of the world.

Developing a storytelling skill is not much different than driving a car and often comes naturally to humans. Some just get on and start with it, while some need professional training and practice to develop this skill, which just like driving demands simultaneous attention and focus on multiple aspects. But once learned, this skill cannot be unlearned, simply because it takes very little effort to continue practising it.

To make this storytelling process relatively easier and much more efficient, I have designed the 'story wheel framework', which will jump-start the storytelling process by leading you to the core of a strong story.

THE STORY WHEEL: ENHANCE YOUR CHANCES TO WIN

When playing a board game, if you are able to strategize and plan your attack, you are certain that your chances to win increase. All you need is an understanding of the game, knowledge of other players and a little guidance to nudge you in the right direction.

The story wheel framework (Figure 3.1) provides this direction to help plan and strategize through the battle with data.

Figure 3.1 The Story Wheel

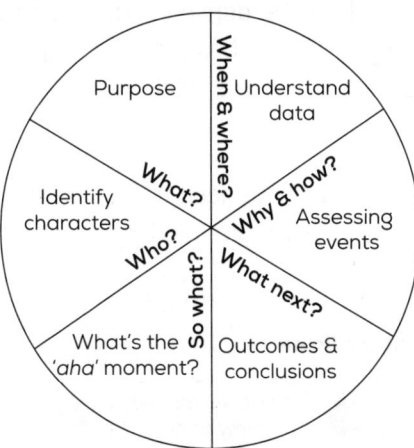

The story wheel, through its orderly set of analytical questions—divided into six parts—helps convert 'data' into 'story elements'. The first two parts focus on developing a broad understanding of the objective, audience and available data. The third and fourth parts give the main story components in the form of characters and events that drive the story. The last two parts compel us to find those elements that can help make a story interesting and worthwhile for an audience.

KNOWING WHERE YOU'RE GOING

Selection of an accurate destination address is critical to find the best route. A good road sense has never been one of my strong pursuits, and, like a lot of people, I heavily rely on GPS. But it requires me to add a destination first. Even a small error in the address can change the route, possibly leading to a wrong destination. And if somehow I still manage to reach the right destination, then it comes at its own cost—waste of time and fuel, which none of us is interested in, right?

Likewise, defining and understanding the purpose of the story from the start are pertinent. All forthcoming story elements will depend on this and will be derived and led by the purpose we identify at this very first stage. Misunderstanding or losing sight of the purpose can put us off the track, resulting in an ineffective end product.

For going on this journey, we need to plan the route with a GPS and break it into three parts, as stated in Figure 3.2.

Figure 3.2 Planning the Route

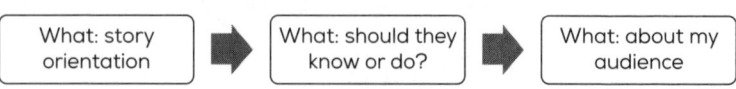

SCOPING THE FIELD

All data stories have a predetermined orientation, which is based on the kind of enabling function that the audience expects it to provide. The application of all other story elements can be simplified and generalized to a large extent using this understanding.

The kind of data stories we tell in business can broadly be divided into the following four story types:

1. **Reporting stories:** Most reports and presentations prepared by businesses are intended to provide an update or information on data movements pertaining to various business aspects during a certain period—weekly, monthly and quarterly. Typically in the form of standard reporting formats, they are the most heavily consumed data stories by both internal and external stakeholders.

Reporting Story Examples

A business performance update by the finance department; a financial market update or fund performance update prepared by an investment bank or mutual fund house; an investor presentation prepared by a corporate investor relations team; an HR manager's report showing recruitment and attrition trends; a presentation to the corporate's treasury department detailing monthly outstanding loan balances; a production manager's report on costs incurred during a month.

---

2. **Decision stories:** The audience—both internal and external stakeholders—often rely on us to help them

make the right decisions. Such stories provide a complete set of analytical insights with a concluding decision or recommendation.

Decision Story Examples

An equity research report providing a buy/sell/hold recommendation on a particular stock; a credit appraisal proposal recommending the approval of a certain loan disbursal by a bank; a project report recommending a new capital investment or joint venture; an investment proposal to participate in a private equity transaction.

3. **Probing stories:** Businesses are always looking to cut costs and improve efficiencies, revenue and profitability; looking for new growth opportunities; and assessing the future of the business or simply evaluating the business impact of a certain dynamic. In this endeavour, exploratory analysis is regularly carried out across different levels at organizations to find avenues which can help achieve this.

Probing Story Examples

A strategy team's presentation on competitive analysis; an investment research report exploring macroeconomic impact on the country's stock market; a marketing team's presentation on strategies to improve customer satisfaction for a bank; an automobile industry report to understand future business implications; a report investigating disparate regional performance; a presentation on methods for improving cost efficiencies.

4. **Pitching stories:** The abundance of data gives us opportunities to use data analytics and insights to add credibility to any of the ideas we propose or products we want to sell. They use data-backed storytelling to help get a better buy-in from the audience.

Pitch Story Examples

An investment advisor, portfolio manager, wealth manager or mutual fund relationship manager's presentation to attract a new client; a business plan or an investment pitch prepared by a start-up to attract funding from investors; an IPO pitch book prepared by an investment banker; a marketing pitch to a new or existing client; getting a buy-in on new or innovative ideas from the company's business heads.

Understanding of the story orientation is a beginning point that gives us a generalized guide, but this needs to be narrowed down to a specific purpose that should be achieved by a given story for a certain audience.

ADDRESSING AUDIENCE'S NEEDS

Explicitly spelling out a specific objective is extremely helpful when it's done at the beginning. Do we want the audience to take some action or simply create awareness on a certain topic?

Reporting and probing stories often provide knowledge that can facilitate decision-making, while decision and pitch stories have a clear intention of making or recommending a decision to the audience that compels them to take an action.

Getting a grip of the purpose is fairly straightforward in decision and pitch stories, as it typically has one clear objective. In decision stories, the objective could be a specific investment decision, while in pitch stories, it could to be to secure a new client, funding or sell a product or idea.

* * * *

The purpose is frequently overlooked in reporting stories, which often leaves them as mere data dumps. The audience ends up spending more time trying to find their way through the data mesh rather than appreciating the message behind it. This problem is further compounded by the usage of standard presentation formats. The following table shows how identifying the message correctly can help enhance impact of such reporting stories.

Reporting Story	Stop Reporting	Start Concluding	Audience Impact
Business performance update by the finance department	Revenue and profit numbers across products and regions	Best and worst performing products and regions	Enable business decision-making
Financial market update by a sell-side analyst	Historical price levels and returns across markets and assets	Best and worst performing markets and assets along with performance drivers	Enable investment decision-making
Presentation to corporate treasury	Loan repayment schedule for a given month	Periods with higher repayment	Enable better financial planning

The excitement of discovering intriguing insights often makes us lose sight of the purpose and message that needs to be conveyed through a probing story. With data in front of us, our mind automatically starts uncovering seemingly interesting patterns, without giving due consideration to the role it plays in our story. The result is an end product which might not serve the audience's purpose. Every data piece should be evaluated in context of the purpose before deciding its place in the story.

Giving the audience what they need is critical to maintaining their interest in the story, but to be able to do this we will first have to build a rapport with them to understand their background and preference.

BUILDING A RAPPORT WITH THE AUDIENCE

Social gatherings and parties are a good way to network and meet new people. When meeting a distant friend or cousin, we intently begin discussing our common links; or when a friend is trying to set you up with someone, the conversation intertwines common personal attributes; or on spotting a potential business connect, we enlighten them about our professional background and achievements.

A storyteller's mere existence is defined by the presence of an audience. Knowing the audience is thus the critical step to scout for relevant data and determine an apt presentation style.

To know an audience, we need to focus on two things:

1. **Understand their background:** As a storyteller, we need to assess the audience's existing knowledge base to present information that falls within their bandwidth while also focusing on 'what they don't know' to provide 'new' information in those areas that haven't been explored by them.

2. **Knowing their preference:** It is important to fully understand our target audience and their specific needs and preferences as this influences the 'depth of analysis' (e.g., brief versus detailed analysis), 'presentation style' (e.g., written versus visual) and 'formatting choices' (e.g., font and colour choices).

The following table discusses examples showing audience's influence on storytelling decisions.

Story	Audience	Background and Preference Considerations	Story Implication
Financial market update	Retail investor	• Limited market knowledge • Lack of time to monitor markets regularly	Snapshot of easily understandable financial market terminology
Presentation to corporate treasury	Chief financial officer	• Seniority of experience and knowledge • Need to make funding decisions • Presentation and formatting preferences	Brevity with key highlights
Business performance update	Senior management	• Seniority of experience and knowledge • Need to make business decisions • Presentation and formatting preferences	In-depth analysis in preferred presentation style
Mutual fund investment pitch	Institutional investor	• Seniority of experience and knowledge • Need to make investment decisions • Evaluating multiple proposals	Compelling story using advanced financial market terminology and analytics

Understanding the purpose and audience are the most critical parts of building a good story which are often overlooked by most people. Building a rapport with the audience guides our data-selection decisions and goes hand in hand with befriending the data.

BEFRIEND DATA

Roughly 2.5 quintillion bytes of data is created in the world in just one day. With this data abundance, there is scope to churn out innumerable insights. But the abundant data creates one big problem and the most common dilemma is: Where to begin?

Figure 3.3 Get to Know Them

When and where: does the data take place?		When and where: does the data become important?

Swimming in the sea of data is like being a warrior in a battle-ground surrounded by thousands of soldiers. You know you have the ability to fight them, you know you can win, if only you knew where to begin. If you are able to strategize and plan your attack, you are certain that one by one, you will take all opponents down. All you need is a little guidance to nudge you in the right direction.

The 'when and where' (Figure 3.3) come in handy when we want to befriend and know more about our data. When applied in the context of the purpose and audience identified in the first stage, it helps narrow down the data range we need to work with in order to build a certain story.

Answering these paired questions leads us towards a point, typically a cell in the Excel sheet or any other form of tabular data. One should focus on narrowing down the data from a whole spreadsheet to a relatively smaller set of cells spread across a few rows and columns. The 'data overload' problem and the 'where to begin' dilemma are now resolved to a large extent, as in the end we are left with smaller refined data tables or structured data buckets which are likely to be the main focus area of the story.

* * * *

The purpose of the presentation to a corporate's treasury department is to enable financial planning in the month of May. The available data set consists of loan outstanding data spread across 10 columns and 200+ rows. The rows list all loans raised by the company and the columns represent different parameters for these loans including issue date, issuing bank, amount outstanding, loan type, due date and more.

Filtering this data set through the lens of the purpose helps narrow down the data range as follows:

- *When and where does the data take place?*
  - Required row range: 20 rows comprising of loans that mature in May.
  - Required column range: amount outstanding, due date, lender bank.

Author's note: Although loan issue date and loan type offer scope for some interesting analysis, they fall off the purview since they do not enable the financial planning decision. On the other hand, providing weekly outstanding balances might be of immense help to plan ahead. Since this column was not a part of original data, we added a column that converted due dates into the week of the month.

- *When and where does the data become important?*
  - Relatively higher repayment obligations across due date, week and bank.

★ ★ ★ ★

DEALING WITH LARGE DATA SETS

Identification of the 'when' and 'where' can be a little tricky for stories with a wider scope, where data comes from multiple sources. And while pinpointing the actual data sets might be an exhaustive job here, one should try to identify the when and where in terms of broad themes that make the story.

Data decision for an automobile industry report might be guided by two aspects: One would provide industry background in terms of products and players, and industry growth trends along with drivers. The other would identify future growth drivers such as higher usage of shared vehicles and launch of electric vehicles.

A private equity investment can similarly be classified into themes: (a) standard requirement including financial summary and fundamental business analysis, (b) analytical insights which drive the decision and influence the audience. These could include a new innovative product, solid growth in a short time or even a strong founder story and (c) investment valuations along with potential exit routes.

The bottom line: Leverage upon the understanding of the purpose and the audience to narrow down the scope of data while also bringing structure to large data sets.

Having narrowed down the data set doesn't complete the job. From within this data, we need to identify the characters and events that form the core of our story. From within these characters, we will then find the story's 'aha' moment.

WHO'S THE STAR?

It's been over a decade that I haven't touched my favourite book, Ayn Rand's *The Fountainhead*, but the moment I think about it, I can immediately visualize and reconnect with Howard Roark, a young individualistic architect and his fight against collectivism and populism. The thought of *Titanic* once again enthrals you into Jack and Rose's love story. You still remember when and where they met, you remember Jack's painting of Rose, you remember the ship's collision with the iceberg, and you remember how Jack froze to death while he tried to keep Rose alive. If you are a *House of Cards* fan, I'm sure that Jack Underwood and his theatrics to reach and maintain his position at the Oval Office have kept you awake many a nights.

Figure 3.4 The Story Drivers

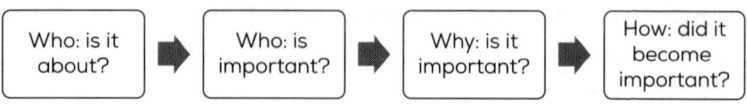

Now, let's think about your favourite fictional novel you haven't been able to pick up in a while, the one that's been gathering dust somewhere in your library or desk. What is the first thing you remember? Every time we think of a story, the first thing we remember is the person/protagonist/character—in other words, ask yourself the question: 'Who' is the story about? The second thing we think of is something unforgettable, impactful or interesting that happened with this character. Asking the question 'Why this character becomes important?' leads us to a list of events which when connected evolve as a story (Figure 3.4).

And while our favourite stories consisted a multitude of characters and events, we remember only a few because the storyteller made us pay attention to them. The identification and focus on 'the key characters and events which drive a story to attain a specific purpose for a given audience' thus become important elements of the storytelling framework.

'Data characters' are typically 'data categories' or 'data series', and these are the things for which we have numbers. The events that these characters (read: data category/series) go through are most commonly found in the movement of the underlying numbers. The event can be a noticeable change in a single number, a change in numbers over time, a correlation between the two set of numbers or a number that sits like an outlier. An event can also be found in a number that hasn't changed over time. Events that drive a story forward are typically in the form of a key relationship between data categories (read: characters) or in the trends and patterns formed by the numbers within these categories.

* * * *

Using These Questions for Presentation to the Treasury Department

Who is it about? This data is about the outstanding loan amounts distinguished by their due dates and lender banks. This gives us four characters: the bank, the due date, the week in which the due date falls and their respective outstanding amounts.

Who is the important character? HDFC Bank, 28 May and week 4 are the most important characters.

Why is the character important? They have a high outstanding balance.

How did this character become important? Outstanding balance for these characters is relatively higher than the rest of the characters.

* * * *

Using These Questions for Private Equity Investment Proposal

Who is it about? This data is about fundamental analysis and investment evaluation criteria for a UAE-based hospital chain.

Who is the important character? Market leadership, financial profile and growth prospects are the most important characters.

Why is the character important? These factors depict business strength, directly supporting the investment decision.

How did this character become important? Market share is high, financial ratios are strong and the company has a strategic growth plan in place.

The bottom line: From the refined data, identify important characters and events that drive the overall story while also leading towards the conclusion.

MAKE AN IMPRESSION: THE 'AHA' MOMENT

To make an impression on the audience, bring out a fascinating piece of information that makes the audience go 'aha'!

The 'aha' moment of a data story is the high point at which the audience's engagement levels reach a peak. This typically happens at a point when they are amazed or surprised with the new, different or unexpected information and insights presented by the story. With time, the audience might forget details, but they will remember the point which made them go 'aha'. The 'aha' moment can be found by digging deeper into data to find an intriguing piece of analysis. Strive to unearth data layers and keep asking the question 'so what' (Figure 3.5) with respect to important characters and events.

Stifling through data is like going on a treasure hunt, every finding is a new clue that leads us closer to the treasure. The story's treasure is that piece of analysis which will make an impression on the audience.

* * * *

HDFC Bank and 28 May were identified as the first set of important characters in the treasury presentation due to their relatively higher outstanding obligations. Following up this insight with a 'so what does it mean?' the answer is: It helps plan for

Figure 3.5 Finding the 'Aha' Moment

| So what: does it mean? | So what: does it imply? |

higher payments. Next we ask: So what does it imply? It implies that they need ways in which they can plan better the company's finances. This led us to find a new way to plan better—converting due dates into weeks where week 4 had highest payment obligations. This becomes the 'aha' moment of the story since it is a new insight (not directly available in raw data) which better facilitates financial planning by providing a week-wise snapshot.

* * * *

The key reasons driving the private equity investment recommendation are the important characters and events—market leadership, strong financial profile and growth prospects. Asking the question 'so what does it imply?' leads to the answer: These factors will drive higher future business valuations, hence strongly support the investment decision. The defining moment will come when the story clearly shows 'the numbers depicting its market leadership and data that casts an impression for a strong financial profile, and shows how the future growth plans are expected to materialize'. These collectively leave a strong impression that higher future value can be unlocked through this investment, thus becoming the 'aha' moment of the story.

The bottom line: Dig deeper into the important characters and events to uncover new and intriguing insights that make an impression on the audience.

Finding an interesting 'aha' moment might feel like an accomplishment on its own, but its full impact will be felt only when it is tied together to a conclusion and followed with a 'what next'.

SHOW THE WAY FORWARD

After the hidden identity of his identical twin brother is revealed, Cameron Black's career as the world's greatest illusionist is destroyed and his brother is sent to the prison on a framed murder charge.

In an attempt to free his brother and find the mystery killer, Cameron starts working with the FBI where he uses his skills of deception to solve high-profile criminal cases in this fast-paced show. When he finally catches the mystery killer, she cuts a timely deal with the FBI to seek her release, leaving his brother locked behind bars. The season ends with a distraught Johnathan Black deceiving Cameron to switch places and teams up with the mystery killer on a quest to find his great grandfather's hidden treasure.[9]

And while I wait for the second season, I am wondering: What will happen to Cameron? Is Johnathan just playing a game to catch the mystery killer? Will he come back for Cameron once he finds the treasure?

The season finale episode of every good show leaves its audience on a hook by introducing an unexpected twist in the tale, and we longingly wait for the next season to find out how it will all turn out. Human curiosity is not easily satiable; we want more. With stories, we want to know what happens next.

While fictional entertainment stories often keep us waiting to find out 'what next', data stories should address the 'what next' part before closing. A business audience relies on this closure to guide them in their way forward by enabling effective decision-making. This closure could be a simple, clear conclusion or a detailed action plan.

We have all sat through presentations and read reports that left us baffled and we failed to understand what was the point being made? Sometimes people get so caught up in the whole act of

---

[9] Story of *Deception* TV series, created for ABC by Chris Fedak.

providing information to an audience that it makes them miss the main point—the 'message' that needs to be provided. If the conclusion does not register in the audience's minds, the whole storytelling exercise can go waste.

This message, as identified in the first stage, guided the entire story-building exercise. We began with the message we wanted to provide, identified all elements that helped us show how we arrived at the message and finally ended the story by clearly spelling out this desired message.

* * * *

Reporting stories' 'what next' aspect is a clear conclusion summing up the message behind the presented data. The 'what next' for the treasury department is the clear conclusion stating all repayment amounts they need to plan in the month of May across days, weeks and the banks to which these amounts are due.

In decision and pitch stories, the 'what next' are clearly guided by the recommended decision or recommendation. For example, buy ABC stock at ₹250; approve 500 million term loan; invest in capital expansion project; invest in private equity transaction at 5.3x EBITDA multiple; invest in mid-cap equity mutual fund; invest ₹100 million in Fintech.

In probing stories, the 'what next' is often in the form of a suggested course of action. In the automobile industry report, the 'what next' can come by identifying clear business opportunities and weaknesses in the light of the changing industry dynamics. When evaluating regional performance disparity at a corporate, the 'what next' is the identification of emerging countries as the next growth opportunity.

The bottom line: Close the story with a clearly spelled out con-clusion that provides a future direction. The conclusion answers the question raised in the purpose, while stages two through five show how we arrived at the conclusion.

SHOWTIME!

Getting to the core of the story using the story wheel framework typically doesn't take more than few minutes. Once you are done with analysing all the data, take a few moments to fill out the story wheel as shown in the examples below. Since the storyteller is already well versed with their data, even a brief structured outline as shown in Figures 3.6 and 3.7 can help a great deal in building a powerful data story.

Story Wheel Example 1: Presentation for the Treasury Department

Figure 3.6 Completed Story Wheel: Treasury Department

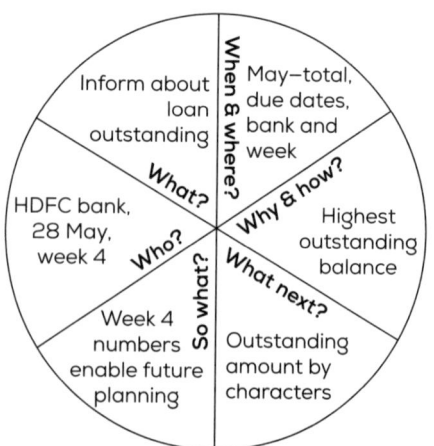

Story Wheel Example 2: Private Equity Investment in a UAE Hospital

Figure 3.7 Completed Story Wheel: Private Equity Investment

Note: The above data has been generated for explanatory purposes only.

Just like a producer on set, the story wheel gives us the direction to identify all components that come together to form a story. But the job isn't done yet. It's now time to wear a director's hat and show the actors when and how to perform a scene which will then be emoted by these actors. The forthcoming chapters will guide you on planning a strong narrative, followed by crafting an impactful story.

4 Planning Is Everything

As a child of the 1990s, *The Lion King* was the first large-scale cartoon animation movie I was exposed to and the *Toy Story* was the first 3D cartoon animation experience. Did you know that the base of both these epic movies lies in sketched drawings? While the *Lion King* was completely hand-drawn on paper, the *Toy Story* characters were first computer-drawn before transforming them into lifelike 3D characters we all came to love.

* * * *

Vincent van Gogh (1853–1890), the creator of renowned paintings like *The Starry Night* and *Café Terrace at Night* is among the most famous and influential figures in the history of Western art. In just over a decade, he created 2,100 artworks including around 860 oil paintings, the vision for which was sketched out before he started creating these paintings, which today adorn famous art museums.

* * * *

Every time I read the *Harry Potter* book series, I contemplate that how could its author, J. K. Rowling, manage to write an intricate story rolling in with so many twists and turns? How did she retain her sanity in demarcating such complex scenes and plots, which took the world by storm and went to become a revolution in the domain of fantasy novels?

The massive following of the *Harry Potter* book series, since the first book in 1997, has marked the entry of Rowling in the list of the world's most successful authors of all times. And as surprising as it may sound, the building blocks for this brand are believed to lie in hand-drawn spreadsheet plans outlining various plots, subplots, characters and the inter-linkages between them. One such fascinating spreadsheet shared below was released by the author in 2010.

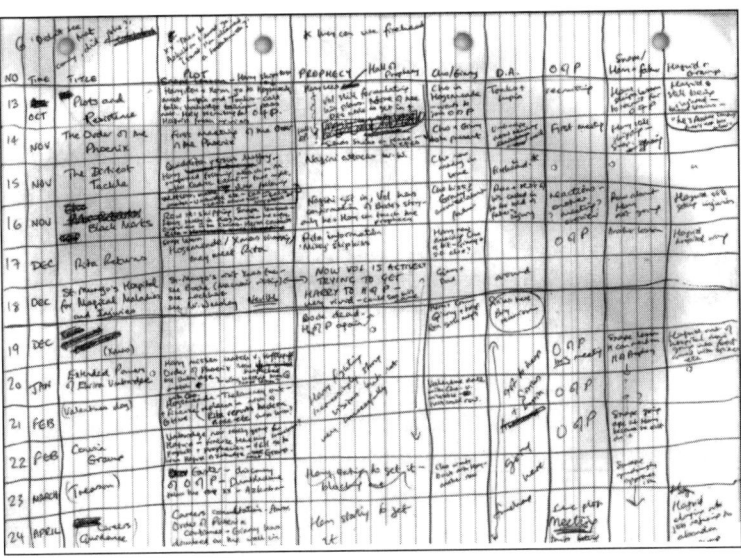

Source: http://harrypotter.wikia.com/wiki/File:Revision_of_the_plan_of_%27Order_of_the_Phoenix.jpg (accessed on 15 November 2018).

Note: The above hand-drawn spreadsheet explains the concept of storytelling.

DATA STORYTELLING ISN'T MUCH DIFFERENT

While we are not expected to churn out a bestseller with our data stories, most of us would agree that even without all the drama, data complexities can be equally overwhelming. All we need is the right planning and scoping of the story, which can go a long way in reducing data complexities within the story while ensuring that the message comes across exactly as we intended it to be.

There should ideally be a pause between the data analysis and data communication at which point one can think and plan on 'what message we want to provide to an audience and how should we go about doing it'. This planning bridge ensures that the story portrays the underlying analysis as desired, thus connecting the two platforms of data storytelling. The story wheel helped us identify the message we want to provide, and in this chapter, we delve into planning the narrative to effectively communicating this story.

He who fails to plan is planning to fail.

—Sir Winston Churchill

SAY IT LIKE YOU MEAN IT!

Following a successful bull run fed by yield-hungry post-credit crisis investors, Chinese financial markets started seeing their first cracks in 2011. On one occasion during this period, I analysed a Chinese real estate company, leading to an overall conclusion that irrespective of the recent market turmoil its fundamentals were still strong and thus we retain a 'Buy' on the company's bonds. I prepared and sent this report to my boss—head of Asia credit desk in Singapore. It was quite a contrarian call for that time, and he immediately phoned to discuss my rationale. After being satisfied with all my reasoning, he said only one thing: 'Then, say it like that.'

Sounds familiar?

Those five words taught me a very big lesson that day. What we think doesn't always come across in the way we think it does.

Our thoughts need to be structured and aligned before they are presented to an audience to ensure that they see it in the same way as we do.

THE STORY SHOULD DO THE TALKING

Today, when I check trainees' written or visual exercises, I frequently find myself in situations wherein I'm compelled to request for an oral explanation to facilitate understanding of the underlying story. They usually begin with explaining the objective along with their thought process to make the story clear. This results in another request from my side: 'The storyteller shouldn't do the talking, the story (visual or writing) should.'

I have commonly found that while most people are well versed with their data and analysis, they do struggle to communicate their message effectively because somewhere their thought processes lose the desired structure and order, making the narrative weak, and the message loses its steam. Planning the narrative beforehand acts as a blueprint to ensure that we don't go off the track when crafting the story.

Most people are well versed with their data and analysis, but they struggle to communicate their message effectively.

A narrative is a plan which outlines when and how all the events and characters unfold in front of an audience. The story arc and story map discussed in this chapter are two effective tools that help plan a strong narrative.

THE STORY ARC

As a child I remember taking a lot of road trips with my family, most of them in interior regions of the country. This was long before the advent of satellite-based navigation systems and I recall my parents relying on printed city maps for directions.

Whenever we began a journey, my father would mark the starting point and the destination first, then outline the potential routes we could take to reach our destination. When he had decided on the final route we were to take, he would highlight it with a red marker. This red line was now our guiding light to lead us to the destination.

Figure 4.1 The Story Arc

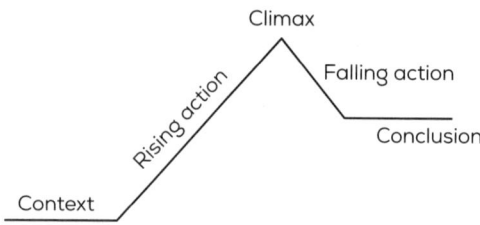

The story arc (Figure 4.1) plays exactly the same role as my father's red route highlighter. It provides a road map for the story's journey by literally showing how the story flows from beginning to end while also identifying milestones it needs to achieve when moving along the story path. Think of any book, movie, show or interesting conversation you had with a friend and you will notice that every story builds up in a similar manner.

CONTEXT MATTERS

Did I tell you how our favourite sandwich was invented? In 1762 London, at very late hours one night, English nobleman John Montagu, the fourth Earl of Sandwich (1718–1792), started feeling hunger pangs, but he was too busy gambling to take a break for food. Wanting to eat something while playing, without getting his hands greasy, he ordered a waiter to bring him roasted beef between two slices of bread, a snack he could consume without getting distracted from his gambling activity! But as he took the first bite, he cringed a little and ordered the waiter to add some condiments to satisfy his taste buds. And that's how an aristocrat's whimsical demand resulted in the birth of modern age's most sought-after quick-food item, we now know as 'sandwich'.

Every story begins with setting a context to the upcoming information. It typically introduces the topic at hand while also providing any background information where necessary. It is essential to set the context correctly, as the audience might not be able to understand or relate to the upcoming information. Moreover, a strong context enables the audience to align with our perspective and thought process. The context also often defines how the audience will perceive a given story. This aspect becomes quite important in pitch and decision stories, where it is essential to set the right tone at the very beginning. As a storyteller, the whole storytelling effort might go in vain if the audience is unable to grasp the basic premise of our story because of a weak beginning.

Let me ask another question. If on a lazy Sunday afternoon, you and your friends decide to binge and watch the *Game of Thrones* or *Suits*, the food and drinks are already laid out on the table, the mood is all set and as the show starts playing on your new 54-inch TV, you suddenly realize that your laid-back friend has forgotten to download the pilot episode! But you have already picked your cosy corners with a cold drink can and chips and so just decide to go ahead and begin watching from what you have available! Do you think you will be able to follow anything of what's going on?

* * * *

The rhetorical question used at the beginning of the sandwich story introduced you to the topic. The first half of the second sentence provides background information about the story. Without this background information, you might be tempted to pass this person as a gambling addict and form a negative impression about the key character, thus resulting into a negative cloud over the whole story. But the fact that he was a 1762 London aristocrat makes it amusing to picture him living up to his whims and fancies.

The bottom line: Set a context to introduce the topic and characters, provide background information and set the right tone to align audience's perspective with yours.

The context sets the tone for the upcoming action in the story and is typically followed by the rising action part.

THE RISING ACTION

Four-year-old Mishti was walking home timidly one day; she had gotten into a little scuffle at school and knew well enough what awaited her at home. Walking into the house, she innocently started saying:

Mumma, I am your brave girl; today I helped a friend. Rohan was troubling Krisha and she started crying. Since it was lunch break the teacher was not around and so I told Rohan to stop doing it. But then he started saying bad things to me so I pushed him away. Did I do anything wrong mumma? I was only helping my friend!

Like all stories, Mishti's story was also meant to provide a conclusion, but jumping to it right away was sure to result in some undesired scolding. Instead, discussing the chain of events that led to the conclusion (read: the rising action) gave her story a momentum, also making it amusing by influencing the reaction garnered from her audience (her mother).

This rising action part is typically the biggest chunk in most stories. It is literally where all the action is—where all the important events are unfolding. All of the key data analysis and insights that drive the desired conclusion find place in this section of the story. The placement of the rising action within the story and the analytics within the rising action are critical to make an impression and build the right momentum. Preceding the rising action with the context ensures that the audience gets the relevant understanding of the unfolding story, and following it up with the conclusion makes it all worthwhile. To achieve flow and linking of events within the rising action, we rely on planning their chronological order of appearance in the story map discussed later in this chapter.

* * * *

The first rising action event for the Earl of Sandwich is his hunger. The natural order of things would be to eat, which leads to the subsequent event that he was too busy gambling and hence did not want to break for food. What can he do then? He thus wanted something that was convenient to eat while gambling. One after the other, these events seamlessly link together, bringing us closer to the climax and the conclusion.

The bottom line: Bulk of the story gets built in the rising action. The order and link of the rising action events are critical to lead to the climax and conclusion.

While the context sets the stage for the rising action, the rising action gives momentum that leads to the most important parts of the story, which are the climax and the conclusion. The climax becomes important because of its role in engaging an audience, and the conclusion becomes important because of its ability to enable them.

CLIMAX

After you finished narrating the story, if someone were to ask your audience about the one or two things that they take away or remember from the story, what do you want their answer to be?

The answer to these questions is the climax of the story. The audience might forget about the storyteller, the data, and even when and where the presentation was made, but in a well-told story, the climax sticks with them. It is the defining moment of the story and it appears at that point in the story where audience engagement levels are at the peak. While the story wheel helped us find the story climax—typically in the form of the 'aha moment'—the story arc guides us on how to position it in our story to unlock its highest potential.

The events discussion in the rising action portion of the story keeps the audience engaged while also generating a host of emotions that grip their attention. They continue to build up the story's curiosity and surprise factor, making them more and more interested in the story. The point at which we have displayed all our rising action events, leading the audience towards their peak engagement levels, is the right time to show the climax.

A friendly game of poker suddenly becomes intense and exciting when there are only two opponents in the race for a pot full of money. It is now time to show your full hand. As you start opening your cards one after another, it is turning out to be a very close game. With every card you open, there is more curiosity, more surprise and more anticipation in the onlookers' minds. Engagement levels are at peak when the third card is about to open. 'Opening the last card—the biggest surprise and the deciding factor for your win or loss—is the climax that keeps them gasping for more'. If you win, you will hear some clinking of glasses and if you lose the game, some foul words are sure to float around.

* * * *

The Earl of Sandwich's dilemma to solve two problems at one time has got you involved, and you are waiting in anticipation to see how he solves this problem. The climax is his solution—the specific food order, which also leaves you surprised, literally thinking: aha ... so that's how he solved his dilemma by discovering a new snack altogether!

With their depth of information, data stories can be home to multiple climaxes. In situations where multiple pieces of analyses come together to form a common story, we can have a climax for every theme identified in the story map, discussed later in this chapter. At the end of the story, there is a grand climax that links together all the mini climaxes witnessed before.

The bottom line: The climax is the defining moment of your story. Use the rising action to build audience engagement to a peak and position the climax at this point.

The climax has a heavy bearing on the upcoming conclusion and in an ideal situation, we would want the climax to lead straight to it, but life isn't always ideal and most stories have some form of a falling action that comes between the climax and the conclusion.

THE FALLING ACTION

The whole purpose of a data story is to provide a conclusion and more importantly show how we arrived at this conclusion. While the rising action and climax move the story ahead in the direction of the upcoming conclusion, sometimes we come across data insights that are not completely in sync with the conclusion; they don't exert a meaningful impact on the conclusion, or go against it in some way. Typically identified as risks or challenges in data stories, these represent the falling action. The number of events in the rising action part of the story far outnumber the events being discussed in the falling action part.

For the conclusion to hold true, it is very important to quickly recover from this falling action. If a quick recovery is not in sight, it can also impede engagement, interest and perception of the audience. The climax will lose its sheen and might suddenly start feeling alien if the falling action starts playing a lengthy role in the story. While it is pertinent to present a true picture of the data, when presenting the story, falling action events need to be presented with this recovery in mind. More on this has been discussed in Chapter 7.

★ ★ ★ ★

We all believed that the Earl of Sandwich would be content with that new discovery that helped him fulfil hunger without disrupting his gambling activity. But there was a twist, since now he wanted to satisfy his taste buds too! This new challenge became the falling action of the story, which he quickly recovered from by ordering the addition of taste-enhancing condiments. This recovery is essential to support the upcoming conclusion.

The bottom line: Falling action events go against the conclusion in some way. For the conclusion to still hold, a quick recovery from the falling action is critical.

CONCLUDING THE STORY

You have worked very hard on a certain report or presentation, even pulling in some full nights. After reading the report or sitting through the presentation, just imagine how you would feel if your boss or colleague completely misses the point you are trying to make? Happens often? You know exactly how irritating and frustrating that can be.

* * * *

When you are watching a suspense thriller, you absolutely do not want to know who the killer is in the very first scene because that will completely ruin the story for you. But a hint on the possible suspect(s) right at the beginning makes you more intrigued and involved in the upcoming story. The Sherlock Holmes in you comes to life and you start actively participating in the story.

* * * *

When presenting data stories, it is pertinent to present a clear conclusion, since without it the business audience's purpose does not get addressed. For maximum impact, as with all other milestones of the story arc, the placement of the conclusion is equally important. Since we use a narrative to specifically 'show' the audience how we arrive at a certain conclusion, its best position is at the end after all the events have played out. It is thus driven from and led by the rising action, climax and falling action. Yes, the falling action is important too, as it shows us how the conclusion holds true in spite of the challenges. In addition to clearly stating the conclusion at the end, I generally prefer to give a glimpse of the conclusion, and sometimes even the climax, when setting the context of the story as it can play a key role in generating curiosity and interest in audience's minds.

* * * *

My use of the rhetoric question at the beginning of the sandwich story not only sets the context but also provides a glimpse into the story's conclusion. Were you not amused and curious to learn more about it? Did it not make you more alert and attentive to the upcoming information? In the end, when you read the complete conclusion, you would have clearly understood how all the linked set of events resulted in the discovery of the sandwich.

The bottom line: The conclusion finds a permanent place at the end of the story to show the audience how it is arrived at. A glimpse of the conclusion provided in the context generates audience's interest and curiosity.

ONE SIZE DOESN'T FIT ALL

While all stories need to achieve the same milestones to make them impactful, they don't necessarily follow the same route from context through conclusion. To address the different types of journeys that data stories can take us on, I have adapted the standard story arc into five types of story arcs (Figure 4.2) that I believe are most applicable to data storytelling. These story arc types are taken from 'The Shapes of Stories' by Kurt Vonnegut.

An upward sloping arc leads to a positive conclusion with some risks or challenges in tow, while a *downward sloping* arc leads to a negative conclusion even after a few positive attributes. The *sharp V* focuses on a recovery from the bottom to lead to a positive conclusion or coming back to a status quo. The premise of the *growth arc* is rising from zero or building from scratch to lead to a sizeable positive conclusion. *Hills and valleys* typically represents a struggle to maintain the status quo.

And while reporting and probing stories could take the shape of any of the above story arcs, decision stories typically fit into upward sloping, downward sloping or growth arcs because of their stronger need for an impactful conclusion, and pitch stories fit into the upward sloping and growth arcs due to their strong need for a positive conclusion to support a given sale.

* * * *

Figure 4.2 Story Arc Types

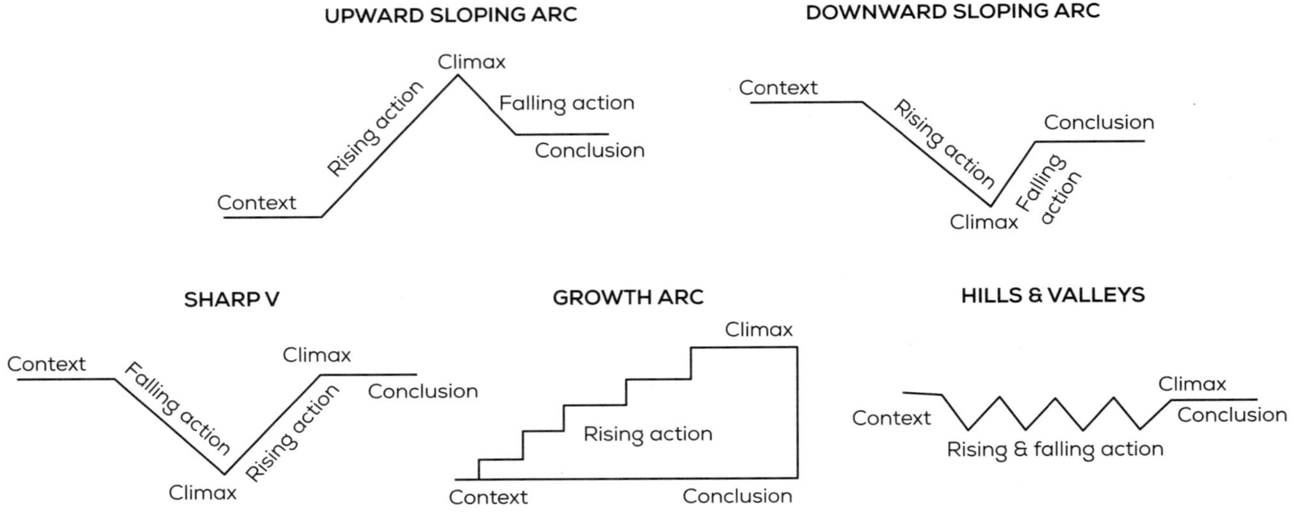

UPWARD SLOPING ARC

Context
Rising action
Climax
Falling action
Conclusion

DOWNWARD SLOPING ARC

Context
Rising action
Climax
Falling action
Conclusion

SHARP V

Context
Falling action
Climax
Rising action
Conclusion
Climax

GROWTH ARC

Context
Rising action
Climax
Conclusion

HILLS & VALLEYS

Context
Rising & falling action
Climax
Conclusion

A private equity analyst recommends their client to invest in a UAE hospital chain, based on its performance assessment that depicted positive results across a host of evaluation criteria. This data story gets translated into an upward sloping story arc as depicted in Figure 4.3.

Figure 4.3 Upward Sloping Story Arc

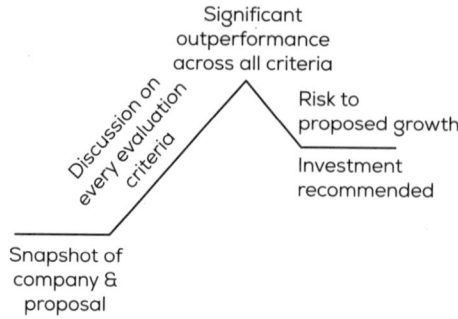

Context: A snapshot of basic company information along with proposal details provides an introduction and background information, which is essential for understanding the impact of the upcoming performance assessment.

Rising action: A discussion on the company's performance across multiple evaluation criteria is the most important part of the story since it will be the key determinant of the client's decision. Presentation of these evaluation criteria, one after another, builds up the required momentum to keep the audience engaged while leading towards the conclusion.

Climax: The key insight from the rising action part of this story is the company's significant outperformance across all evaluation criteria. Its relevance and importance to the upcoming conclusion along with its ability to garner maximum audience interest makes it the climax.

Falling action: All investments entail risks. It is the analyst's duty to present such risks while using mitigants as a tool to recover from this falling action quickly to move towards the conclusion.

Conclusion: The climax supported by the rising action overcomes the falling action to lead to a conclusion that the UAE-based hospital chain is a strong candidate for private equity investment.

* * * *

An equity research analyst recommends a sell rating on a certain stock because they believe that the risks far outnumber the positives associated with this investment. This data story gets translated into a downward sloping story arc as depicted in Figure 4.4.

Figure 4.4 Downward Sloping Story Arc

Context: A rating change is typically triggered by an event. For the audience to appreciate and agree with this change, an introduction and background on this event is essential and hence becomes the context.

Rising action: It is that part of the story and analysis that supports the conclusion. In this scenario, it is a downward sloping line since it leads to a negative conclusion, that is, a sell rating. A discussion of pertinent risks and challenges that lead to the requisite conclusion falls into this section.

Climax: While risks abound, there is one significant risk that has a higher impact on the conclusion. When this is a new or different information uncovered by you, it deserves the climax spot.

Falling action: When leading towards a negative scenario, the falling action includes positive attributes and hence is upward sloping. The risks drive the sell rating, hence, their mitigants become the falling action. However, the risks still overshadow the mitigants for the sell rating to be meaningful.

Conclusion: The rising action and climax, that is, the risk section of this story, overpower the falling action, that is, the mitigants, hence leading to the concluding sell rating.

★ ★ ★ ★

The marketing department is investigating the impact of discounts on the profitability of a consumer discretionary business. They conclude that while the initial reaction was a negative profit impact, a lagged sales volume recovery supported profit generation. Overall, net profitability impact during this period has not been very significant. This data story gets translated into a sharp V story arc as depicted in Figure 4.5.

Figure 4.5 Sharp V

Context: In probing stories, an introduction to the specific topic is critical because of the wide scope and application of data discussed within the report. Outlining the purpose of the report along with background information about the strategy forms a relevant context.

Falling action: In a recovery story, the falling action comes first. In this case, the initial negative profit impact is the falling action since it goes against the overall conclusion of a zero-profit impact.

First climax: It is the point where the story makes its turn from a downward journey to an upward journey. The reason for this change in course, that is, the volume recovery, is the first climax of this story.

Rising action: Reasons for profit improvement become the rising action as they show the recovery from falling action, thus leading towards the conclusion.

Second climax: The second climax is a desired but unanticipated outcome of this particular story. Showing market share improvement (an independent variable in this case) becomes the surprise element for this story, hence the second climax.

Conclusion: All milestones ultimately lead to the conclusion that overall there isn't any significant profit impact.

★ ★ ★ ★

A mutual fund relationship manager wants to convince a client to invest in a certain fund by showing how the fund has performed and grown over the years. This data story gets translated into a growth story arc as depicted in Figure 4.6.

Figure 4.6 Growth Story

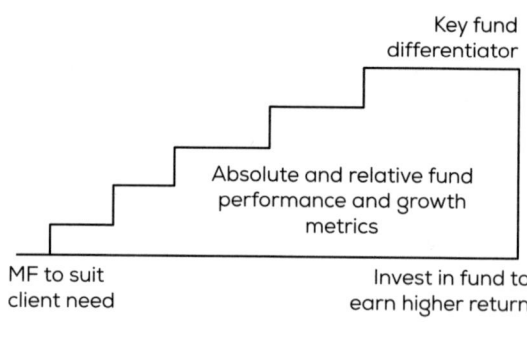

* * * *

Context: Introducing a mutual fund while stating its relevance to a client's needs sets the right tone for the upcoming information while also generating audience interest.

Rising action: Multiple metrics outlining the fund's performance over a period are essential to lead towards an upcoming investment decision.

Climax: Identifying a key fund differentiator right after all the performance metrics makes both the rising action and the climax all the more impactful.

Conclusion: All the positive fund performance discussions lead towards investment decision.

* * * *

An internal business performance update discusses various performance metrics, both positive and negative, that contributed to the overall profit for the quarter. This data story gets translated into hills and valleys story arc as depicted in Figure 4.7.

Figure 4.7 Hills and Valleys

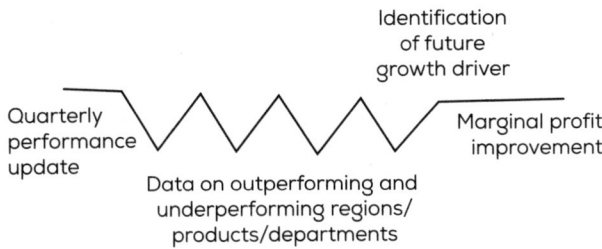

Context: A reporting story's context can be as straightforward as describing the underlying data.

Rising and falling actions: Discussions on all performance metrics form part of the rising and falling actions and are typically aligned together in this type of story. All outperformers become the rising action and all underperformers become the falling action.

Climax: In reporting stories, the climax is often in an insight which goes beyond the purpose of the story. In this case, the identification of the future growth driver adds more meaning to the rising action and conclusion by giving a direction to the audience.

Conclusion: The conclusion is simply the net impact of the rising and falling actions. In this case, it is a marginal profit improvement.

SHOWTIME!

The same story can keep changing its journey every time the underlying events and conclusions change due to their differential impact on the milestones the story is supposed to hit. Figure 4.8 shows the different journeys taken by the discount strategy assessment (first discussed in Figure 4.5) under different scenarios.

The bottom line: The story arc depicts the story's journey and is an essential tool to plan the event order and flow when presenting the story.

Figure 4.8 All in a Glance

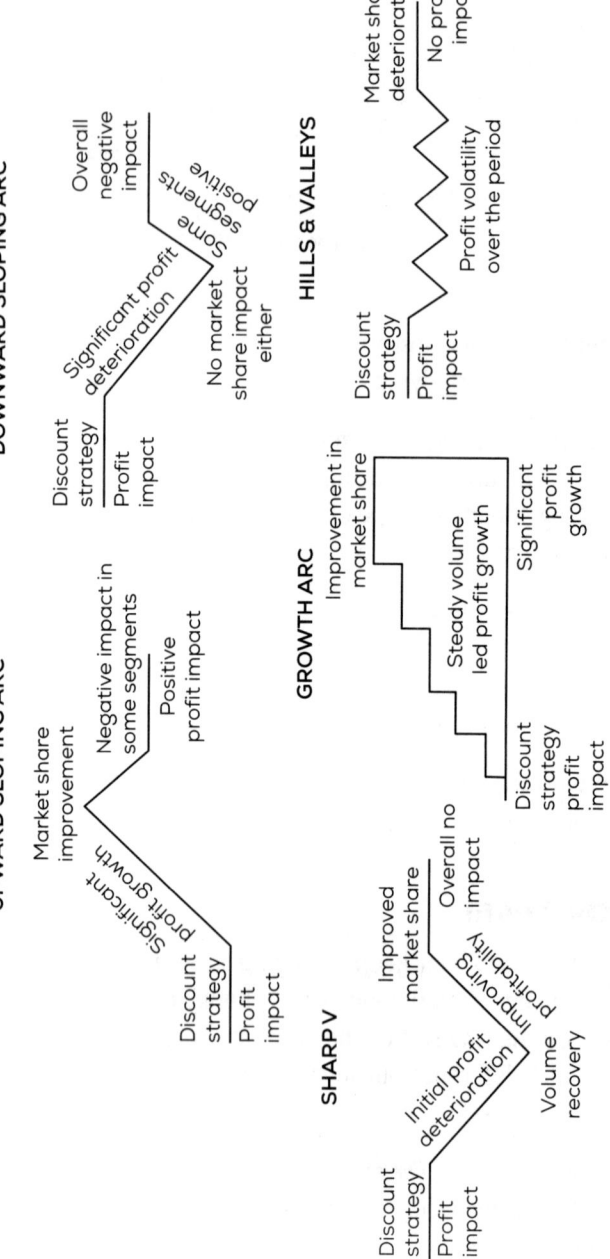

ARCHITECTURAL STORYTELLING WITH THE STORY MAP

'Architecture is a visual art, and the buildings speak for themselves,' said Julia Morgan, a renowned American architect who has designed more than 700 buildings in the USA. Like an architect speaks through buildings, a storyteller speaks through stories. Architecture, I believe, embodies a perfect blend of art and science in building both functional and good-looking structures. The beginning point of any construction site is a blueprint built with scientific precision incorporating artistic design elements, which also serves as a constant reference guide during the construction phase. An architect never loses sight of this blueprint because the risk of straying from the vision can result in heavy costs. Every construction decision is taken on the basis of this pre-planned blueprint to ensure that they build the structure as envisioned.

The story map provides an essential framework upon which the story can be crafted. Through its top-down approach, the story map lists down every essential story component, bifurcated into three logically demarcated layers, which help bring in a narrative structure. The basic premise in building this map lies in the logical grouping of data at these three stages. Data pieces leading to a common insight or conclusion are grouped together to build up to an overall conclusion. The more complex the data set, higher is the need to sketch out the story map.

MAPPING THE STORY

The bottom-up approach used during data analysis and the story wheel help us arrive at the story's conclusion. However, the link from data to the conclusion is often patchy at this point due to the multiple moving parts that were studied at these stages. To display a strong link, we convert this bottom-up analysis into a top-down

Figure 4.9 The Story Map

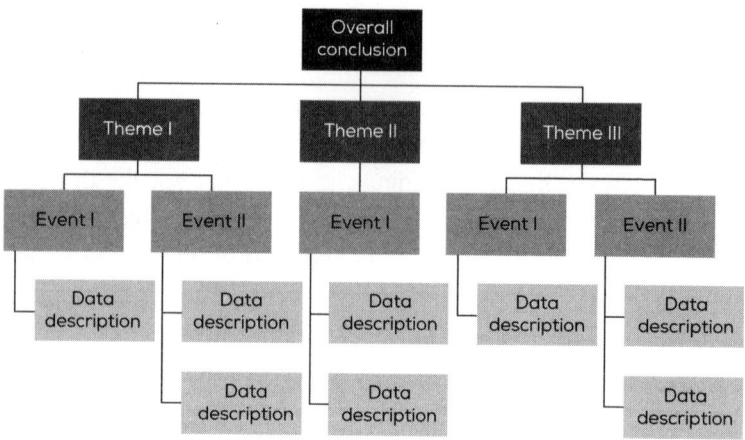

story when mapping it (Figure 4.9), beginning with the overall objective or conclusion filtered down into multiple conclusions, insights and data, which collectively drive the said conclusion.

1. **Themes:** The themes demarcate a story into different sections, each with its own mini conclusion. We can identify the story themes by logically grouping similar events together. A data story typically consists of three to four key themes which drive the overall conclusion.
2. **Events:** The second layer identifies the key events or event groups within these themes, each generating a particular insight and arrived at by logically grouping similar data points together.
3. **Data description:** Every event has specific characters associated with it, which are represented in the form of the underlying data. The third layer lists down the important data description, which together shows the story's journey.

To make a strong narrative, ensure that all the important story components find their place on the map in a desired chronological order of appearance. The journey outlined in the story arc helps guide this feat. Further, identify and highlight any priority events within the map to ensure that they get their due in the final presentation. Of all the events that make a story, there will be some which are more important than the others because they exert a higher influence in leading to the conclusion and thus become priority events.

In addition to bringing in a structure and an order while serving as the backbone of the story, the story map is a great tool to validate your ideas. When our thoughts and ideas come down on paper, they get a voice and start talking to us. The story's links and patterns become real for the first time. We can test our ideas and play around with the order to find the best way to present these links and patterns. Any inconsistencies or mistakes also start coming to fore.

When our thoughts and ideas come down on paper, they get a voice and start talking to us. The story's links and patterns become real for the first time.

The story map is the blueprint of the story; it should show the same links, patterns and conclusions that a completed story would. A well-structured map can thus be shared with a colleague, team or boss to ensure that you are all on the same page and leading towards the desired outcome. In case of a team effort, it is also a great brainstorming tool wherein a group of people can jointly discuss and validate their ideas.

In all storytelling workshops, I sketch out a story map on the whiteboard along with my participants, to ensure that our understanding is clear, and thought processes are in order and aligned. The mapping process typically does not take more than 5–10 minutes and helps save a lot of time by addressing most issues at the planning stage.

SHOWTIME!

A private equity analyst builds a data story to support their recommendation to invest in a UAE-based hospital chain (Figure 4.10). General information about the company, key factors driving the investment recommendation and a discussion on the valuations are identified as the three key themes for this story. An understanding of the company is essential to understand the basis for this investment, while the investment drivers and valuation are pertinent information on which the decision will be based. Within each of these themes, specific events are identified in the third layer of the story map, followed by the data which leads to specific insights derived from these events. Further, market share, key financials and valuation metrics are identified as the key data points (highlighted with a black outline in the story map) as they have a significant impact on the upcoming investment decision. When crafting the story, the information is to be presented in the chronological order as identified by the story map with special emphasis on these key events.

> *The bottom line: Time spent on planning the story arc and story map ensure that we don't go astray and maintain the connection with the underlying data analysis even at the story-crafting stage to ensure that the message comes across exactly as we intended it to.*

With a plan in hand, you can be fairly certain that you are on the right track to achieve the desired objectives for your audience. But on occasions when you simply do not have the time to undertake detailed level planning as this, you can refer to the quick fix offered in the next chapter.

Figure 4.10 Story Map for UAE Hospital Investment

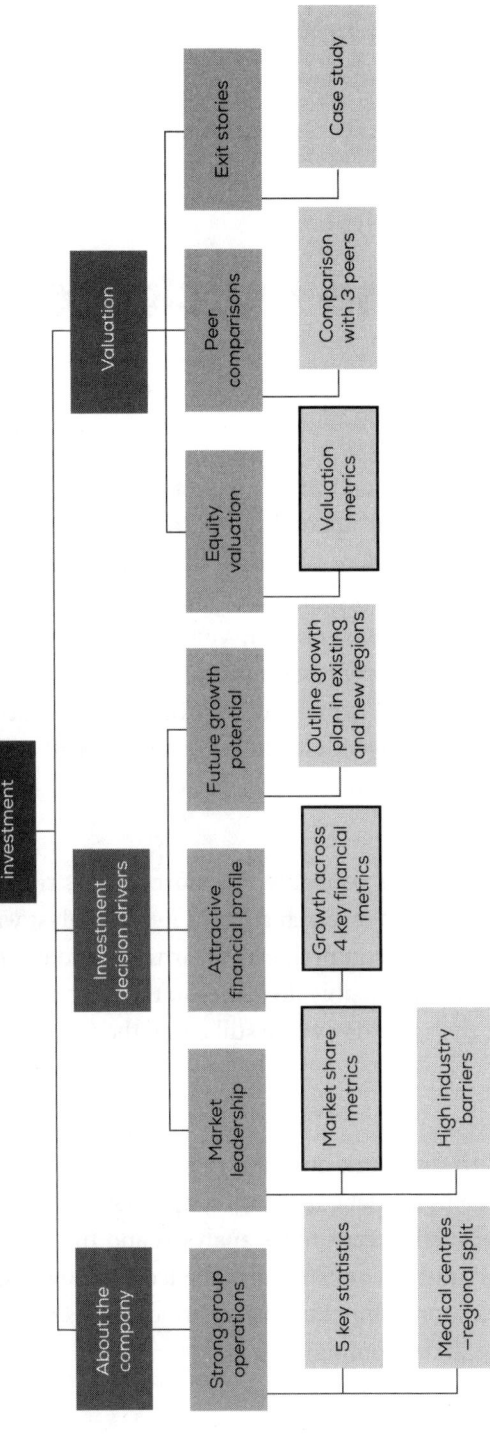

 **The Quick Fix**

After a long and tiring week spent on preparing a presentation for an upcoming board meeting, you finally take a breather when your boss heads into the meeting. But just as you walk up to the breakout area, in the mood for some hot coffee and light conversation, your mobile phone buzzes, it's a text message from your boss, asking you to quickly run over some numbers and send across the printouts. You immediately run to your desk, pouring yourself into the numbers all over again!

* * * *

Earnings season is probably the most chaotic time in the life of an equity or credit research analyst. Every analyst wants to be the first to provide a comprehensive earnings update to their client; but how can you possibly do justice to the multiple companies that report on the same day while still being the first one to report?

* * * *

Your day-to-day work does not require you to bury yourself into bulky or complex data sets; it is simple data—typically in a small table—but it still needs to be analysed and the stories communicated to an internal or external audience. But how can you possibly find all the story elements within two columns of data, consisting of just 15–20 data points?

Most of us have been in similar situations at some point in our work lives when working against a hard deadline does not leave us with enough time for pre-production or where the sheer size of data might not justify comprehensive planning needs, and we dive right into data without considering the overall impact of our data communications. The result, as you probably understand by now, will be an ineffective communication, often nothing more than a data dump. The story triangle discussed in this chapter helps you sail through such situations with ease by providing a quick fix that can bring in a story structure with minimum time and efforts.

THE STORY TRIANGLE

The Ferrari California takes three weeks to manufacture, start to finish, with the process taking place in two different buildings. A Toyota or Ford on the other hand are put together on an assembly line in 30 labour hours on an average. Different types of cars with different manufacturing processes and time still perform the same core function and are made up of the same key components. Every car performs the job of taking you from one place to another; it stands on four wheels and has a battery that makes the machine run, an accelerator that adds speed and a break to bring it to a halt!

Every story also embodies the same core elements irrespective of the time and process spent on building it. The story triangle (Figure 5.1) helps us nail these core elements in a quick and easy way.

Just like the story wheel, the story triangle also begins with understanding the purpose for which we are undertaking the storytelling effort. However, in this case, we jump right to identifying the objective we want to achieve with the story. It's either a message we want to provide or an action we want the audience to

Figure 5.1 Addressing the Core Story Elements

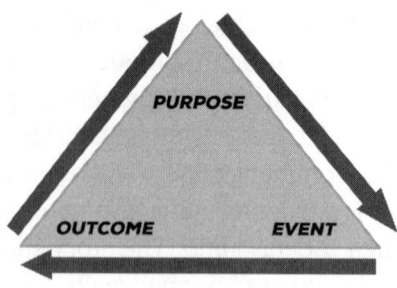

take. Beginning with the purpose ensures that the story provides information that is useful to the audience while also aligning the rest of the story to this overall objective that leaves an impact on the audience.

The events are all the action within data which help us achieve the stated purpose. Using the story triangle, one would have identified three to four key events that lead to an upcoming conclusion. Their presence along with the right chronological order of appearance gives a flow to the story, providing a strong narrative structure. When crafting a story, one should ensure that these key events stand out in front of an audience so that they can appreciate the impact of the upcoming conclusion (more on this has been discussed in Chapters 7 and 8).

The story triangle finally leads to the conclusion, providing a much-needed closure to the story. It is led from and driven by the events discussed within. The story will be impactful only when we can form a strong chain of link: purpose–events–conclusion–purpose. The conclusion should answer the question raised by the purpose while exhibiting a strong link with the events which in turn are identified on the basis of the purpose we want to achieve.

ONE KEY FOR MULTIPLE LOCKS

In addition to the story triangle's crucial time-saving role at the planning stage, the events listing on it can also double up as the story's blueprint. It can be referred to during the story crafting stages, just like in case of a story map, which ensures that we remain on track at all times. I also recommend using it as an editing tool for bigger stories to check that all important story elements have been enveloped. When editing, check if the story still addresses the purpose you set out to achieve, ensure that the key events clearly stand out for the audience to understand and appreciate the same, and be certain that the conclusion is clear. Going this last mile can act as the double knot at the end of an embroidery stitch to ensure that the story's threads don't become loose in any situation.

SHOWTIME!

An Indian shoe company has just announced its annual results for the financial year 2017–2018. Having pondered through the financial statements and earnings released, the analyst uses the story triangle (Table 5.1) to help build a strong story within a short span of time.

Table 5.1 Story Triangle Application for an Earnings Update

Elements	Description	Forming the Story Link
Purpose	Earnings update for an Indian shoe company	Provides an objective
Events	1. Results in line with expectations/consensus 2. Revenue growth lower than peers due to increased competition 3. Cost savings—primarily from change to GST, boosts profitability by 42% 4. Loses market share due to unavailability of key brands like ABCD	Each event identified on the basis of the objective, listed in a chronological order of appearance

(Table 5.1 continued)

(Table 5.1 continued)

Elements	Description	Forming the Story Link
Conclusion	The current profit spike is a result of a one-time event (GST-led cost savings) and until the company resolves its store level product management, competitors will outperform in terms of sales growth	Led by the events, answers the question raised by the purpose

Note: The above example is for explanatory purposes only.

Putting the data through the story triangle compelled us to find the key events and conclusions in light of the purpose. At the story-crafting stages, we will now be able to do full justice to these data pieces that matter most.

* * * *

During my storytelling workshops, I often create a practice exercise using data from Table 5.2 wherein trainees are required to build a visual story. With this simple data set, while everybody comes out with the same analytical conclusions, it doesn't always

Table 5.2 Product Contribution to Revenue

Products	2018–Revenue Contribution (%)	2022 (Projected)– Revenue Contribution (%)
A	40.24	44.18
B	23.03	16.82
C	12.20	08.00
D	10.45	14.17
E	04.60	06.00
F	03.10	03.93
G	02.70	02.89
H	02.70	02.98
I	00.97	01.05

Note: The above data has been generated for explanatory purposes only.

Table 5.3 Story Triangle Application for Small Data Set

Elements	Description	Forming the Link
Purpose	Understand the current and future growth drivers	Provides an objective
Events	1. Product A remains the dominant contributor while also depicting a strong growth 2. Products A and B also portray significant revenue contribution; however, they lose highest market share during this period 3. Product D gains significant market share while also portraying high growth rate	Each event identified on the basis of the objective, listed in a chronological order of appearance
Conclusion	Product A continues to dominate revenue contribution while Product D is fast gaining traction	Led by the events, answers the question raised by the purpose

Note: The data has been taken from Table 5.2.

get translated into an impactful visual story because an understanding of key story elements is missing in most instances. I constantly nudge these trainees to refer to the story triangle during the visualization process to get a grip on these story elements.

A discussion on the current and future growth drivers leads to an analysis of the revenue contribution on both absolute and relative bases. Key pieces of analysis uncovered during this process (summed up in Table 5.3) are as follows:

1. On an absolute basis, Product A has the largest industry contribution, followed by Products B and C in both 2018 and 2022P.
2. On a relative basis (comparing 2022P with 2018), Product A's contribution to the overall market size increases in 2022P, while Products B and C decline.

3. On the other hand, Product D gains a significant market share in 2022P (compared to 2018), although still contributing less than segments A and B on an absolute basis.

When presenting a visual story, these three attributes should register in the audience's minds at the very first glance. All the above three data points (i.e., events) do find their place in the left-hand chart in Figure 5.2; however, their role in the story and impact on the conclusion do not stand out at first glance because most people do not take a moment to identify the story elements and then consciously make them stand out. The audience is compelled to analyse the chart themselves to arrive at this conclusion—a standard problem I see in most charts being prepared across organizations. And while the absolute product contribution is quite clear in this chart due to descending order of the bars, understanding of the relative contribution is a little fuzzy.

The following attributes make this chart ineffective:

1. One begins with comparing the size of the two bars under each segment to understand which one has increased and which one has declined. This slows down the understanding process of the audience.

2. The chart consists of a total 18 bars, which makes it a little crowded. The last eight are barely visible, while the first eight form the key story characters. Excessive information that does not add value to the story diverts audience's attention from these key characters and their associated events.

3. The trend line on the secondary axis showing growth percentage between 2018 and 2022P doesn't intuitively suggest the positivity or negativity of these numbers. Every time one looks at a point on this line, they need

Figure 5.2 Story Visualization for Product-wise Revenue Contribution

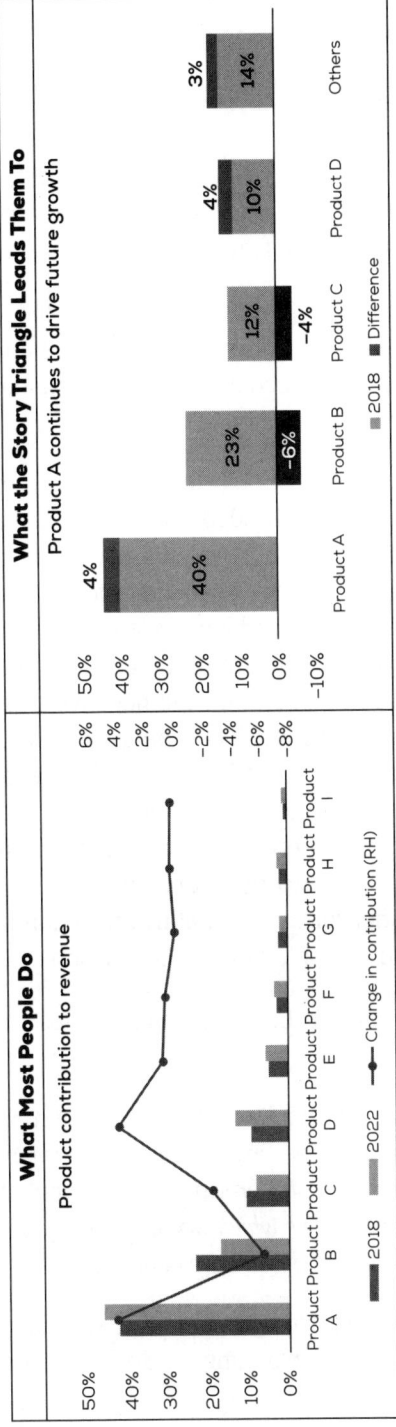

Note: The above data has been generated for explanatory purposes only.

to look on the right-hand side to assess its value and impact.

4. While some might think that adding data labels would solve this problem, it will only make an already crowded chart even more difficult to read.

The right-hand chart in Figure 5.2 leverages on the understanding developed by the story triangle to showcase the three key events in a simplistic manner which can be intuitively understood at first glance and hence the story's impact realized.

1. The length of the bar shows a segment's absolute contribution in both 2018 and 2022P. The light grey bar represents 2018, and the plus dark grey box or minus black box represents the 2022 figure.

2. The dark grey box, which sits above the light grey bars, shows a positive growth and the black box sitting below the light grey bar, and on the negative side of the chart below the X-axis, depicts a de-growth. The size, colour and position of these boxes identify the outperformers and underperformers on a relative basis.

3. Combining the peripheral segments, which do not add significant value to the story under 'others', makes the chart cleaner, further facilitating understanding of the key events and its impact on the conclusion.

Incorporating simple attributes like these helps transform data into a story.

The bottom line: When telling data stories, the core story elements apply at all times, irrespective of their length, breadth and depth. The quick fix provides this essential storytelling framework for situations which do not command the use of detailed story wheel and narrative planning.

Even though the story triangle is not as detailed as the story wheel or the narrative planning, it touches upon the most important aspects of building a story to ensure that the essence of a data story gets portrayed. A host of simple tools come together to make the events and conclusion stand out in our stories (a detailed discussion on these has been provided in Chapters 7 and 8). The important thing is to have an understanding of elements that need to stand out. Hence, using the planning tools discussed in this book is strongly recommended, since without their help, it will be difficult to develop the understanding of the key story elements.

6 Making Good Stories Great!

The range of entrepreneur stories presented in *Shark Tank* has often left me amazed and inspired while also motivating young entrepreneurs to live their dream! Since its launch in 2009, *Shark Tank* has aired 9 seasons and 199 episodes, with an average of four start-up pitches per episode. And while the business proposal itself is key, there are only a few stories that find a deeper connect with both the audience and investors.

* * * *

Movies and books are our avenues to escape the real world and live the fictional story of another. All of us have stayed up nights while on a movie marathon or while reading a book which we just couldn't put down. An average person watches 20–30 movies and reads 4 books in a year. How many of these movies and books can you remember? How many you think have left a mark on you in some way?

IT NEEDS A LITTLE POLISHING

Stories are all around us, but not all stories are equally effective and impactful. Some strike the right chord and hence leave a deeper mark on us than others do. And while every storyteller puts in his best effort to convey a great story, I have often found that the differentiating factor between a good story and a great story lies in giving the last finishing touches while bringing it all together. The story wheel and narrative give us a strong story foundation whose true impact will be realized only when all parts fit together perfectly, with suitable angles adorning the right parts of the structure.

Often, I come across people who are genuinely good with their writing and also make high-quality charts. Naturally, they fail to understand why their stories don't leave a mark! A common answer I have in such situations: 'You have a good story, it just needs a little polishing to make it stand out', which is typically the last 5 per cent of our story-building process. It's like when painting the walls of your home, if you apply only one coat, it might suffice your current need, but there is no guarantee that it will stick until the end of the year. But when you give the second finishing coat, the deep colour shows better and you can be more confident about the colour lasting for a longer time.

The last 5 per cent time spent on polishing the story can make all the difference.

On most occasions, when people create data stories, their focus is only on getting the right 'characters' and 'events' that make the story, which by itself does not guarantee a great story. While important, it is just like the first coat of paint; it isn't enough. How these characters and events unfold in the story makes all the difference. It is the second coat of paint which will determine how well and how long the story will stick.

A data story leaves a mark when it has the ability to engage and enable the desired audience. When it generates and maintains interest throughout the story while also providing new knowledge tools, it calls for a powerful and impactful data story.

In this chapter, we discuss some simple and important aspects which once enveloped in our story can help us achieve just that!

The data analysis incorporated in the story wheel and narrative give the most compelling parts of the story. The factors discussed in this chapter ensure that those compelling aspects exert the power and impact we want them to.

GET THEM HOOKED!

It is every storyteller's dream to tell a captivating story. A smart three-pronged approach (Figure 6.1) can help sail through this feat with ease:

1. **Hitting the target:** A storyteller must cater to the audience's requirements, and this is a mandatory checklist for him/her. This helps in making the audience curious about the theme of the story and what it has to offer.
2. **Keep your story interesting:** Like a movie, you need to maintain the rhythm and continually surprise them with interesting insights.

Figure 6.1 The Three-pronged Engagement Funnel

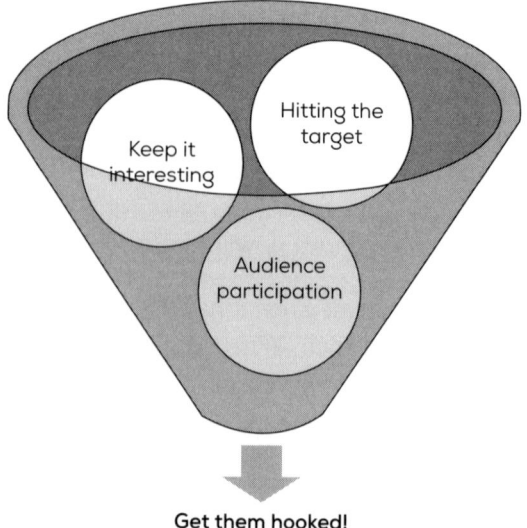

Keep it interesting

Hitting the target

Audience participation

Get them hooked!

3. **Audience participation:** Dragging a point makes no sense, as your audience may just hang up to the boredom of your story. They should participate in the story by agreeing with the conclusions and start thinking from the storyteller's perspective.

HIT THE BULL'S EYE

The simplest way to grab someone's attention is to give them what they are looking for.

On a hot summer afternoon, after running around completing some errands, you stop at one of the local stores and ask for a cold bottle of water. The shopkeeper, a very kind old gentleman, is about to start drinking his hot cup of afternoon tea and for some reason he hands it over to you. You are touched by his gesture, but you respectfully decline because all you can think of in that scorching May heat is a sip of cold water! Very politely, you ask him for a cold bottle of water; he again hands over the cup of tea. After trying another two–three times, you either drink the tea because you don't want to be rude or, irritated with the heat, you simply walk outside and towards the next store in the hope to find what you need so that you can finally quench your thirst!

No matter how good or kind a certain person or their product is, if they don't understand your need and are unable to meet your requirement, they will not be able to get your interest or attention.

The simplest way to grab someone's attention is to give them what they need. Identification of the story's purpose and the audience's understanding developed in the first stage of the story wheel come in handy here. We will have hit the bull's eye when we are able to align our data and story to the audience's need.

An improper assessment of either of these can lead to audience distraction and lost focus and interest.

A problem most compounded in reporting stories is the tendency to report only facts and not insights. This gets further aggravated in situations wherein standard periodic presentation formats haven't changed for years! In such situations especially, it is recommended to periodically review the purpose and audience's understanding to ensure that the data story still remains relevant.

* * * *

The finance and planning department of a diversified conglomerate in India prepares a quarterly presentation that shows management how far the company has succeeded in achieving its budget for the year. An AVP from this team was struggling to leave an impact on the management using the standard data and format where the same factual information was being provided slide after slide. The use of the same line and bar charts throughout the presentation did not help either. My prompt suggestion was: 'Don't simply compare budget versus actual numbers across items. Think about how and why they are likely to use this information. Then try to incorporate those elements in your story' (Figure 6.2).

The management is typically interested in the budget variance so that they can make decisions that help the company stay on course. And while the purpose of this story is not to make this decision for them, when you make this variance, the 'star' of the story while also showing its drivers, you are leading them towards the next crucial step of their decision-making process, thus 'giving them what they need'.

Figure 6.2 Make the Star Shine

What Most People Do

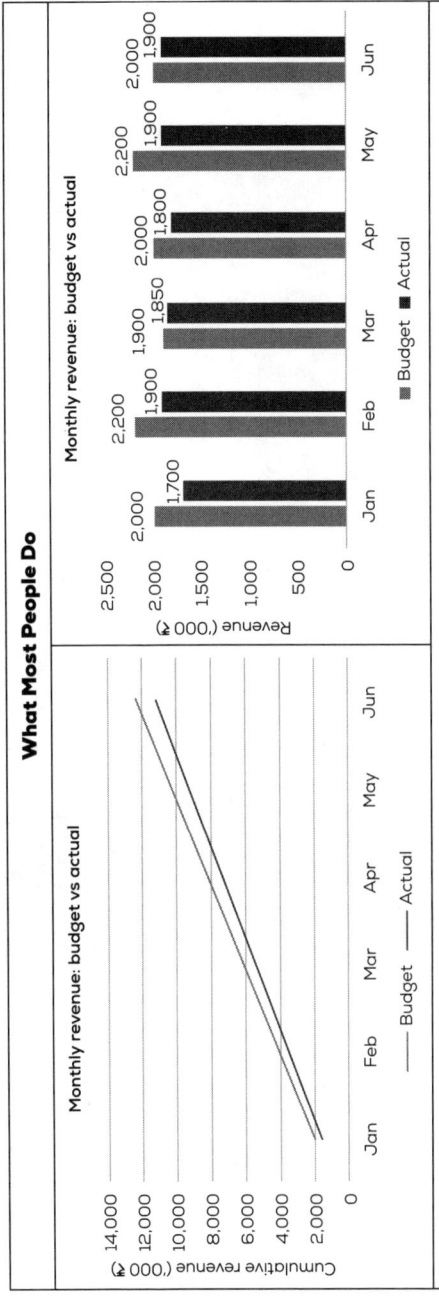

- In the first two quarters of the year, the company recorded a total revenue of ₹11,050,000, which came in lower by ₹1,250,000 when compared to budgeted revenue of ₹12,300,000.
- A negative revenue variance was recorded in every month of 2018. January, February and May recorded the highest variance with revenue shortfall of 300,000, while March had the least negative variance of 50,000.

(Figure 6.2 continued)

(Figure 6.2 continued)

What We Should Be Doing

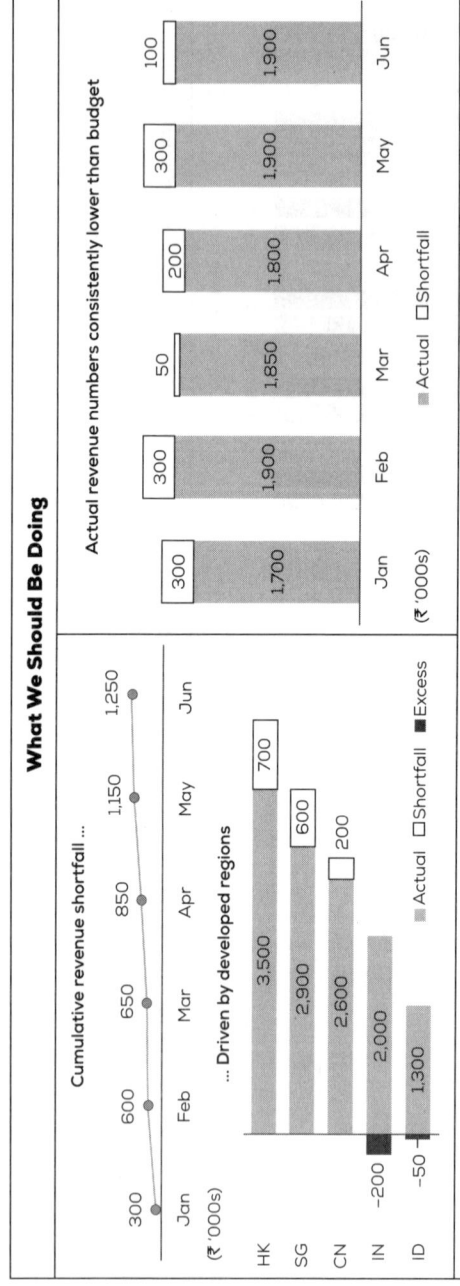

Actual revenue numbers consistently lower than budget

(₹ '000s)

	Jan	Feb	Mar	Apr	May	Jun
Shortfall	300	300	50	200	300	100
Actual	1,700	1,900	1,850	1,800	1,900	1,900

■ Actual □ Shortfall

Cumulative revenue shortfall ...

(₹ '000s)

Jan	Feb	Mar	Apr	May	Jun
300	600	650	850	1,150	1,250

... Driven by developed regions

HK	3,500 / 700
SG	2,900 / 600
CN	2,600 / 200
IN	2,000 / −200
ID	1,300 / −50

■ Actual □ Shortfall ■ Excess

- The company recorded a revenue of ₹11,050,000 in the first half of the year, with a negative variance of ₹1,250,000 from the budgeted ₹12,300,000. And while this poor performance was recorded across months, there are clear distinctions at the regional level.

- Developed regions—Hong Kong and Singapore are primarily responsible for this poor performance, wherein the revenue has come in about 20% lower than their respective budgets.

- Emerging countries like India and Indonesia, on the other hand, witnessed a successful first half with actual revenues surpassing the budget by 9% and 4% respectively.

Note: The above data has been generated for explanatory purposes only.

* * * *

The head of institutional sales at one of the country's top mutual fund houses was once exploring how his sales team, comprising primarily of relationship managers, can improve the impact of their communication with institutional clients. They wanted to achieve this by specifically incorporating a few elements to improve the chances of scoring an investment mandate.

The sales team relies on a common sales pitch when talking to potential clients and investors. It typically discusses various fund categories and their performance and holdings over a period of time. Like any salesperson looking for a grand opening, these relationship managers tend to begin their pitch with the 'best numbers', albeit the difference lies in defining the 'best numbers' for each client.

Going back to the basics, I said: 'Know the investor (audience) and pitch the numbers that would "interest him"'. When following this approach, the biggest change is that a common sales pitch cannot be used by every salesperson across all clients. This generic pitch or presentation deck demands minor changes with every new client to suit their requirements.

When approaching a pension fund investor, we first acknowledge their need for stable returns with low to moderate risk and direct our presentation on funds that fit this bucket. But with a high-net-worth individual (HNI), we change our tactic and focus on diverse investment options to gain high portfolio returns.

Table 6.1 gives a snapshot of how the information order can change to meet the needs of different clients.

* * * *

While reviewing credit appraisal proposals written at one of India's top private banks, I was slightly taken aback when reading this statement in the very beginning of a proposal: 'The company's name is derived from three words abcde + fghij + Ayurveda and

Table 6.1 Sequence Matters

Standard Presentation		Pension Fund Client		HNI Client	
1.	Fund performance table—all products	1.	Fund performance table—core funds	1.	Fund performance table—all
2.	Core funds—all	2.	Core funds—all	2.	Tactical funds
3.	Peripheral funds—all	3.	Peripheral—dividend yield	3.	Peripheral—mid-cap
4.	Tactical funds			4.	Core funds—all

the name was conceived by the grandfather of director xyz.' In decision stories, like the credit appraisal proposal or equity research report, one should include only those factors—both positives and negatives—which will enhance the audience's decision-making ability. If a certain piece of information (like the statement above) does not lead the audience towards making a decision, it does not have a place in the story.

* * * *

In probing stories, one should be vigilant to present a complete picture and not just a one-sided story. Since, by nature, such stories offer new information, the audience might not be able to catch hold of the missing information, but they will find loopholes. When probing regional sales performance at a corporate, the strategy team was leading to a conclusion that 'emerging markets are the next big opportunity to drive sales'. A complete picture in this scenario includes not only the positive revenue growth of these regions but also an increase in their relative sales contribution while also discussing potential challenges to growth along with mitigants.

The bottom line: Leverage the understanding of your audience to identify and focus on those aspects which help serve their purpose best.

INTRODUCTION MATTERS

On one of my long and tiring airport waits, I encountered an amusing incident that taught me a big lesson on human behaviour.

In the seating row opposite me was a young mother trying to spoon-feed her child while he constantly kept getting distracted by the wide open space that he was using as his own little runway. Exasperated, the mother showed him a big bar of chocolate, telling him that he will get it the moment he finishes his food. She held the chocolate in one hand, feeding with another. All the while, the child's eyes remained transfixed on the chocolate. He quickly finished the food, snatched the bar from his mother's hand and ran away, leaving a content look on her face and an amused smile on mine.

Getting attention from your audience is not very different from getting a child's attention, wherein you want them to first listen to you and then do as you tell them to. When you first show them what they are getting at the end of it all, they are likely to pay more attention.

Breaking the norm and beginning the story with the most important part, which could be your 'aha moment' or a glimpse into the conclusion, can get the audience hooked.

Most people have a habit to present information in a chronological order, something I do not always agree with. Beginning the story with the most important part—which could be a taste of your 'aha moment' or the conclusion—and then leading to the rest of the analysis helps keep the audience gripped. An introduction, typically in the form of a headline or title, is the key to grab initial audience interest. In data storytelling, there is no place for jargons and proverbs. Using catchy titles without supporting them with relevant discussions in the upcoming story will not help either. Hence, beginning with an important piece of information is the best bet to get them hooked.

* * * *

Don't introduce yourself as a salesperson, but walk in as a solution provider for the client's needs.

Pitch stories rely heavily on attractive introductions because there is high competition in effectively using the audience's 'brain time'. The introduction is particularly important for sales-persons, and I always recommend introducing themselves as solution providers. Begin by showing the client that you under-stand their problem or issue and are there to provide solutions for the same. When pitching the mutual fund to an HNI, one could begin with: 'We have a special recommendation for our HNI clients which can enable them to earn high returns by taking only a moderate risk exposure....' For the pension fund, one could begin as: 'We understand your need for stable returns and limited risk-taking capacity, and we have a unique fund offering which will help you achieve just that....'

* * * *

By their nature, probing stories have a wide scope, and hence it becomes pertinent to set the right context at the very beginning so that the audience can get on to your thought trail. When probing regional growth opportunity, if we use an introduction as 'Hong Kong contributes 31 per cent to 2017 revenue and reported a drop in revenue by 2 per cent at \$118 million in 2017 versus \$120 million in 2016...,' the audience might perceive this story as a performance update for Hong Kong and may be other regions.

But when we begin with 'Hong Kong and Singapore continue to dominate regional sales; however, losing some ground to emerging countries…,' we give them an indication that this is not just a performance update, but it also gives clear conclusions of disparate performance across regions which can be perceived as a road to decision-making.

* * * *

The need for setting the right context and tone at the very beginning is quite important in decision stories, wherein I recommend using a summary at the very beginning of the report, as is commonly done in most equity research reports. Reading a summary is like peeping through a window to gain knowledge of everything that's going on inside. Using the story map as a backbone of this summary ensures that all the key themes, events and conclusions have been mirrored in.

The bottom line: Begin with the pertinent information which you believe will hook your audience and make them eager to learn more from your story. Leverage on the findings from the last two stages of the story wheel.

Table 6.2 First Impressions Matter

Introductions—Best Avoided	Introductions—Preferred
Monthly revenue: Budget vs actual	Actual revenue numbers consistently lower than budget
FMCG market in India is expected to grow at a CAGR of 22.6% and is expected to reach $113.9 billion by 2020 from $50 billion in 2016	Favourable demographics and rise in income level to boost India's FMCG market which is expected to grow at a CAGR of 22.6%
ABC reported 6% cigarette volume decline and 8% EBIT growth on QoQ improvement in cigarette demand	ABC reported 8% EBIT growth driven by improved cigarette demand, wherein volume decline came in at a lower 6% (earlier 8%)

Note: The above data has been generated for explanatory purposes only.

MAINTAIN THE PACE

Movie trailers, book titles and newspaper headlines can all be attractive and enthralling and have often sucked us into giving time to their respective stories. But so many times, in the first few minutes itself, we realize that there is no meat to the matter! After the introduction, the story just falls flat.

An exercise used in my storytelling training sessions requires the trainees to critically evaluate a few data stories. One such story has a very catchy title that trainees find interesting: 'Unkind Cut after Note Ban'. But as they start moving along the story, their interest starts waning as the multiple GDP growth rate comparisons make the story rather confusing and all pieces just don't fit together.

To ensure that the story keeps the audience hooked all throughout, we need to constantly keep feeding their requirement while also providing new information at every stage. Even one piece of information—like describing the meaning of the company's name—which does not serve the audience's purpose, will be enough to set them off into their dream world. The thematic structure developed in the story map serves as a blueprint to help achieve this.

* * * *

The corporate banking division of a bank presents corporate loan appraisal proposals in the monthly credit committee meeting, wherein at least 8–10 proposals are reviewed within a span of 4–5 hours. The credit analyst from a top Indian bank wanted to understand how he could convey this story and receive an 'approval stamp' within a limited time frame while also leaving a mark for himself as a good analyst.

Presenting the fundamental analysis of a company in this case becomes quite a challenging task because of the multiple aspects that go to either support or contradict an overall recommendation. This is further compounded by the quantum of information required to make a responsible business decision. A perfect solution-oriented approach here is to use a thematic structure to break down the story into multiple sections with new insights and conclusions at each stage as depicted in Tables 6.3 and 6.4.

Table 6.3 Keep It Coming: Corporate Credit Proposal

Theme	Potential Insight	Link with Overall Conclusion
Corporate Background	Diversified business with long vintage and stable earnings	Supports approval recommendation
Business Operations	• Stagnating revenue from key region • Planned product facelift to support future growth	Mitigant reduces impact of identified risk, hence supporting approval recommendation
Financial Performance	Liquidity strong, leverage manageable in spite of stagnating revenue	Supports approval recommendation
Industry Analysis	Mature industry. However company has constantly re-invented its products to stay ahead of the curve	Mitigant reduces impact of identified risk, hence supporting approval recommendation

Table 6.4 Keep It Coming: Regional Performance

Theme One: Dominant regions	Hong Kong and Singapore continue to dominate regional sales, however losing some ground as 2017 revenue dropped by 2% and 3% respectively, reducing their revenue contribution to 53% in 2017 from 57% in 2016.	New insight: Dominant regions lacking in growth
Theme Two: Future growth drivers	Emerging markets such as India, Malaysia and Thailand, on the other hand, recorded strong revenue generation with an annual growth between 14% and 19%, thus increasing their revenue contribution to 24% in 2017 from 21% in 2016, also making them the future growth drivers for the company's revenue generation.	New insight: These regions to be centre of attention

(Table 6.4 continued)

(Table 6.4 continued)

Theme Three: No impact, for information purposes only	China maintains its significance with a marginal 4% revenue growth, while Indonesia and Vietnam perform poorly on both absolute and relative grounds.	**New insight:** These regions do not have much significance for future decision-making

Note: The above data has been generated for explanatory purposes only.

> *The bottom line: Leverage the thematic structure from the story map to maintain the pace of the story by providing new insights for every theme.*

KEEP THE DOPAMINE FLOWING

Providing a constant doze of new and interesting information is the best way to keep the dopamine flowing and grip the audience's attention. We have all at some point experienced those thriller movies which made us sit at the edge of our seats and we wouldn't want to bat an eyelid. A data story doesn't have to be dramatic in the above sense, yet it should be so effective that the audience is engrossed.

GIVE YOUR AUDIENCE SOMETHING NEW AND DIFFERENT

The first step is to ask 'What does the audience not know?' and focus on providing information in that area. In addition to the overall 'newness' of the story, focus on providing fresh information at each stage of the thematic story structure. By the time their interest starts waning, they would have most likely reached a new section where they will again get something new to re-grab their interest.

* * * *

The biggest investment banks publish hundreds of equity research reports among themselves daily, most of which come out with the same recommendation for a given stock, albeit at different target prices. One equity research analyst from a well-known Indian investment bank was worried how he could make his report stand out from the rest. The answer lies in providing a new and compelling piece of analysis that can directly impact the decision-making.

In equity research reports about ITC Ltd, while every analyst discussed the segmental revenue mix of the cigarette and FMCG businesses in the light of waning cigarette demand and increasing FMCG sales, there was one analyst who introduced a new angle to ITC's diversification story and hence the basis of the stock recommendation.

This particular story provided an insight into the government's tax collection, leading to an inference that tax collected from the cigarette industry did not make any significant contribution to the exchequers tax collections, which was only 2 per cent. Further, this contribution has been falling over the years and thus the government is not dependent on cigarette taxes as a major source of income. The report concluded that expectations of higher cigarette taxes in light of the country's fiscal stress are overstated and thus unlikely to translate into higher tax expense for ITC.

Give an 'Aha' Moment

Another guaranteed way to keep the dopamine flowing is to give them an 'aha moment'—information presented at this point makes the story interesting and irresistible. Going back to the fifth stage of the story wheel, the most important part of a story is that part of your data analysis which is not obvious to the audience.

I'm often asked a question: 'What if there is nothing new in my data? My data is the same MIS I pull every month and there is really nothing new in that data!'

When one thinks that 'there is nothing new in their data; it's all the same month after month', they are focusing on the characters and not the events. The characters could remain the same, but events don't remain the same because the numbers keep changing. To find newness even in the regular monthly MIS, we begin by unearthing the data layers and start linking the 'whats' to the 'whys'.

> *There is always something new in data. If the number changes, it is new information and if it doesn't change, it is still a new event on which a story can be built.*

* * * *

I once sat down with a gentleman working in the home loan department of an Indian housing finance company to tackle this problem of 'nothing new'. We had in front of us an MIS report, in the form of a table detailing home loans sold in India across a few states, further granulized by income, profession and ticket size. To him, it seemed like a sea of numbers in which he was drowning. Worried, he asked me: 'I have to make a presentation with this data and I don't know how to go about it. How to give them a good story when there is nothing new in my data?'

After a few leading questions, we were able to come to a logical assessment of the management's purpose from this task. A requirement for analysing periodical sales data first translates into a performance assessment, further leading to insights into future growth opportunities.

The first aspect here is very straightforward and, hence, the key focus area of most stories. The second aspect on the contrary is never obviously stated nor directly visible from the data; but it is there if you can find it. This will prove to be the 'new' factor which you possibly discovered as the story's 'aha' moment during the story wheel.

A quick run through the numbers and in less than 10 minutes, we had identified a particular Indian state with a relatively higher sales figure for the performance assessment. Bulk of these sales were concentrated in the small–medium ticket size, even for the higher income groups—this identified the opportunity as a potential to grow large-ticket-size loans for higher income groups.

Old Wine in a New Bottle

If there is nothing new in your data, then simply present the same data in a new attractive way, at the same time not shocking the audience by doing something completely different.

In every training programme, trainees show me their work presentations comprising slides full of similar looking charts, with a hope that we could give them a facelift. Even with simple changes to the chart types, we are often able to present a fresh story in a new format (Figure 6.3).

Reporting stories are often in need of a facelift because finding a new story each month might become challenging. And while we are bound by the standard corporate templates and formats, there is still scope to make them appear new. We can do this through either selection of different chart types or use of props to showcase the 'aha' moment or the 'star' of the story. More on this has been discussed in Chapter 8, but to put it in two lines, we can use titles, shapes and colours on charts as props that can help highlight certain key aspects and bring out something different in the same charts.

The bottom line: Focus on new information; dig deeper to uncover data layers or simply present the same information in a newer format.

Figure 6.3 An Attractive New Packaging

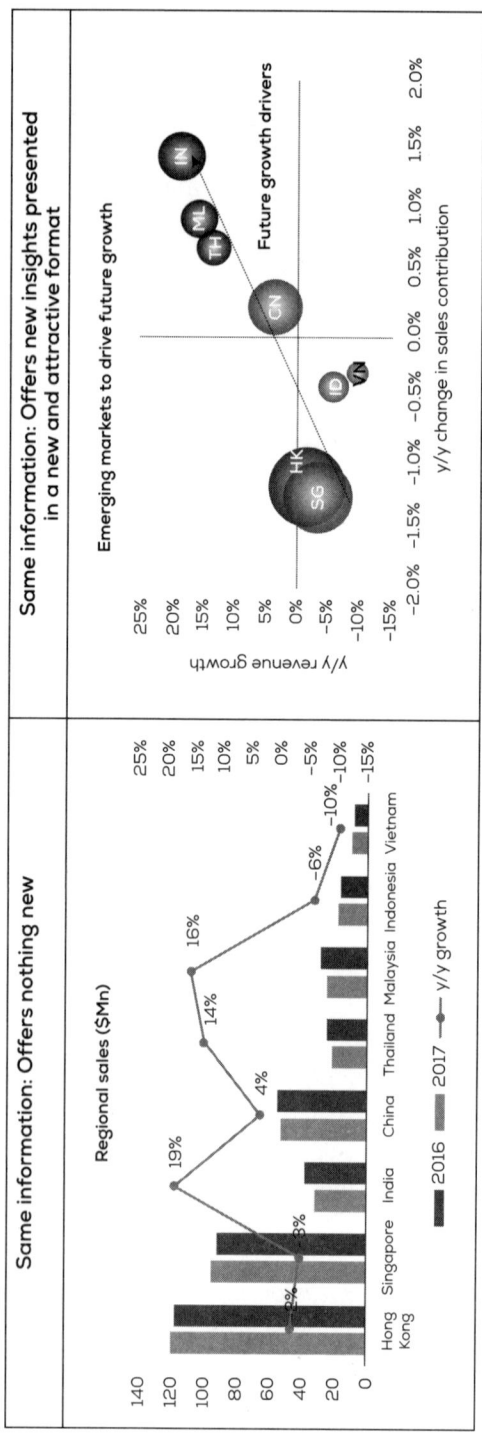

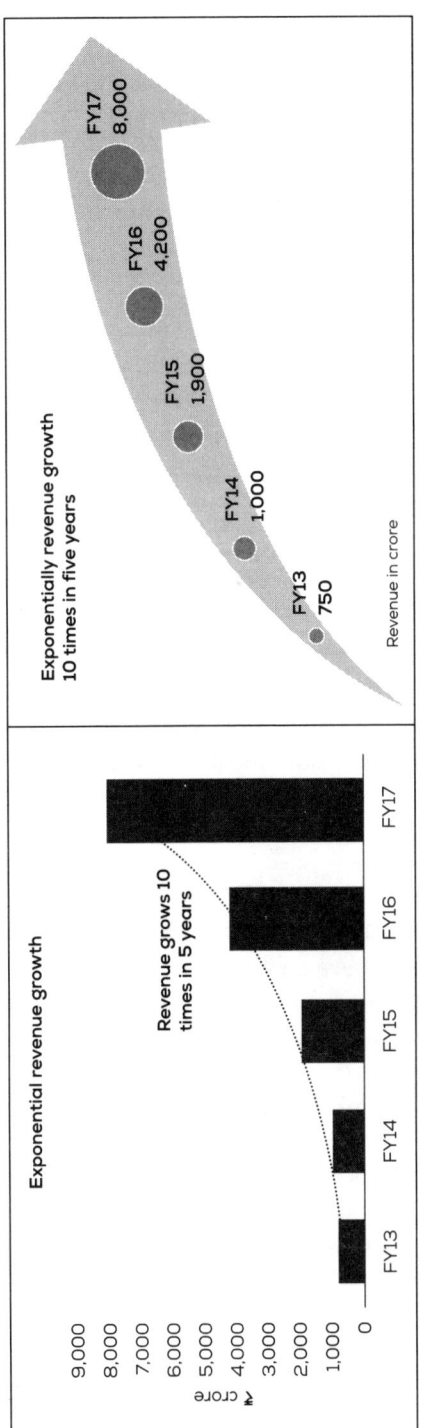

Exponential revenue growth

₹ crore

9,000
8,000
7,000
6,000
5,000
4,000
3,000
2,000
1,000
0

Revenue grows 10 times in 5 years

FY13 FY14 FY15 FY16 FY17

Exponentially revenue growth 10 times in five years

FY17 8,000

FY16 4,200

FY15 1,900

FY14 1,000

FY13 750

Revenue in crore

Note: The above data has been generated for explanatory purposes only.

INTRODUCE AN ELEMENT OF EMOTION

Antonio Damasio, a Portuguese–American neuroscientist, as part of his breakthrough research, famously coined the phrase:

> *We are not thinking machines. We are feeling machines that think.*

Emotions are an integral part of all stories as they help the audience connect better with the story and the storyteller. Emotions come in different forms, all of which meet the same purpose, that is, connecting and engaging your audience while also influencing their thought process.

When we think of emotions, the first things to come to the mind are 'happy', 'sad' and 'angry', and hence people often find the idea of emotions in a data story a little absurd. They are used to seeing data as dry figures and facts and hence struggle to appreciate how these emotions can become a part of data stories. And while data stories might not arouse these core feelings and emotions, they have immense potential to trigger associated layers and branches of these emotions.

To help navigate through this not-so-straightforward element and make its application easier, I have developed 'The Circle of Emotions' (Figure 6.4). This works as a guide with respect to different types of emotions which can be introduced in data stories along with associated situations which can trigger the emotion.

Curiosity and surprise are two emotions that are easy to envelope in data stories and find a deep connection with the audience. To generate curiosity, focus on bringing out the story's 'aha' moment or provide a glimpse into the story's conclusion. Curiosity will make the audience want to know more, getting them hooked on to the rest of the story.

'Curiosity' plays a relatively bigger role in pitching and probing stories since getting the audience hooked from the very beginning

Figure 6.4 The Circle of Emotions

is pivotal to ensure that they appreciate and hopefully agree with our idea or product. When the mutual fund relationship manager begins with: 'We have a special recommendation for our HNI clients which can enable them to earn high returns with only moderate risk exposure....,' he is able to address the investors' key concern, which makes them want to know more about this 'special recommendation' and thus make them attentive and interested.

Story titles help a great deal in generating curiosity even in standard reporting or decision stories. Titles such as 'Three Cost Control Strategies to Improve the Bottom Line' or 'Emerging Markets to Lead the Next Growth Cycle' from the strategy and analytics team; 'Higher Attrition in South Region Becoming a Cause of Concern' by the HR reporting team; 'India Equities: Macro Headwinds Cloud over Earnings Recovery' or 'ABC Ltd—Healthy Cash Flows to Unlock Value' by an equity research analyst, all play a similar role in generating audience curiosity.

At the time of generating curiosity with titles, ensure that the upcoming story has sufficient information to validate the point you made.

'Pitch and probe' stories by their nature have a wide scope to 'surprise' an audience, as the topic itself is new on most occasions. Adding an element of surprise, however, becomes pivotal in the standard reporting and decision stories. An HR manager probing attrition rates across regions was able to surprise the audience by bringing a compelling new insight, suggesting that the attrition rate was specifically higher in the 0–3 year experience vintage (largely campus recruits), further recommending steps to lower it.

* * * *

Pride or disappointment can be achieved by showcasing positive or negative aspects which an audience can associate with. The moments when you felt proud or were disappointed are hard to forget. You are even likely to remember the reasons and circumstances that led you to feel those emotions. 'Remember the praise your boss showered on you during a town hall meeting?'

Typically, performance figures for a character that the audience identifies with can generate pride or disappointing emotions. It could be the positive or negative profit and sales performance of a company or department, profit or loss on an investment portfolio, lower or higher attrition rates or even the GDP performance of a country.

Underachievement reported in the quarterly budget update by the financial planning analyst first disappoints the management. While this lingers on their mind, the positive emerging market performance shows them a way out. This act of finding a solution to overcome a setback instils a feeling of pride and accomplishment.

* * * *

Admiration can be triggered when someone has overachieved their objective or benchmark. Admiration for something or someone makes us want to be like them and hence learn everything about how they achieved it. This strong desire to learn gets the audience hooked. To trigger this emotion, one needs to diligently outline the overachievement along with the road map that led to this overachievement.

Securing the audience's admiration can translate into a big win for a pitch story. When trying to sell an idea or a product to a prospective client, if we can get them to admire our product or idea, it gets us much closer to sealing the deal.

In 2016, the technology head at an Indian private bank made a recommendation to increase investment in artificial intelligence. As the world moves towards fintech, the necessity of this investment proposal was a no-brainer, but including bank case studies in the presentation was a game changer. This story instilled higher confidence in the management team, as they now admired the results that were achieved with such an investment.

* * * *

An evident risk makes the audience 'cautious'. The gravity of the situation with potential negative consequences makes them more attentive. When the crux of the story lies in any material risks that the audience should be wary about, it is prudent to highlight them upfront so that the audience becomes alert and attentive from the beginning.

Probing, reporting and decision stories can often have a negative connotation, wherein we want to caution the audience about something. The strategy and analytics team can raise caution to the management on the over-usage of discounts to increase market share by showing how discounts hurt profitability. The use of the right title 'Discounts—Top Line Positive but Detrimental on Bottom Line' immediately cautions the audience and thus makes them attentive and engaged.

Figure 6.5 Emotional Journey of a Data Story

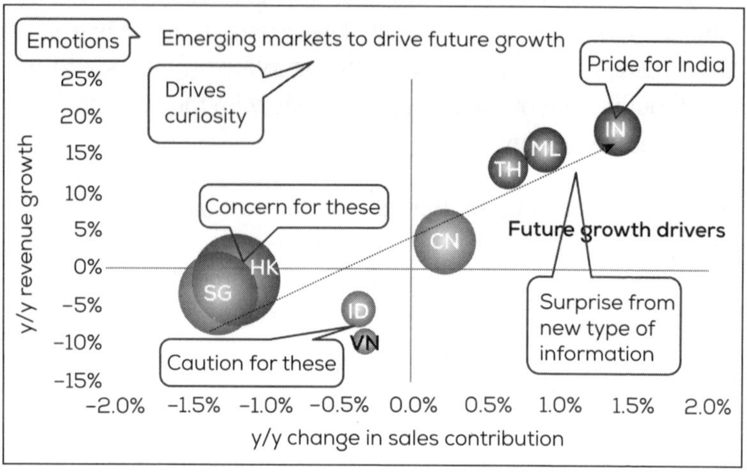

Note: The above data has been generated for explanatory purposes only.

In an equity research report, the caution generated through the report should be visible in the summary as well. For ITC Ltd, the key risk of falling cigarette demand is an elephant in the room that should be addressed right upfront, as this feeling of caution will keep the audience attentive.

Figure 6.5 shows how these emotions get generated through a data story.

> *The bottom line: Use the circle of emotions to find and incorporate story aspects that help generate emotions in the story.*

FORM DATA PATTERNS

Humans are the world's best pattern recognition machines with an ability to transform these patterns into concrete, actionable steps. When the flow of information allows the audience to form patterns, their brain can better process such information and relate it to an upcoming conclusion. Resulting in 'coupling of minds' where the audience's thought processes are aligned with the storytellers, it encourages audience participation and thus engagement.

The right analytical or logical flow of information can be achieved when one piece of information intuitively leads to the next. All pieces together lead to an upcoming conclusion. The groundwork for this has already been done in the story map's thematic structure.

Figure 6.6 Patterns Change Perception

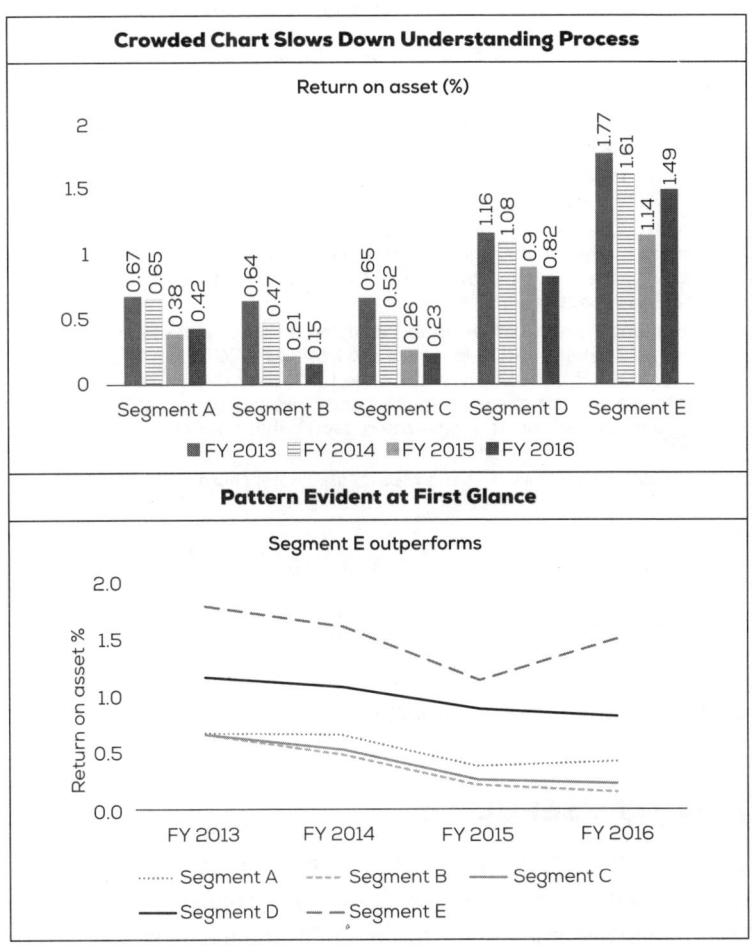

(*Figure 6.6 continued*)

(Figure 6.6 continued)

Only Information Being Presented
• Return on assets (ROA) of Segment A declined from 0.67% in FY 2013 to 0.42% in FY 2016.
• Segment B witnessed the highest decline in ROA compared to all other segments to a mere 0.15% in FY 2016 from 0.64% in FY 2013.
• A steep decline was also seen in Segment C where ROA declined from 0.65% in FY 2013 to 0.23% in FY 2016.
• Segment D's ROA decline was contained to 0.82% in FY 2016 from 1.16% in FY 2013.
• ROA of Segment E increased to 1.5% in FY 2016 from 1.14% in FY 2015; however, it is still lower than the 1.77% recorded in FY 2013.
Clear Themes Can Be Understood
• ROA across all segments have decreased over the past few years with the highest impact seen in Segments B and C, where almost half of the ROA was wiped off from FY 2013 to FY 2016. During this period, ROA at these segments reduced from 0.64% to 0.15% and 0.65% to 0.23% respectively.
• The ROA reduction at Segments A and D was largely contained, driven by their wide regional presence. During FY 2013–FY 2016, ROA for these segments reduced from 0.67% to 0.42% and 1.16% to 0.82% respectively.
• Segment E, on the other hand, recorded a slight recovery in the last year, wherein ROA increased to 1.5% in FY 2016 from 1.14% in FY 2015, albeit still lower than the 1.77% recorded in FY 2013. Adherence to strict service norms and presence across select regions only is believed to be the reason behind this recovery.

Note: The above data has been generated for explanatory purposes only.

In a visual story, presentation and decoding of these patterns become fairly simpler as all the information is presented at the same time. As storytellers, all we do is direct the audience towards the patterns we want them to find. Something that can be easily achieved with the use of simple props.

MAKE IT USEFUL

Since ancient times, stories have been used as tools to teach lessons and make messages stick. This enabling function of storytelling becomes all the more significant in data stories where

Figure 6.7 Problem-solving Funnel

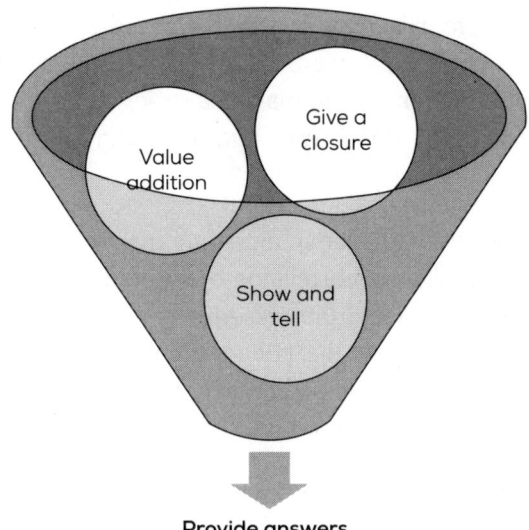

Provide answers

the business audience comes with clear expectations to either increase their knowledge or aid their decision-making.

A similar three-pronged approach (Figure 6.7) helps stories don the role of problem-solvers, providing answers to a business audience:

1. **Value addition:** Let your audience go back with a feeling of having enhanced their existing knowledge.
2. **Give a closure:** Don't leave your stories open for interpretation. Make a clear conclusion to give them a closure.
3. **Show and tell:** Make your conclusions stick by getting the audience to agree with them.

Value Addition

At the end of the story, if the audience goes back thinking 'That was something new and interesting', 'This will help me in...', 'I did not know about this', 'I did not look at it from this perspective before', then you have enabled them by enhancing and adding value to their pre-existing knowledge. When the audience leaves with such an emotion, they are likely to be satisfied with the time spent on the story. The key to making a strong value addition is to focus on what they don't know and addressing that with clear conclusions.

Showing a positive variance in emerging markets by the finance team, focus on negative correlation between discount and profit by the strategy team and the reason behind the higher attrition in region 4 discussed by the HR reporting team are all simple insights which provide value addition to the audience.

Give a Closure

When the story does not have a clear conclusion or outcome, it may feel unfinished and leave the audience frustrated, often raising the questions: So what does this mean? 'Is this the right interpretation?' 'What does this imply for my line of business?' A conclusion gives them a closure, enables some form of decision-making and makes their time well spent.

A conclusion could be something as simple as a conclusive statement: 'Strong revenue generation recorded across all segments' for reporting stories; it could be an exploratory conclusion: 'Negative budget variance driven by developed regions', or a result-oriented conclusion: 'Discounts while positive for top line are detrimental to the bottom line' in reporting and probing stories. It could also be a decisive conclusion: 'Buy XYZ stock for a target price of 140 and 20 per cent price return' in decision and pitch stories; it could be a detailed action plan: 'Fintech investment recommended in a phased manner beginning with...' in pitch, decision and probing stories.

Show and Tell

Stories influence an audience when they 'show' why and how we arrived at a certain conclusion and don't just 'tell' or state the conclusion. They also add credibility to our own work as an analyst since they enable audience participation and agreement to our point of view.

In spite of the whole industry buzzing about fintech investment, the technology head will be unable to impact an audience by just stating, 'This investment is the future of the business'. They will be able to drive this point better by showing linkages with potential monetary benefits of such an investment, thus focusing on the why and how.

The bottom line: Back up an interesting beginning with a strong and insightful analysis that provides a value-add and leads to a conclusion. It is important to give a closure with a conclusion and also show why and how you arrive at the conclusion.

SHOWTIME!

Figure 6.8 Attributes That Make a Great Story

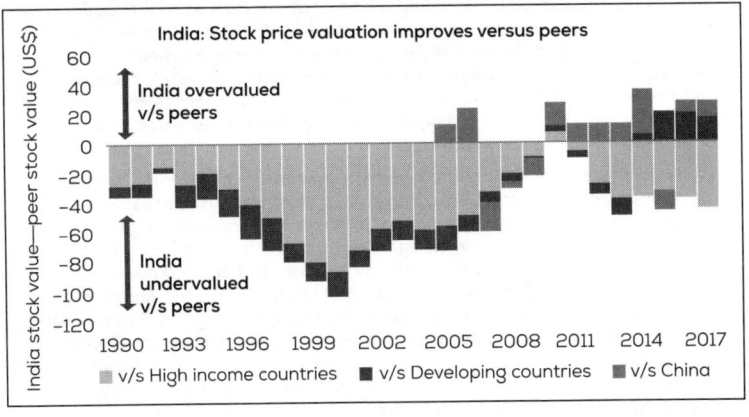

(Figure 6.8 continued)

(Figure 6.8 continued)

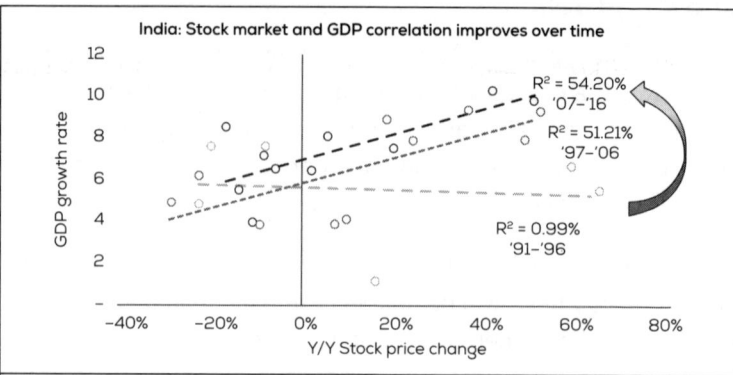

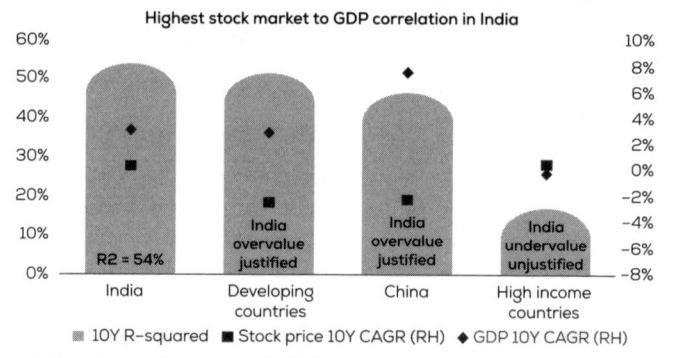

India: Improving Stock Valuations versus Peers Justified

The NIFTY 50 closed 2017 recording a gain of about 89% with S&P BSE Sensex in tow at an annual return of about 78% in 2017. As all-time high index levels were breached during the year, investors' worry of overheated and overvalued stock market valuations are not completely unjustified, especially in a year where government policy initiatives took a toll over the country's GDP. In this report, we take a deep dive to assess how India's stock valuations compare to other regions in the world.

Indian stock valuations show improvement over the last 25 years, wherein from being largely undervalued compared to most regions in the 1990s, they are now overvalued compared to China and other developing markets while the undervaluation ratio to high income countries has reduced in the last decade. We further find that not only has the correlation between stock market returns and GDP growth improved in India, but at an R-squared of 54.2% (2007–2016), it is also the highest among all the regions. This leads us to believe that the Indian stock market overvaluation compared to China and other developing countries is justified, whereas the noticeable undervaluation compared to high-income countries is not justified on the back of decoupling between the stock valuations and fundamentals in such regions.

Source: data.worldbank.org; www.nseindia.com

Note: The above data is for explanatory purposes only.

WHAT MAKES THE STORY POWERFUL AND IMPACTFUL?

1. Directly addressing the audience's key concern, which is understanding the story behind India's stock market valuations.
2. Title and attractive visuals with an interesting introduction also generate curiosity.
3. An introductory paragraph gives a complete context and background information about the topic.
4. The three different visuals supported with the write-up continually offer new information, adding an element of surprise while maintaining the pace throughout the story.
5. The titles generate curiosity, followed by surprise through the new insights and pride and admiration for India's improving valuations relative to other countries.
6. The order of information presented through the three visuals and in the write-up follows a logical link that leads to the conclusion. The story shows clear patterns on why and how we reached the conclusion.
7. There is value addition through the new information at every step of the story, which facilated with the concluding titles gives a complete closure to the audience.

By the time we approach the end of any report or presentation, it is natural to feel tired and exhausted and leave out that little part at the end, thinking that it will not make any difference either way. But if your experience has been anything like mine, you will be quick to agree that it is those last few minutes and the final finishing touches that 'do make' all the difference. To ensure that the last-minute pressure doesn't make you miss out on these important aspects, it is prudent to develop an understanding of these at the story-building stages so that they start getting incorporated right from the initial stages when crafting the story.

 Writer to Storyteller

It has often been said, 'Stories have always been shared over a good meal.' Have you ever wondered the reason behind the strong camaraderie between the two? Cooking is a therapeutic creative act just like writing, which is another important form of art. I love to whip up my family's favourite dishes. But I don't follow any standard recipes with fixed ingredients and quantities. My cooking is pretty much driven by our personal preferences and ingredient availability. And while I do pride my cooking skills, the food taste can vary from one time to another. A chef-prepared dish, on the other hand, tastes great and even looks perfect every time you order it. The difference I believe lies in the chef's diligent use of a perfectly made recipe to tantalize our taste buds. Given an option, most of us are more inclined to relish a chef-prepared dish.

* * * *

The eagerness of playing with a new toy is reason enough for a child to tear open a gift packet in hand. And when the toy is their favourite superhero figure, the excitement and anticipation is at another level! But the new superhero I gifted my nephew came with a twist—it was a DIY kit with multiple body parts which needed to be assembled together to form the figure which came with a detailed photographic instruction list to help complete this task. While he struggled initially because the excitement didn't allow him to focus on the instructions, he soon realized that the only way to get the desired result was to patiently follow the set instructions. It's no surprise that he was now able to complete the task in a matter of minutes! Uncovering intriguing data analytics can be equally exciting but without a set method, we will struggle to communicate this analysis.

ARE YOU A STORYTELLER OR A WRITER?

A regular writer is like a cook, who goes about the act without any particular method, tools or techniques. On one day, his output might be great and on another it might lack the most basic flavour. A storyteller, on the other hand, is like a chef who has learnt, developed and perfected a skill. This skill relies on set methods, tools and techniques to produce a higher-quality output on every occasion. And just like an excited child, detaching ourselves from these set methods will only take us backwards on our storytelling efforts.

You don't write because you want to say something, you write because you have something to say.

—F. Scott Fitzgerald

We don't write because we have data to write about, we write because we have a story to tell. To be a successful data storyteller, we need to first and foremost adapt to this mindset, wherein we stop getting bogged down by data and start envisioning a story. Use the story map and the story arc as the blueprint of the broader vision we want to present to an audience. The data is simply the tool which fills up the blank spaces of this blueprint to transform into a written story.

UNIMPRESSIVE VERSUS IMPRESSIVE STORYTELLING

If there is a tussle between unimpressive and impressive story-telling, who do you think will win? I'm sure that the latter will get 100 per cent votes for itself. But the real question is: How do we implement the art of 'impressive storytelling'? With all my writing and training experience, I have found that there are three primary reasons which make any writing unimpressive, which are as follows:

1. **There is no clear structure:** A complicated TV drama with twists and turns but no clarity will make one switch it off. The audience is also in a similar predicament. A complex looking data set gets nothing more than a cursory glance. A reluctant reading effort might also not get any result because of the sheer lack of clarity. It becomes difficult to nail down on the story's major components, sections or themes. A clear, visible story, on the other hand, is more appealing and easily understandable.

2. **There is no visible pattern:** The base of a strong story is its linked set of events; when the order in which information is presented doesn't show a strong link or connection, it makes the story look fragmented or hap-hazard, making it hard for the audience to decipher patterns and understand the story. If the murderer in a story is caught before the crime is committed, or the boy falls in love with the girl before meeting her, the audience will struggle to understand the ramifications of each of these events, leaving them confused and disengaged.

3. **Audience has no understanding of the key story event:** If the audience is not able to comprehend the key story event, then this is because it does not stand out, making it difficult to form a strong link with the conclusion. While a group of events together lead to an upcoming

story conclusion, there are always one or two key events which have a relatively higher impact on the conclusion. The story will not leave an impact on the audience unless a strong link between the key event and conclusion has been clearly established.

A perfect solution to this comes by adopting the storyteller's mindset that can completely outdo these issues in a very short span.

To give wings to your understanding, let me explain this with an example. Think of the colourful blocks kids play with. If you empty a bucket full of blocks in different shapes and colours, you might find it hard and too complex to sort through them and make a castle for your child. But if these blocks are sorted and placed in piles organized on the basis of shape or colour, your task becomes that much easier. When you want to start building something, you will definitely choose the sorted pile rather than the dumped lot. Coming out from the kid's world, let's look at a practical business example shared ahead for your reference in Tables 7.1 and 7.2.

Table 7.1 Data in Action Regional Revenue Performance

An Unimpressive Data Story
Regional Performance Summary for FY 2017
• Hong Kong contributed 31% to 2017 revenue and reported a drop in revenue by 2% at $118 million in 2017 versus $120 million in 2016.
• Singapore, the second biggest revenue contributor, also showed poor growth, falling by 3% y/y to $92 million in 2017 from $95 million in 2016.
• India recorded highest revenue growth of 19% y/y to $38 million in 2017 from $32 million in 2016. Thailand and Malaysia also showed strong growth of 14% and 16% respectively. Revenue contribution of these countries increased to 24% in 2017 from 21% in 2016.
• Revenues from Indonesia and Vietnam declined by 6% and 10% respectively, while China gained slightly by 4%, recording a revenue of $55 million in 2017 versus $53 million in 2016.

(Table 7.1 continued)

(Table 7.1 continued)

An Impressive Data Story
Emerging Markets: Future Revenue Growth Drivers
• Hong Kong and Singapore continued to dominate regional sales, however losing some ground as 2017 revenue decline (2% and 3% respectively) reduced their overall revenue contribution to 54% in 2017 from 57% in 2016. • Emerging markets such as India, Malaysia and Thailand, on the other hand, recorded a revenue growth between 14% and 19%, increasing their revenue contribution to 24% in 2017 from 21% in 2016 while also making them future growth drivers for the company's revenue generation. • China maintained its significance with a marginal 4% revenue growth, while Indonesia and Vietnam performed poorly on both absolute and relative grounds.

Note: The above data is generated for explanatory purposes only.

Table 7.2 Data in Action: FMCG Sector

An Unimpressive Data Story
FMCG Sector in India
E-commerce, like with all sectors, is causing a disruption in the FMCG sector as well, leading to the next growth spurt in the sector which is expected to grow at a CAGR of 22.8% from $50 billion in 2016 to $113.9 billion in 2020. This is also supported by favourable demographics and rise in income levels. The sector is dominated by household and personal care which contribute towards 52% of the total market size, followed by hair care (22%) and food and beverages (10%).
Consumer spending in the country is expected to increase to $4.7 trillion by 2020 and per capita income is estimated to grow at a CAGR of 5.02% during 2012–2021, supported by the country's large youth population. Over 50% of India's population is below the age of 25 years. Online users in India are expected to touch 950 million by 2022 and are likely to push the share of modern retail from 12% in 2017 to 32% in 2022. Modern retail is expected to grow at a CAGR of 18%, while traditional retail is expected to grow at a CAGR of 8%.
Hindustan Unilever dominates the market with its 42% market share; however, consumers are openly accepting newer brands and products, giving rise to a new FMCG major—Patanjali—in the Ayurveda segment.
An Impressive Data Story
FMCG: Indian Youth Boost Sector Growth
FMCG, the fourth largest sector in the Indian economy, is poised for further growth with an expected CAGR of 22.8% from 2016 to 2020. Favourable demographics and rise in income levels are the primary drivers for this growth push, which is expected to increase the industry market size from $50 billion in 2016 to $113.9 billion in 2020.

(Table 7.2 continued)

(Table 7.2 continued)

With more than half of its population under the age of 25 years, India is home to the world's largest youth population, whose changing preferences and dynamics coupled with a growing per capita income are projected to grow at a CAGR of 5.02% during 2012–2021. This is expected to increase consumer spending to $4.7 trillion by 2020, thus giving a boost to the country's FMCG sector.

E-commerce, like with other sectors, is causing a disruption in the FMCG sector as well, wherein the growth of sales through modern retail segment (CAGR 18%) is likely to outpace the growth through traditional retail (CAGR 8%). The rising number of online users in India is expected to touch 950 million by 2022 and is likely to push the share of modern retail from 12% in 2017 to 32% in 2022, leading to a spurt in the sector's overall growth.

The sector is dominated by household and personal care which contribute towards 52% of the total market size, followed by hair care (22%) and food and beverages (10%). And while Hindustan Unilever dominates the market with its 42% market share, consumers are openly accepting newer brands and products, giving rise to a new FMCG major—Patanjali—in the Ayurveda segment.

Note: The above data is generated for explanatory purposes only.

Both the above examples clearly show how a story with the same facts and figures can be made impressive with the simple key of a better presentation. The next step is to learn the art of presenting and weaving your story.

WEAVE IN A STORY STRUCTURE

Glued to your favourite TV programme, what do you prefer—episodes or scenes or dialogues? Sounds like an absurd question? You would ask: How can you differentiate and pick one of these when they are all co-related, forming part of one complete structure? That's my point. A producer has to first weave in a structure, which has a story plot, with episodes, episodes with scenes and scenes with dialogues—all the three components are inextricably linked and presented in the best possible manner to produce a good show. So now that you have clicked the switch in your mind and become a storyteller cum producer, let's start thinking like one. To make this smooth transition, let's think of the

Figure 7.1 Story Map to Story Structure

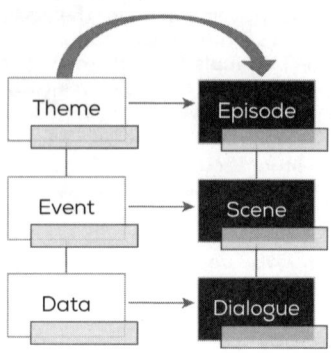

story write-up as a show that is unfolding in front of an audience. The story lies in the episodes, scenes and dialogues of this show. Start writing, not about the data but about events and characters that appear within these. The backbone of this strong story structure (Figure 7.1) lies in the three layers of the story map.

The Episode

The huge choice of shows available on Netflix or Amazon Prime can sometimes be as overwhelming as the abundant data itself. Since most shows do not have trailers, to help me select a good show, I like to see information about all the seasons and episodes to get a peek into it. I have noticed that every episode has its own title and description which provide a glimpse into the activities that unfold within the episode, representing the 'theme' of each episode.

Our data story also needs to be crafted into these episodic themes to give the audience a clear understanding of the insights or conclusions provided by the underlying activities and for the whole story to become more comprehendible. These themes or report sections are already identified in the first layer of the story map.

To weave in an episodic structure in your writing, ensure the following:

1. All themes are written about in different and dedicated sections or paragraphs or different slides of a presentation.
2. Each episode contains a similar set of information which together lead towards a common insight or conclusion.
3. When dedicating sections to an episode, section titles are used to provide a glimpse into the upcoming action.
4. Each episode while independent in its own right is linked to other episodes through the flow of information within them.

Incorporating an organized episodic structure in the writing breaks down the complexity of ideas while also maintaining audience engagement levels as new information keeps flowing with every episode. The presence of clear insights and conclusions at different stages of the story also make the story more impactful while increasing its recall ability.

* * * *

The regional performance data story consists of three episodes divided into three bullet points, each consisting of a similar set of information leading to its own insight and conclusion while getting linked to the overall story.

Episode	Similar Set of Events	Insight/ Conclusion	How It Gets Linked
1. Developed regions	Performance data of developed regions	Declining absolute and relative performances	Overall performance is broken down at a regional episodic level
2. Outperforming emerging regions	Performance data of outperforming emerging regions	Strong absolute and relative performances	The first episode discusses underperformers, second discusses outperformers

Episode	Similar Set of Events	Insight/ Conclusion	How It Gets Linked
3. Other emerging regions	Performance data of other emerging regions	No significant performance impact	and third discusses insignificant performance

★ ★ ★ ★

The FMCG data story consists of four episodes divided into four paragraphs, each consisting of a similar set of information leading to its own insight and conclusion while getting linked to the overall story.

Episode	Similar Set of Events	Insight/ Conclusion	How It Gets Linked
1. Context	Industry background	Significant growth and growth drivers	It sets the stage for all upcoming episodes
2. First growth driver	Factors supporting higher consumer spending	High consumer spending boosts sector growth	Detailed discussion on growth driver stated in the first episode
3. Second growth driver	Data showing positive e-commerce impact	E-commerce will also drive future growth	Detailed discussion on growth driver stated in the first episode Secondary impact of youth population discussed in the second episode
4. Other relevant industry information	Market share of products and players	Identification of dominant products and players	More details on sector introduced in the first episode

Scenes and Dialogues

While the episodes offer a structure to the story presentation, the scenes are where all the activities are. The activities within these scenes are presented in front of an audience through dialogues. The unfolding 'events' within the scenes along with dialogues, that is, the 'data description', identified in the second and third layers of the story map respectively, determine how the story takes shape.

Assigning right data within scenes and scenes within episodes is critical for the episodic structure to show clear themes with insights. A story is technically written scene by scene; hence, the flow and linking of these scenes and the data within are essential to show an overall pattern in the story. We can rely on the bucketed data lists from the story map and its journey from the story arc to help us nail down both these aspects when writing the story.

* * * *

The first two episodes within the regional performance story consist of two scenes—absolute and relative performances. The episodes first discuss the absolute performance scene/event, including requisite data, before moving on to relative performance scene/event and dialogues/data. This correct grouping and data make the episode's insights clearly visible.

* * * *

The second episode (paragraph) of the FMCG data story includes three scenes and requisite dialogues within. The first discusses youth population in India; the second talks about improving income levels; and the first and second scenes together lead to the third scene, which is the resultant growth in consumer spending. The appropriate grouping of data within the scenes shows the link; the appropriate grouping of scenes within the episodes provides a clear insight.

DRAW THE RIGHT SPOTLIGHT

A typical 1980s Bollywood song is playing on your big screen TV. The leading pair performs their moves surrounded by a host of dancers and colourful props. And yet your eyes only follow the movements and expressions of the hero and heroine? It is not something that happens by chance. The filmmakers have put in an effort to ensure that your eyes follow 'only' those two. It is the camera focus, the choreography, even the make-up and clothing that put the spotlight on this duo, ensuring that your focus doesn't shift.

The audience will see what you show them. They will focus where you tell them to. They will think in the way you nudge them to.

While writing a story, one also needs to don a director's hat and ascertain how the information should be packaged and presented in front of an audience. To influence audience's perception of the story, priority, events and climax need to shine and stand out, while the falling action bit could use some camouflaging to assure a quick recovery.

When writing, do we use glitter to make the data shine or bushes to hide the unimportant data?

How to Make Your Data Shine?

1. **Literally give more space:** As a storyteller, you should actually give more space in terms of number of words, sentences or paragraphs to the information that needs to shine. More space means that it's a longer scene and the audience spends more time on it; the insight is thus likely to register better.

   The important scene commands relatively more space compared to others. Avoid using excessive words and becoming repetitive to write a lengthy scene.

2. **Begin an important scene on a new paragraph:** Wherever possible, dedicate a separate paragraph or section to that scene. This will ensure that it stands tall among all the other scenes and thus seeks higher

audience attention. The mind gets a short break just before a new paragraph begins and can thus focus more on this piece of information.

3. **Incorporate the important scene/event/data in report or section titles:** Titles are read first and play an important role in grabbing audience's attention and generating curiosity. Not only does such information register better in audience's minds, but it also enables higher engagement levels.

4. **Add visuals for highlighting scenes/events:** Visuals lead to higher levels of interest and attention from the audience and thus result in better retention and recall. Therefore, it is good to add visuals, wherever possible.

∗ ∗ ∗ ∗

In the regional performance data story:

1. The second paragraph discussing the outperformers is more important and gets relatively more space (higher word count).

Figure 7.2 Adding a Visual Impact

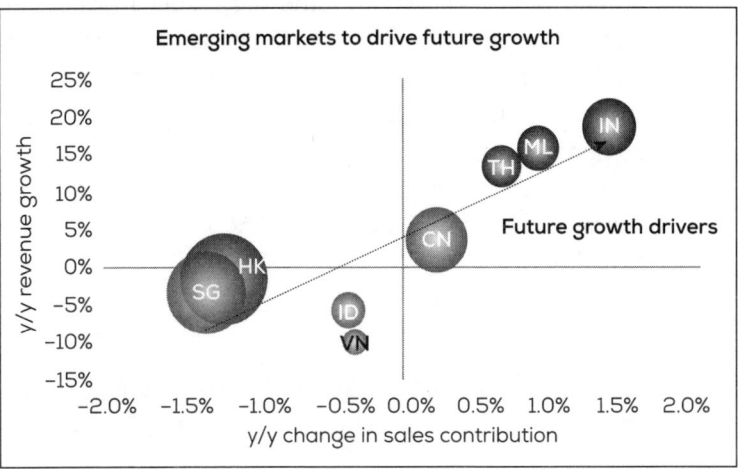

2. Every episode begins on a new paragraph.
3. Adding the visual (see Figure 7.2) makes the story much more clear and impactful.

∗ ∗ ∗ ∗

In the FMCG data story:

1. The second and third paragraphs are the most important as they discuss the reason behind the sector's growth story and are literally given more space (higher word count) compared to the other themes.
2. Every episode begins on a new paragraph.
3. The title clearly spells out the most important scenes, that is, the Indian youth-related data and how they drive the sector's growth.

How to Camouflage a Scene?

1. Firstly, don't let the reader spend a lot of time on that scene or information. To achieve this, 'literally give it less space' in the writing in terms of number of words, sentences or paragraphs.
2. Include such information at 'the end of a paragraph, section or report'. By the time the reader touches the end of the paragraph, his mind has already processed a lot of information and it is preparing for a break. The information that comes at such times is least likely to get etched into audience's memory.
3. 'Precede or follow' a falling action scene with a rising action scene to dilute its ability to contradict the conclusion.

∗ ∗ ∗ ∗

The falling action for declining developed region's revenue in the regional data story has been mitigated by a rising action data, stating that these regions are still dominant contributors in the overall revenue generation.

* * * *

The least pertinent information that does not play any significant role on the conclusions of both the FMCG and regional performance stories have been placed in the last paragraph.

MAKE IT ANALYTICAL

I received a call one day, my best friend sobbing on the other side. She had just broken up with her long-time boyfriend and was inconsolable. I kept asking her how it happened and why she broke up, to which she quipped that I was only interested in the story and not her current state! Immediately realizing my mistake, I empathetically apologized while telling her that I am always there for her!

When a certain fact is presented, human curiosity makes us want to know more about all behind the scene activities. In data stories, the audience is more interested in the 'why' and 'how' the numbers came to be what they are. When writing, ensure that all insights and conclusions are supported by the rising action part which discusses this 'why and how' to make the story more analytical and appealing to a business audience.

* * * *

The second episode of the regional performance story discusses absolute and relative performances of certain emerging regions, which is the reason (the 'why and how') they become 'future growth drivers'.

* * * *

The first episode of the FMCG data story discusses the sector's growth. The next two episodes and the biggest chunk of this piece are dedicated to discussing 'why and how' this growth is likely to be achieved.

GIVE A BEGINNING AND AN ENDING

Remember those times when you got stuck in traffic and missed the first 20 minutes of the movie? Or that time when you had to leave the movie half an hour early because your child got sick?

When you missed the beginning, did you struggle to keep pace with and understand everything that kept coming up in the movie? When you missed the ending, did you feel like it was an incomplete experience?

When crafting a written story, ensure that your words do justice to the context and conclusion.

Set the Context at the Beginning

The first sentence of a paragraph, first paragraph of a page or first section of a report introduces the 'story topic' so the audience can get a fair idea of what to expect from the story. Data stories command the use of simple and yet intriguing introductions which come straight to the point while also generating interest and curiosity. Titles and headings come in handy as their word count limitation provides a window to say something without saying too much.

And while most people focus on providing an introductory context only at the beginning of the story, I think that every theme or episode needs its own context to support understanding of the particular sub-topic while also maintaining audience engagement levels by generating fresh bouts of interest and curiosity. If the report format allows for it, section titles are a good tool to set such a context. In other instances, a previous episode or the beginning of the current episode could set the requisite context.

* * * *

Emerging Markets: Future Revenue Growth Drivers

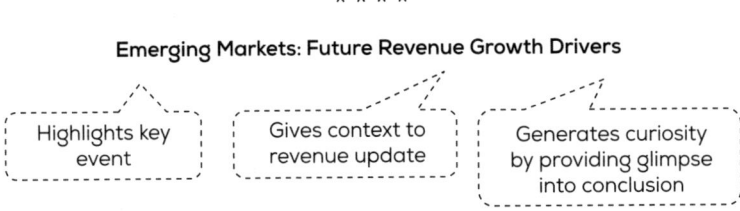

| Highlights key event | Gives context to revenue update | Generates curiosity by providing glimpse into conclusion |

Regional performance data story. The title of the impressive regional performance story gives a clear insight while setting a context to the story. The first line sets the context by using the words 'dominate regional sales' which give the audience an understanding that this story is about regional sales performance. The relative comparison early on by using words 'losing some ground in 2017' generates curiosity and interest to learn more about it.

The title of the unimpressive regional performance story only describes the data while providing no background or insight. The story itself begins with discussing Hong Kong's performance by itself, thus not giving a clear picture of the broad scope, which is the presentation of the entire regions performance.

* * * *

FMCG data story. The impressive FMCG story's heading sets a strong context while also generating enough curiosity. The unimpressive FMCG story, on the other hand, begins with the use of the word 'E-commerce' creating ambiguity about the main topic of the story.

Provide Relevant Background Information

All the hard work and time spent in analysing data and building the story can go waste if the audience does not have the requisite tools or background knowledge to understand the topic at hand.

If we have the slightest reason to believe that a certain terminology or topic might create ambiguity in the audience's mind, then it is worthwhile to spend a little extra time and space in clearing that ambiguity at the outset.

Depending on the length of the written story, its relevance and importance, we can use either of the following ways to provide background information:

1. Make it a part of the story where the background information is relatively more important.
2. Add an appendix in bigger reports where the background information is good to have but not essential for understanding.
3. Use footnotes in smaller stories to provide crisp explanations while avoiding excessive usage of footnotes in one story.

* * * *

Here's how I provide background information in the FMCG story:

1. The two words 'modern and traditional retail' might not have been self-explanatory by themselves, but in the context of e-commerce industry, these terms make intuitive sense.
2. The first paragraph discusses growth at the industry level, providing background information to the next two paragraphs, which discuss the details with respect to the growth drivers.

Simple Issues Create 'Big Impact'

In addition to explanatory requirements, simple oversights often result in missing or incorrect background information, which can impact the audience's story-grasping ability. We tend to focus on the bigger issues, often letting the simple things slip because of the constant stress and pressure; however, these can have a devastating impact on the story and even the storyteller's credibility. Keeping an eye out for these is thus recommended:

1. **Correct and consistent use of denominations and nomenclature:** While it may seem obvious and insignificant, it is a very common and fatal mistake. For example, using 'billion' instead of 'million', 'USD' instead of 'INR' or '1.0 billion' instead of '10 billion', the entire meaning behind the numbers and the message from the story will be lost.

   In the FMCG story, the currency with amounts follows a standard practice throughout, that is, currency–amount–space–denomination (e.g., $50 billion). Inconsistencies can be distracting and might require more time to understand and interpret that piece of data.

2. **Use relevant short forms:** Some people have a habit of converting every big term into a short form as they believe that it makes their paragraphs smaller and hence their writing concise. Short forms can be used only for industry-accepted terminology such as GDP, USD, INR, PAT, EBITDA and the likes. We may use short forms for a long name of a company, product, segment or region if it gets repeated multiple times in a write-up. In such instances, write both the full form and the short form together when using it for the first time.

3. **Adhere to appropriate font styles:** Report title, section title and body command a different and dedicated use of font styles and sizes. When these principles are strictly adhered to, a cursory glance will let the audience ascertain which part of the report they are looking at. Inconsistencies can distract the audience while also commanding more time to decipher simple information.

THE CLOSURE

Without a clear ending, the data story will appear to be abrupt. The audience will feel lost and will not know what they were supposed to take back from the story. To ensure that the audience leaves with a feeling of having learnt or accomplished something new through the story, spell out a clear conclusion, not only at the end of the story but also throughout the story's multiple episodes, which together help arrive at the overall conclusion of the story.

Importantly, this conclusion should be intricately weaved into the story wherein it directly flows from the rising action scenes and dialogues, representing a clear link between the analysis and the conclusion. Writing analytically, while focusing on the 'why and how', makes the conclusion appear as a part of the story and not a loose end added as an afterthought.

* * * *

Conclusions Provided in the Regional Performance Story	
Paragraph One Conclusion	Developed regions though dominant losing ground
Paragraph Two Conclusion	Some emerging regions recording strong growth
Paragraph Three Conclusion	Some emerging regions are not performing well, and they don't drive any significant impact on the overall performance

* * * *

Conclusions Provided in the FMCG Data Story	
Paragraph One Conclusion	Favourable demographics and rise in income levels are the primary drivers for the growth push
Paragraph Two Conclusion	Favourable demographics and rise in income levels together are expected to give a boost to the country's FMCG sector
Paragraph Three Conclusion	This is leading to a spurt in the sector's overall growth
Paragraph Four Conclusion	Consumers are openly accepting newer brands and products

Adhering to and incorporating these storytelling elements can ensure that the data story's structure, themes, links and patterns are clearly visible and easily understandable by the audience. An understanding of essential writing principles can help a storyteller further leverage upon this story structure.

BASIC MATTERS

For one house party, I made my famous seven-layer taco dip and served it in a see-through glass bowl with the seven different colours standing out beautifully, just like a rainbow. After clicking a few pictures of my creation as I took the first bite, I realized that one layer was lacking in salt while another had excessive lemon! After a long tiring day, I had worked hard to make this perfect-looking dish but that was no excuse to feed this unappetizing dish to my friends no matter how sweet they are. So I pulled out another bowl and began all over again!

Focusing on the story aspect alone does not absolve us from the responsibility of adhering to common writing essentials. No matter how simple or basic these might appear, overlooking these can be devastating for the entire storytelling effort. A self-committed crime, as I call it, is often responsible in murdering the story!

Bigger issues always get our attention, but the constant stress and pressure make us slip on basic matters which can be a death nail for the story's impact and the storyteller's credibility.

Clarity: No Room for Chinese Whispers

Achieving clarity in writing implies that the reader should understand what we are trying to tell them, exactly as we want them to. If there is some gap in their understanding, namely what we intended, then they will not be in complete sync with the story. Resulting in decoupling of minds and lower participation and interest, which can lower engagement levels, thus making the story less effective and impactful. So then, how do we achieve clarity in writing?

Clear writing starts with clear thinking: Writing often mirrors the thoughts in our head; if the thoughts are clear, then so will be the writing; but if the thoughts aren't in sync, then the same will reflect in the writing. The entire planning exercise from the story wheel to the story arc and story map thus become crucial because it helped us get the desired clarity of the story we want to present, without which it is impossible to get any clarity in the writing.

Write in relatively short sentences: There is a limit on the quantum of information that can be processed by the reader at one go. After a certain point, the human mind might continue reading, but it stops processing the information because it simply gets tired. The use of punctuation marks gives the audience's mind a much-needed break. Even if it is just for a fraction of a second, it is enough for the mind to get back into an active alert position.

The 'full stop' plays a critical role in paragraphs. The ideal writing style to achieve clarity is through a right mix of long and short sentences. This ensures that the reader gets just enough breaks to aid information processing while also enabling pattern formation. Using full stops miserly implies that we are writing in very long sentences which might contain excessive information that the mind cannot process at one go.

In data stories, I recommend judging the size of a sentence, not just by the number of words used in it but also by the quantity of information or insights presented in the sentence. While a short sentence consists of only one piece of information, a long sentence can go up to three–four pieces of information.

* * * *

Short Sentences versus Long Sentences

Example—short sentences: Emerging markets such as India, Malaysia and Thailand recorded a revenue growth. This growth was between 14 per cent and 19 per cent. They also witnessed an increase in their revenue contribution to 24 per cent in 2017 from 21 per cent in 2016. They are also the future growth drivers for the company's revenue generation.

Example—long sentences: Emerging markets such as India, Malaysia and Thailand recorded a revenue growth between 14 per cent and 19 per cent, which increased their revenue contribution to 24 per cent in 2017 from 21 per cent in 2016 while also making them future growth drivers for the company's revenue generation.

Example—mix of long and short sentences: Emerging markets such as India, Malaysia and Thailand recorded a revenue growth between 14 per cent and 19 per cent. This increased their revenue contribution to 24 per cent in 2017 from 21 per cent in 2016 while also making them future growth drivers for the company's revenue generation.

Follow a structured and organized writing approach: When the story follows a structure and is broken down in clearly visible sections with related information kept together, it becomes easier for the audience to understand the stated message. The episodes, scenes and dialogues framework will play a significant role in bringing structure into the writing and providing a dose of clarity to understand the various components of the story.

Use simple English language: In every training programme, I always make it a point to tell my participants that when writing a data story, the audience is not judging you on the basis of your English language skills. If anything they are interested in, then it is your analytical and storytelling ability. Thus, do not go overboard with the use of complex English language words, phrases and jargons. On most occasions, it can backfire as it either takes away from the essence of the story or makes audience's interpretation difficult.

Concise–effective Use of Real Estate

A constant feedback that most people get is to make their writing 'concise'. In my training programmes when I raise the question, 'What do you understand by concise?' an answer I often get is that concise means 'writing in short', a common misconception nonetheless. If we simply start cutting information to make the write-up shorter, we risk making it incomplete, which in turn makes it unclear.

Writing concisely means saying everything we have to say, but doing it with the least possible words. The golden rule of achieving concise writing is to weigh every word and every piece of information and ask yourself, 'Is this word or information required for the purpose of my story, or is it simply there for sentence construction?' All the time spent in pre-production ensures that most of the unrequired data has fallen off at the earlier stages and weighing every word is not as daunting a task as it might appear to be.

When it comes to weighing in every word of your write-up, the following tips will serve as a good guide:

> *Avoid tautologies:* A tautology means saying the same thing twice over in different words. This is a fault in our style of writing that we might have imbibed unknowingly, but this adds unnecessary words to the write-up. Examples of tautology include the following: new innovation; short summary; close

proximity; in my opinion, I think; adequate enough; future projection.

Unnecessary use of adverbs: Just like tautologies, adverbs sometimes repeat the same thing over, adding only words without adding value to the overall meaning. One should be careful and conscious when using such adverbs which end with 'LY'. Avoid these commonly used adverbs: basically, naturally, obviously, extremely, actually, definitely, expertly and randomly.

No use of idioms: An idiom is an expression, word or phrase that has a figurative meaning, wherein the meaning inferred from the idiom is different from the literal meaning of the idiom's individual elements. In other words, idioms don't mean exactly what the words say and they have hidden meanings. They are long phrases with high potential of being misunderstood and are hence best avoided. Examples: All hell broke loose; Spill the beans; Ahead of the pack; Back to square one; and Go the extra mile.

Show All the Angles

It goes without saying that the writing has to be complete at all times. We should present a full picture of all the variables that go into making the data story. It will be clearly understood and its impact realized only when all moving parts are addressed while receiving their due space. Unwittingly missing out a key piece of information, no matter how simple or basic it might appear, can make the story fall flat by making it appear patchy or broken. Following the story map blueprint ensures that every required piece of information finds its due place when crafting the story. Cutting information to make the write-up short is the most common mistake that makes the writing incomplete. This typically happens at the editing stage where we have cut our ties with the blueprint.

* * * *

Does This Story Still Leave Any Impact?

Changing preferences and dynamics of the youth population are expected to increase consumer spending in the country to US$3.6 trillion by 2020, further aided by rising per capita income which is estimated to grow at a CAGR of 4.94 per cent during 2010–2019, both of which together are expected to give a boost to the country's FMCG sector.

CONNECT THE DOTS

Having the full list of information dumped into words does not make a data story. To get a good story, all pieces of information and insights need to fit together and find their connection to form links and patterns that the audience can understand. The linked episodic structure helps attain a cohesive writing.

★ ★ ★ ★

How to Make the Writing Cohesive	
Data/Information	**How It Gets Linked**
FMCG, the fourth largest sector in the Indian economy to gain...	Introductory statement
Favourable demographics and rise in income levels are the primary drivers...	Gives reason behind growth and defines it through market sizes
With more than half of its population under the age of 25 years...	Sets context to the upcoming theme, i.e., details on growth drivers
Changing preferences and dynamics of this youth population...	Delves into detailed impact of this youth population
Both of which together are expected to give a boost to the country's FMCG sector	Provides conclusion to the theme
E-commerce, like with all the sectors, is causing a disruption...	Sets context to the upcoming theme, i.e., additional growth push

How to Make the Writing Cohesive	
Data/Information	**How It Gets Linked**
The rising number of online users in India is expected to touch 850 million...	Gives conclusion by relating macro impact to industry growth
The sector is dominated by household and personal care...	Sets context to the upcoming theme, i.e., sector-specific information
And while Hindustan Unilever dominates the market...	Continues with sector-specific insight

THERE'S NO ROOM FOR ERRORS!

I probably don't even need to mention this, but I must! At all times, all the information, analysis, insights and conclusions presented should be correct, as stated in the following table. The reason I put this very obvious point in black and white is because of the innumerable times I have seen people make silly mistakes in simple things which become the death nail for a story's impact and effectiveness.

Often, an oversight caused by the constant pressure can result in negligence over some smaller aspects. Hence, no matter how strict a timeline we are working against, keeping time aside for editing and checking the work is critical to avoid such mistakes. Common mistakes include the following: incorrect nomenclature, incorrect data points, missing titles and sources, and drawing incorrect inferences.

* * * *

What Can Make the Data Story Incorrect—Mistakes We Are Likely to Make	
Incorrect Version	**Correct Version**
CAGR of 20.6% from 2016 to 2025	CAGR of 20.6% from 2016 to 2020
Consumer spending in the country to US$3.6 billion	Consumer spending in the country to US$3.6 trillion
Giving rise to a new market leader—Patanjali	Giving rise to a new FMCG major—Patanjali

MAKE IT BETTER!

Like any good student, you might have also incorporated all the storytelling principles and writing essentials in your current work and I am sure that with a little practice you will be writing impactful data stories. To help you in this endeavour, I outline a few points below, an awareness of which will help you make your data stories even better!

Use titles and headings to your advantage: Titles and headings are a very powerful but unfortunately most underutilized tool when writing and visualizing. Most people use titles to 'describe' the content, thus not effectively unearthing its true potential. Titles should instead be used to conclude the story, give away a key message and form the story link, all the while generating interest and curiosity.

★ ★ ★ ★

In my training programmes, I often use a case study wherein trainees are required to build a story on Patanjali's brand strength. In my version of the story, I use the following four subtitles, which together give away the full impact of the story. The written and visual stories in line with these respective titles show the audience 'why and how' I arrive at these conclusions.

1.   Patanjali's revenue grows 10 times in 5 years
2.   Making it the top FMCG brand
3.   Brand strength driven by price strength
4.   Driving a dent in competitor earnings

Come to the point: Respect your audience's time, especially when it is a business audience who is always hard-pressed for time. Focus on your analytical skill rather than literary skill and give them what they need at the very outset. Don't beat about the bush, don't write very long introductions and don't use proverbs or idioms to begin your write-up as they don't help in generating interest and curiosity from a business audience. It is the meat of the matter, your story—your conclusions—that the audience is most interested in.

Questions to ask before and after writing: Before you start writing, ask yourself: 'What do I want to say?' After writing, ask yourself: 'Have I said it?' The first question will give you clarity of thought; the answer to that lies in your story wheel and narrative planning. The second question will check if you have achieved the objective you set out to achieve. These are golden words that can help bring the much-required polishing to your writing.

Write for your specific audience: Always remember—you are writing for an audience and not for yourself. Give the audience what they want and need in the way they want and need it. When writing, ensure that you are meeting the audience's objective and purpose while presenting it in relevance to their background and preference.

Don't take the basics for granted: Knowing and learning the basics come easy to all of us, but remembering and adhering to them even under tight deadlines and pressure situations are the challenge. These are simple things that demand very little time, but if overlooked they can cause chaos in your writing.

Never be content with your first draft: To be a good writer, one needs to be a good editor. Never send out your work without reading and re-reading it. From experience, I can confidently say that every time you re-read, you will make at least one change, no matter how small. I recommend editing the writing at least three times, of which one time should be on printed hard copy. For small write-ups of within one page, two times would suffice. The first time you read, you will be more focused on the overall structure and essence of the story. The second time, the focus shifts towards the relevance of the analysis, insights and other story enablers. The third time is when the eye starts catching smaller mistakes in numbers, nomenclatures and grammar. After reading three times, one can be fairly certain of having put in their best efforts!

Most people get so overwhelmed with the entire data-storytelling effort that they tend to overlook simple aspects that can change the face of their data story. Adhering to writing basics ensures that our effort does not go in vain, as incorporating these writing tips into the story can uplift the overall output and make it more impactful. Don't let the ignorance or oversight of such factors become the death nail of your story!

8 Use Visuals to Your Advantage

It was literally middle of the night at 3:30 AM and we were all tucked into a jeep. The two-hour uphill journey seemed much longer than it was, thanks to the multiple bumps that made every inch of the body sore. Sleepy and irritated when we got out of the jeep around 5:30 AM, it was still dark—all of us wondering what made us endure this tough ride? Slowly as a gleam of light made its way through the clouds and the sun started showing, the sky turned into beautiful shades of orange and red. It was the most spectacular sunrise I had seen in my life! We looked at each other smiling, all thinking the same thing—this scene, this visual made, the whole trip worthwhile!

* * * *

My eight-year-old nephew very excitedly came and placed his entire second grade classwork in front of me one day. Taking my cue, I started going through his work, all the while trying to show genuine interest when suddenly something struck me. All the worksheets consisted a heavy usage of visuals. His school seemed to rely on visual learning as an important teaching technique. He even had a hand-drawn, ruler-aligned bar graph and an original written short story supported with hand-drawn visuals!

* * * *

Let me ask you a question. If you had a table full of business magazines and newspapers laid out in front of you, which one are you more inclined to pick—your daily newspaper or a magazine with attractive visuals on its cover?

Not only do we humans prefer to see good visuals, but we also learn better with visuals.

Our brain is hard-wired to process visual information better and faster than words! When reading words, the brain processes one word at a time, which considerably slows down its ability to consume information. But a visual, an image, allows you to consume and process all information together, at one go. This coupled with human's natural power of vision makes consumption, processing and understanding of visual information much faster and easier.

Marcel Just, the director of the Center for Cognitive Brain Imaging at Carnegie Mellon University, said in one of his interviews, 'The brain can't generate more activity beyond a certain point.' There's an upper limit on the quantum of information it can process at one time. In today's data-loaded world, there is a constant demand on attracting this 'brain time', and using visuals helps utilize it most effectively.[10]

In data stories, visuals play an integral role, not only because of their ability to enhance understanding but also to attract audience's interest and improve retention of the conclusions and analysis thereof. Information processed through visuals and images is believed to enter the brain's long-term memory, unlike words, which become a part of the short-term memory, thus increasing the brain's power to recall and retain information that was absorbed through visuals.

---

[10] Nieman Reports, 'Watching the Human Brain Process Information' (2010). Available at: http://niemanreports.org/articles/watching-the-human-brain-process-information/ (accessed on 29 June 2010).

IT'S ALL IN A GRAPH!

*There is a magic in graphs. The profile of a curve reveals in a flash
a whole situation—the life history of an epidemic, a panic, or an
era of prosperity. The curve informs the mind, awakens the
imagination, convinces.*

—Henry Hubbard

Graphs, charts and data visuals are all tools that ignite life into data. And yet we are surrounded by bad graphs—mere data dumps that provide no clear message. Nobody wants to make a bad graph intentionally, but it happens. The narrative plan does not always turn into an impactful end product because we missed out on something along the road. In this chapter, we will cover various nuances that go into making an impactful visual story.

The first step to putting a plan into action is selecting the right chart type, a common dilemma to begin with for most people. In most situations, I have found that people restrict themselves to using only two–three chart types they are comfortable with. The flip side of this is that the impact and power of the story are often compromised because the standard lines and bars do not always do justice to the underlying story.

The first ground rule here is that the storyteller doesn't decide which chart or visual to use in a particular case; the data and narrative help make this decision for us. This might be a right time to introduce you to one more surprise element: 'visuals' are not restricted to Excel charts alone. Even two shapes, or text boxes, and some pictures combined together can become a visual!

The storyteller doesn't decide which chart type to use. The data decides.

The first-level classification is to view the data as numbers, text or pictures. The analysis and conclusions we want to present to our audience can be both quantitative (read: numbers) or qualitative (read: text). The quantum of numbers and text are essential in telling a story and thus form part of our narrative, which will decide the visual category we should use in the following manner.

1. If the data is number-heavy, use an Excel chart.
2. If the data is text-heavy, or a mix of text, numbers and pictures, use a smart diagram.

Excel charts enable us to plot numbers across horizontal and vertical axes, with an option to add a secondary vertical axis in certain chart types. Its biggest advantage is that there are no limitations on the range and quantum of numbers that can be included in these charts and they offer a variety of standard options which cover a bulk of the charting needs. The availability of these multiple choices, however, makes the chart-selection decision a little tricky.

The story characters and events play a lead role in determining this selection process (Figure 8.1). Characters are the data series; every chart has its own capacity in terms of the data series it can accommodate—too many and the chart will be hard to comprehend, too few and the chart will not display any story. Events represent the activity flowing within the numbers. It can be comparing one number(s) relative to another number(s), that is, the 'relationship' of the numbers, or how one series of numbers

Figure 8.1 Drivers of Chart Type Selection

Characters	Events	Outcome
• Best fit minimum and maximum number of characters, i.e., data points for a given chart type	• Relationship or trend among the characters, i.e., data points	• Is the outcome clearly showcased on the selected chart type?

compares over time, that is, the 'trend' of the numbers, or to show how the trend of one series of numbers compares with the trend of another series, that is, both 'trend and relationship'. The event could also be an anomaly or outlier in the desired relationship or trend.

This event classification, in terms of relationships and trends, directly leads to Excel chart selection.

At this stage, the chart we create is still in a draft mode; it will most likely need a couple of iterations and a lot of 'touch-up' to make it that perfect data visual that tells a powerful and impactful story.

In the following diagrams (Figures 8.2 and 8.3), I present an inclusive list of most common chart types along with situations in which they best fit. They offer a guideline to chart selection, which can help save valuable time. That said, there can be one-off situations where a deviation from this guideline can also result in good visual stories. There are about 10 most commonly used chart types in Excel. Any complex or creative visual we set out to make will be based on one of these basic chart types. It is hence imperative to understand the fundamentals of the 'best fit situations'.

Using the chart-selection logic (Figures 8.1–8.3) to find the 'best fit' chart situations considerably simplifies the data-visualization process as it is expected to give the right result in the first attempt. This also reduces the number of iterations that might come up at a later stage and makes the visualization process much more efficient. Figure 8.4 discusses how we can apply the chart-selection logic in practice.

Smart Diagrams: The Smart Way!

Any thought or idea can be converted into a visual to make the underlying message impactful. Especially with text-heavy data on presentation slides, I recommend converting them into some

Figure 8.2 The Role of Events in Chart Selection

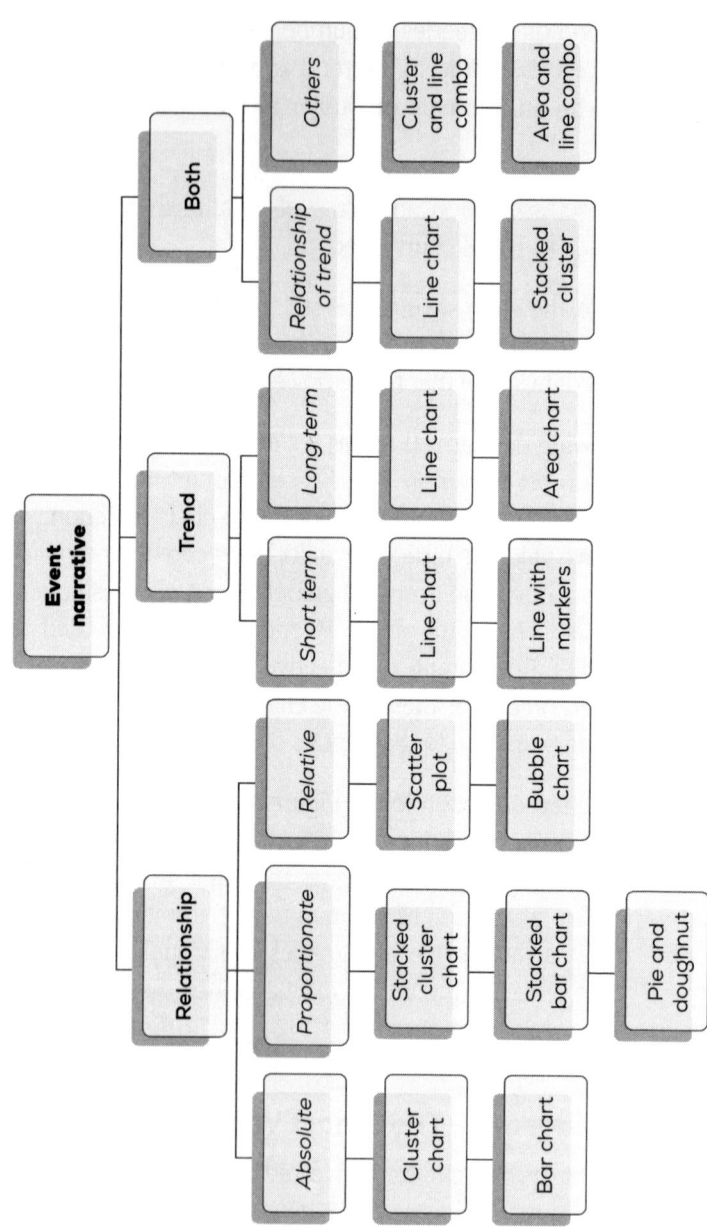

Figure 8.3 The Role of Characters in Chart Selection

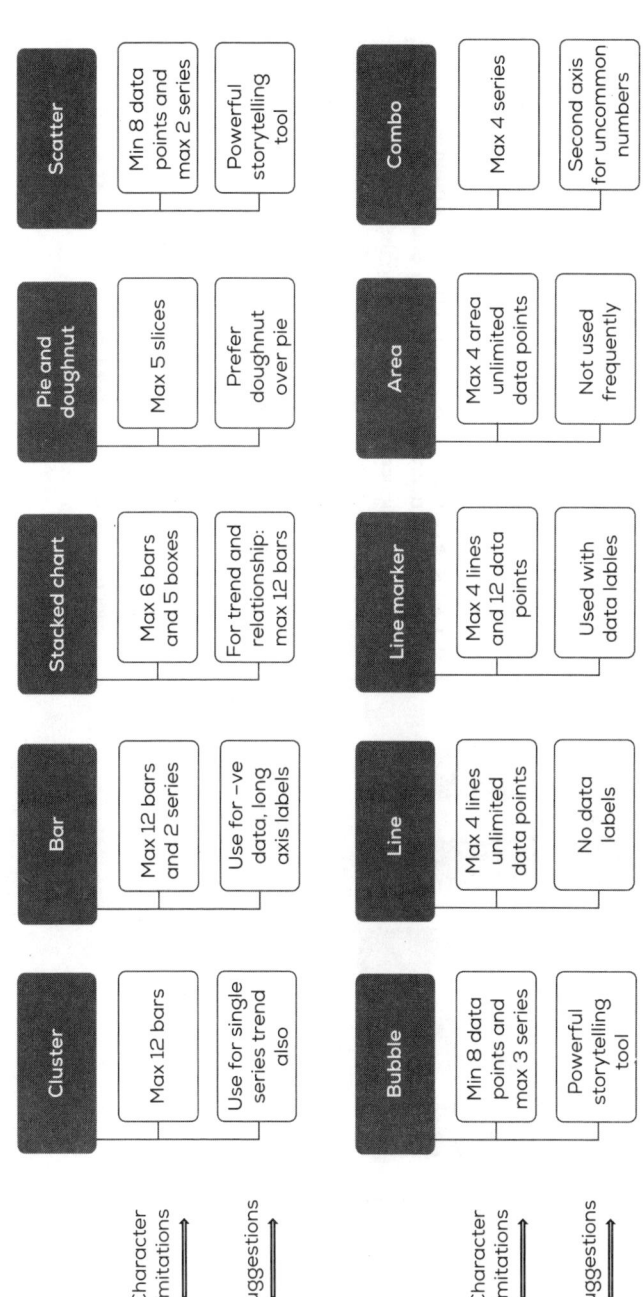

Figure 8.4 Chart Selection Logic in Practice

Chart Selected in Specific Situations	Selection Logic
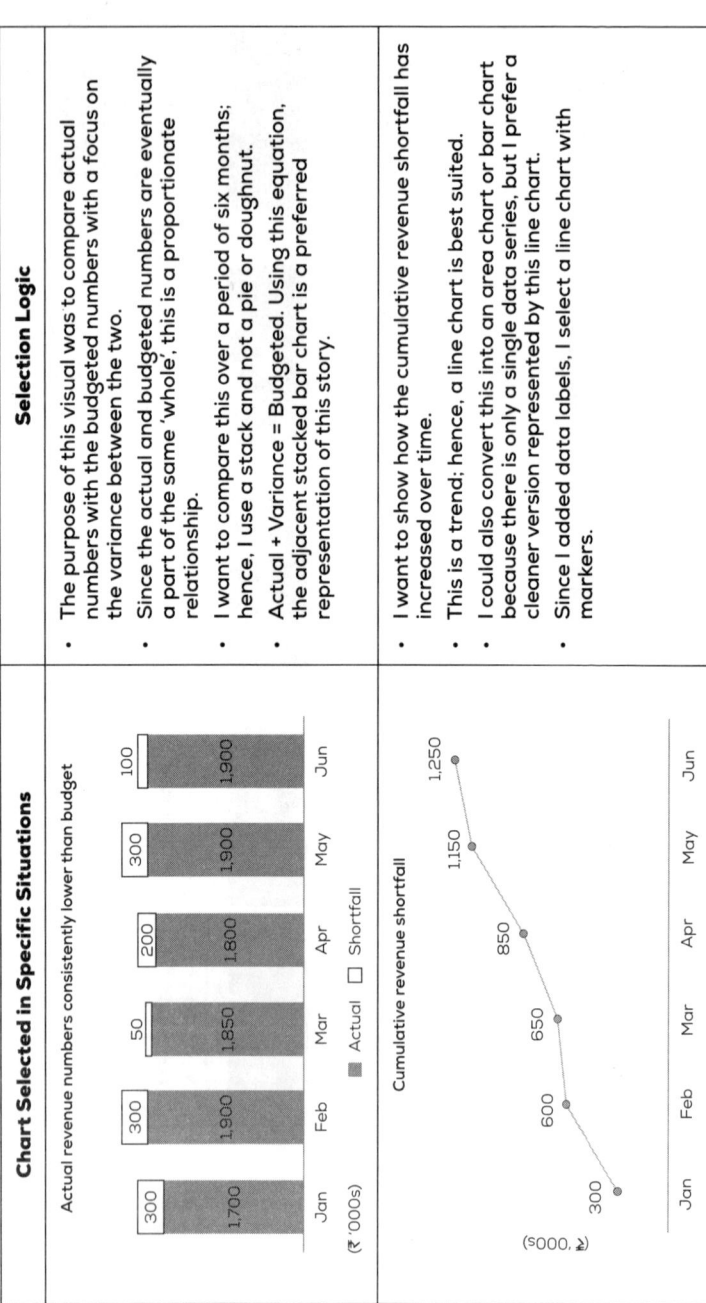 Actual revenue numbers consistently lower than budget	• The purpose of this visual was to compare actual numbers with the budgeted numbers with a focus on the variance between the two. • Since the actual and budgeted numbers are eventually a part of the same 'whole', this is a proportionate relationship. • I want to compare this over a period of six months; hence, I use a stack and not a pie or doughnut. • Actual + Variance = Budgeted. Using this equation, the adjacent stacked bar chart is a preferred representation of this story.
Cumulative revenue shortfall	• I want to show how the cumulative revenue shortfall has increased over time. • This is a trend; hence, a line chart is best suited. • I could also convert this into an area chart or bar chart because there is only a single data series, but I prefer a cleaner version represented by this line chart. • Since I added data labels, I select a line chart with markers.

(Figure 8.4 continued)

(Figure 8.4 continued)

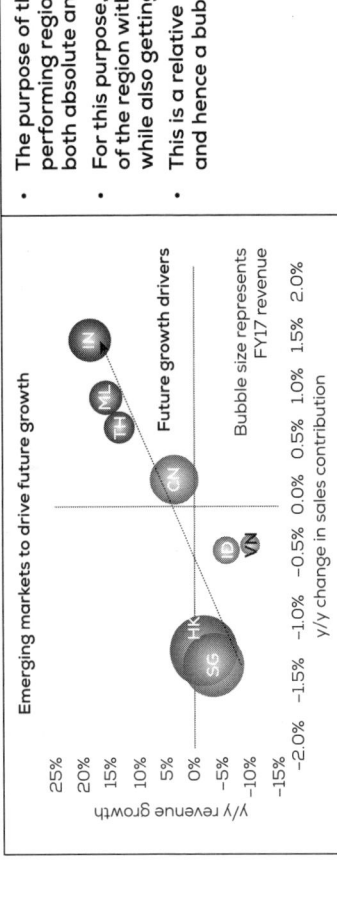

- The purpose of this data story is to identify the best-performing region. My interpretation of performance is both absolute and relative.

- For this purpose, I need to compare y/r revenue growth of the region with its change in total sales contribution while also getting an idea of the actual sales level.

- This is a relative relationship between three data series and hence a bubble chart is best suited in this situation.

Note: The above data has been generated for explanatory purposes only.

form of a visual rather than listing bullet points. Any amount of shapes, pictures, text and numbers can come together to form a smart diagram and, thus, it's quite an impossible task to list down standard formats and provide a detailed guideline like in the case of Excel charts.

Smart diagrams demand a higher creative vision, and I have often found that the ready templates under the SmartArt tab in MS Word, PowerPoint and Excel serve bulk of the needs when it comes to creating a smart diagram. We can add some pictures or combine visuals together to convert the SmartArt into an impactful visual story. At this point, I will encourage you to start thinking of situations where you can convert textual information into a smart diagram and take inspiration from the example in Figure 8.5.

* * * *

I was conducting a training for the relationship managers of a mutual fund house and wanted to show them how they can

Figure 8.5 Illustration of Smart Diagram: Explaining How a Mutual Fund Works

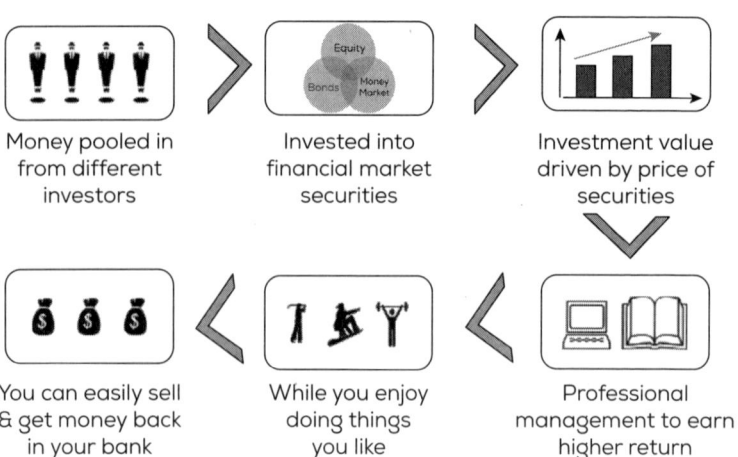

Money pooled in from different investors

Invested into financial market securities

Investment value driven by price of securities

You can easily sell & get money back in your bank

While you enjoy doing things you like

Professional management to earn higher return

incorporate visuals in their client conversation to make the selling job much easier. A lot of their retail and institutional clients do not have a basic understanding of the mutual fund product itself, and I recommended using the visual as below to facilitate its explanation and understanding.

Explanation: The visual above is a combination of six text boxes, which together explain the working of a mutual fund. Supporting these with relevant images (to be sourced on the basis of copyright considerations) and linking them together on a step-by-step basis using arrows transform it into a smart diagram.

Most reports we make are likely to be dominated by Excel charts, because data does primarily consist of numbers, and thus the suggested ratio of Excel charts to smart diagrams should not be more than 5:1. This means that we can have not more than one such creative visual for every five Excel charts. Over-usage of such diagrams can make the whole report complex or too 'showy' at the least, taking away from the overall story impact. These visuals find a relatively higher usage in pitch and probing stories due to the wide scope presented by their story purpose.

WEAVE IN A STORY

Remember the hare and the tortoise? Just because someone wins the first round, it doesn't mean they won the race or the championship. Similarly, just because we got the visual selection right, it doesn't mean we got the story right! What we have at this stage is more of a draft, and a story still needs to be weaved in. On some occasions, this weaving might need more threads and beads to make the end product stand together and appear attractive, while at other times just one double stitch or a single bead might do the job.

A context, a spotlight and an ending are the essential components that need to be consciously weaved into a story.

Set the Context Right

Think of the context as an introduction which facilitates the understanding of an unfolding story. Axis titles, legends and data labels play a vital role in introducing the ensemble of characters being presented on the visual. And in spite of being part of default chart-formatting options, these are often overlooked.

Where did we go wrong?

1. Legends that read 'Series 1' and 'Series 2' because the series name is not selected in the source data
2. Unclear axis labels and data labels due to non-intuitive alignment or overlapping
3. Ambiguity in interpretation of axis titles and legend names

The ambiguity issue is quite prevalent, especially in situations where raw data is subjected to analytical calculations before being included into the source data. For example, when we calculate the difference between two series of numbers, it can be interpreted as a growth, a differential, a shortfall, a variance or a deviation. All of which mean different things but are frequently used interchangeably, resulting into the aforementioned ambiguity. Our familiarity with data often makes us overlook these smaller issues, but this ambiguity could be the death nail of the story, as an incorrect introduction will not facilitate the correct understanding of the story (Figure 8.6).

Things to keep in mind when setting the context of the visual story:

- Provide legends and axis titles where needed.
- Legends and axis titles should have complete clarity.
- Axis labels should be clearly visible.
- Is the denomination of the axis value clearly understood or stated?

- Can you clearly decipher the series for each data label value?
- You can also use pictures instead of axis labels and markers.

Figure 8.6 The Importance of Context

Can you understand the stories and agree with the conclusions made in the visuals?

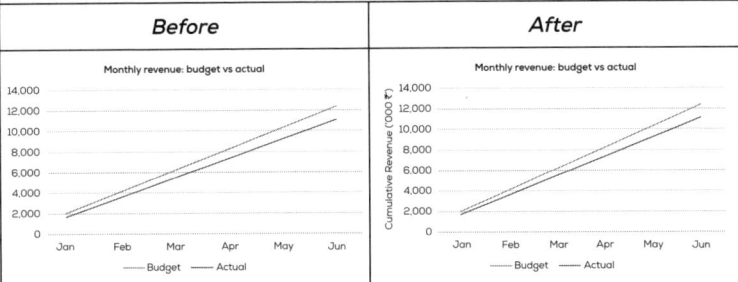

Explanation: With only two lines, the left-hand chart above is fairly simple; however, the understanding of the story is not complete and clear because we do not understand the denominations of the budget and actual figures. It could be rupees or USD or it could be millions or billions. The use of the vertical axis title on the right-hand side clarifies the currency type and value, making the chart completely clear.

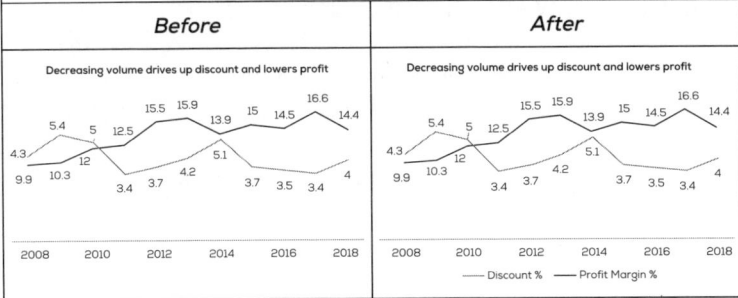

Explanation: The left-hand chart is a fairly simple line chart, but the audience still cannot understand what the story is because they do not know which line stands for discount and which for profit, or does one of the lines depict volume. When looking at the chart on the right, they can easily grasp the relationship between profit and discount because the legends help identify the respective lines.

Note: The above data is generated for explanatory purposes only.

Draw the Spotlight

The most important element of a data story is the priority event that directly impacts its conclusion. If the event does not stand out on its own, we need to direct audience attention to that part of the visual by drawing a spotlight. This makes the story enabling by showing the audience why and how we arrived at the stated conclusion. Using props that can range from shapes such as arrows, lines, boxes and circles to even a simple choice of colour can change the way the audience perceives our story (Figure 8.7).

In data analytics, the 'why' becomes more important than 'what', and hence supplementing the event highlight with an event discussion can make the story more impactful. When drawing the spotlight on increasing revenue, for example, the event discussion could crisply identify the reason behind this growth. This event discussion can be displayed on the chart through the use of titles and props like text boxes or shapes; or an upcoming visual could provide the discussion (read: analysis) into this event.

With your priority event in mind, ask yourself:

1. Does this event draw audience attention?
2. Will their eyes capture this part of the visual at first glance?
3. Can they appreciate its impact and role in the story?

If you have answered 'Yes' to all, you can move ahead; if not, then there is more work to be done here!

Figure 8.7 Spotlight Techniques

Example 1: A consumer products company reported a significant drop in the quarterly sales volume. An equity research analyst, analysing the significance of this volume decline, wanted to tell his investors that there is nothing to worry about since the company's market share is intact and it is only a temporary phenomenon led by macroeconomic factors.

Without an Event Highlight

Demonetization led drop: market share intact

	2008	2010	2012	2014	2016	2018
	250	272	274	297	291	303	324	310	298	368	337

Volumes (Mn units) — Market share (%) RH

Explanation: The audience will start reading the chart from left to right and will not realize the significance of the priority event that holds the story.

With the Event Highlight

Demonetization led drop: market share intact

8% YoY drop

2008	2010	2012	2014	2016	2018
250	272	274	297	291	303	324	310	298	368	337

Volumes (Mn units) — Market share (%) RH

Explanation: The call-out and arrow highlight the event. The audience will first look at the right-hand corner and appreciate the story impact at first glance due to the use of a downward sloping arrow, which intersects with a horizontal line and call-out.

(Figure 8.7 continued)

(Figure 8.7 continued)

Example 2: The company is assessing how well it has fared in the current year post a recent dip in revenues.

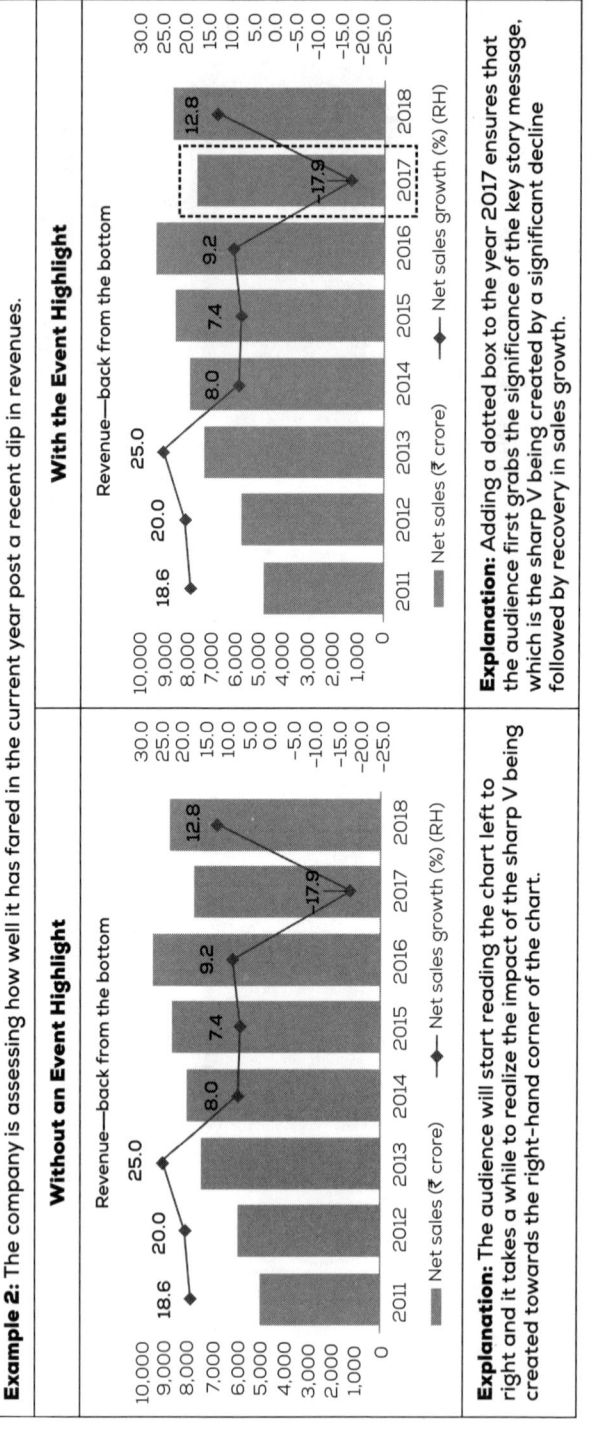

Without an Event Highlight

Revenue—back from the bottom

Explanation: The audience will start reading the chart left to right and it takes a while to realize the impact of the sharp V being created towards the right-hand corner of the chart.

With the Event Highlight

Revenue—back from the bottom

Explanation: Adding a dotted box to the year 2017 ensures that the audience first grabs the significance of the key story message, which is the sharp V being created by a significant decline followed by recovery in sales growth.

Example 3: The Indian arm of a global bank is making a presentation to the global management team to show how India has performed vis-à-vis other countries with an objective to showcase India's importance in the banks' overall business.

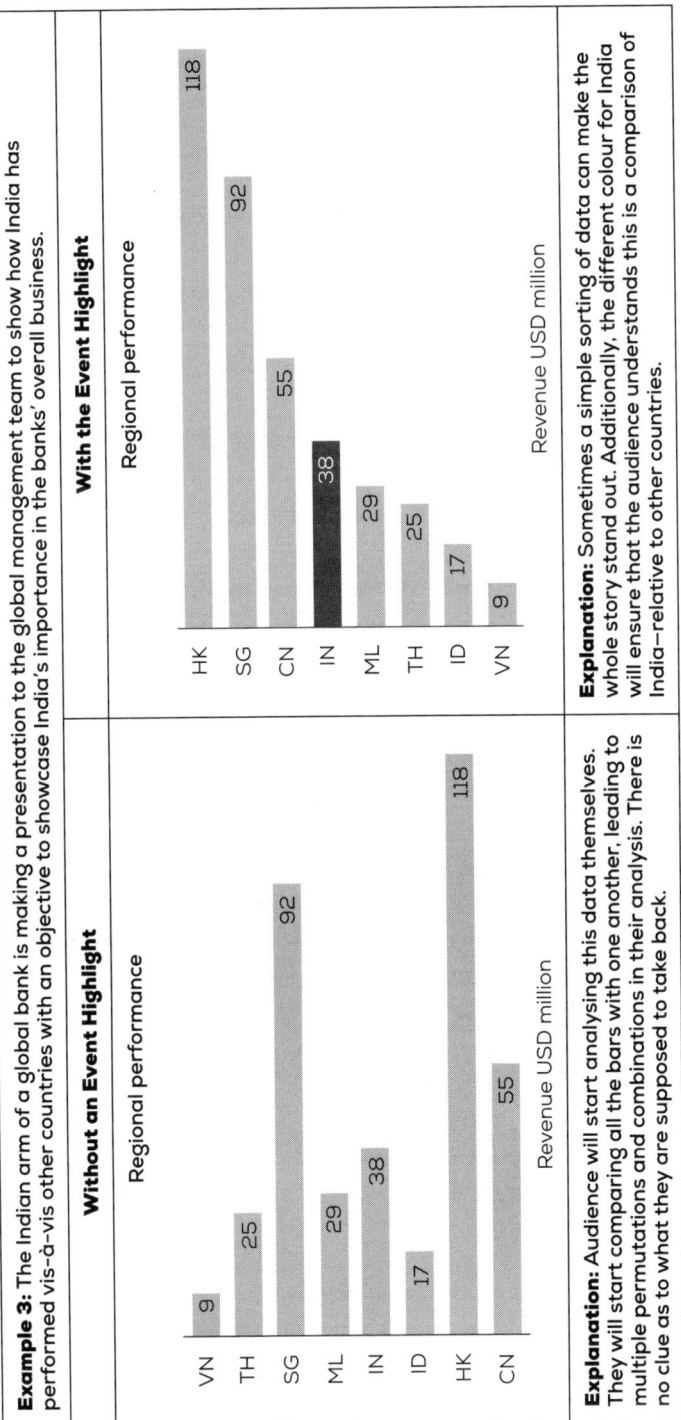

Without an Event Highlight

Regional performance

Revenue USD million

With the Event Highlight

Regional performance

Revenue USD million

Explanation: Audience will start analysing this data themselves. They will start comparing all the bars with one another, leading to multiple permutations and combinations in their analysis. There is no clue as to what they are supposed to take back.

Explanation: Sometimes a simple sorting of data can make the whole story stand out. Additionally, the different colour for India will ensure that the audience understands this is a comparison of India–relative to other countries.

Note: The above data has been generated for explanatory purposes only. For coloured figures refer to colour plate A.

How to make the event stand out:

- Use arrows to showcase trend events.
- Use shapes—squares, rectangles, circles—to highlight relationships.
- Use different colours for characters or events that need to stand out.
- Adjust minimum and maximum values on the Y-axis to depict a trend.
- Sort data ascending or descending to highlight relative relationships.
- Divide scatter plots into quadrants and define the relationship in each.
- Use call-outs and text boxes for event discussion.
- Use titles for highlighting events and event discussion.

End with a Bang!

A story is not complete until it does not enable the audience by providing a clear message or conclusion. A chart gets converted into a data visual only when the priority event and conclusion stand out in a way that grabs audience attention (Figure 8.8). The audience should not have to spend one additional second to analyse the data and arrive at the conclusion themselves. Giving the audience everything ready on the platter will make them spend less of their 'brain time' in trying to comprehend the story and its message while leaving more time to absorb its impact.

A chart gets converted into a visual story only when the priority event and conclusion stand out while depicting a strong link between the two.

Not spelling out the conclusion clearly also leaves it open for interpretation. The audience will arrive at a conclusion using their own perspective. We humans have a tendency to interpret the

Figure 8.8 The Impact of a Conclusion

Example 1: A credit analyst is trying to convince the credit committee that the business performance of a commodity producer is likely to be supported by recovering volume demand, which in turn supports the approval recommendation to disburse the loan.

Without Conclusion	With Conclusion

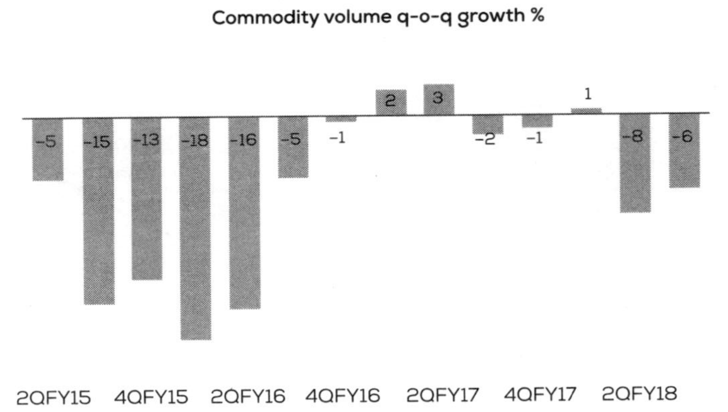

Commodity volume q-o-q growth %   (Without Conclusion)

Commodity demand recovering   (With Conclusion)

Legend:
- Commodity volume q-o-q growth %
- ------ Average growth rate (%)

Without Conclusion x-axis: 2QFY15 4QFY15 2QFY16 4QFY16 2QFY17 4QFY17 2QFY18

With Conclusion x-axis: 2QFY15 4QFY15 2QFY16 4QFY16 2QFY17 4QFT17 2QFY18

Explanation: Reading from left to right, we see precisely three quarters with positive numbers with the most recent quarters being negative. There is no way the audience will interpret this as a recovering demand, and hence a positive.

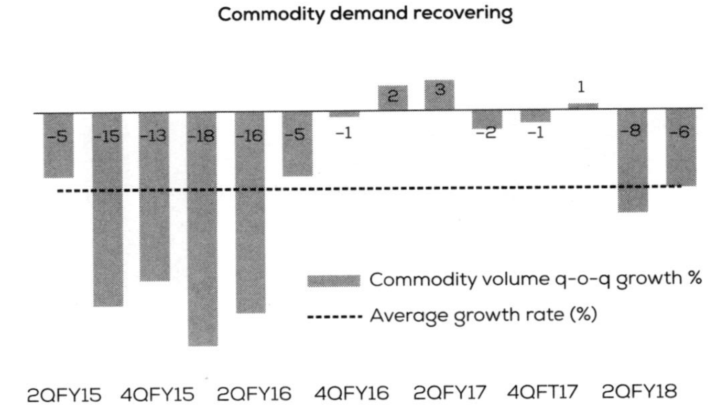

Explanation: First, the title makes the conclusion stand out. Second, the addition of the dotted line for average shows that for most quarters within this period, the bars have been above the average line. The mind can now interpret this as a recovering demand, and hence a positive.

(Figure 8.8 continued)

(Figure 8.8 continued)

Example 2: The company's management wants to know about its growth trend and the driver of this growth.

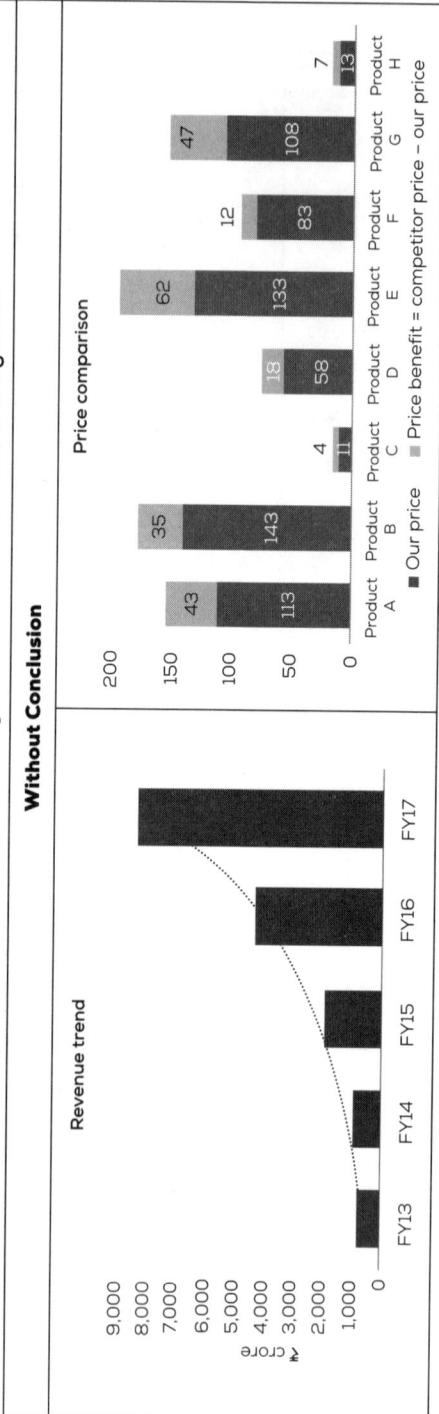

Without Conclusion

Revenue trend

Price comparison

■ Our price ■ Price benefit = competitor price − our price

Explanation: The above two charts are simple and easy to understand. Yet the audience will have to spend a few additional seconds to analyse this data to arrive at the conclusions and assess the impact of these numbers.

With Conclusion

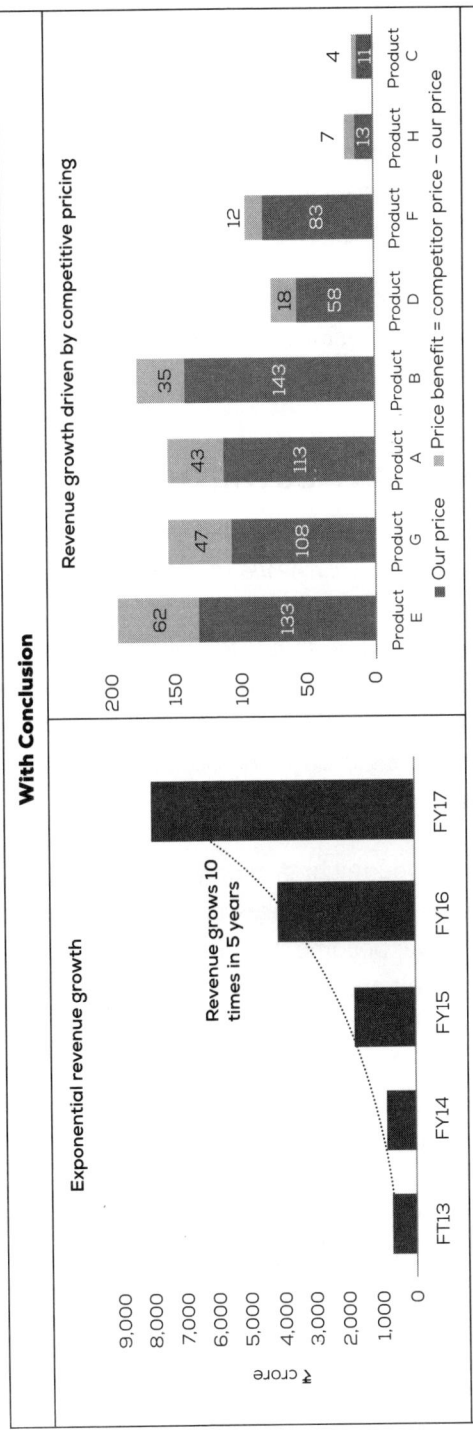

Exponential revenue growth

₹ crore

9,000
8,000
7,000
6,000
5,000
4,000
3,000
2,000
1,000
0

Revenue grows 10 times in 5 years

FT13 FY14 FY15 FY16 FY17

Revenue growth driven by competitive pricing

200
150
100
50
0

Product E Product G Product A Product B Product D Product F Product H Product C

- 62 47 43 35 18 12 7 4
- 133 108 113 143 58 83 13 11

■ Our price   ■ Price benefit = competitor price – our price

Explanation: The titles not only conclude each individual visual but also link them together and provide a conclusion for the full story. Addition of the text box adjacent to the trend line in the left-hand chart above makes the growth impact clear. On the right-hand side, sorting the bars by the size of the price benefit makes the key impact stand out, doing full justice to the title above.

Note: The above data has been generated for explanatory purposes only.

exact same things in different ways because we all come from different backgrounds with different perspectives. If I want to ensure that my audience takes back exactly the same conclusion as I want them to, it is best to spell it out clearly.

Titles are the most valuable tools when it comes to displaying the conclusion on the story. On occasions, props such as text boxes and arrows also come in handy.

THE POWER OF VISUAL AESTHETICS

A mountain range in front of you, brown and green from below turning into the lightest shade of blue-white as its ice-caped peaks touch the sky above. Among the lush greenery on one side, a small waterfall of melted ice runs down, merging into the lake below. The lake's still water reflect the beautiful blues of the sky. From the far corner, you see a boat moving into the lake. All you want to do is stand there, absorb the whole view, close your eyes and store it in your long-term memory forever!

When surfing the Internet, you might give only a cursory glance to a plain-looking website with no images and no colours, but sometimes you might have become transfixed on a website because of its exquisite look and feel. Occasionally, you might have chosen to use one mobile app over another simply because you like the look and feel of it. When in a retail store, how many times have you preferred to buy a product because it had an attractive packaging compared to another?

We humans like things of beauty. Good-looking data visuals also have a similar impact on the audience. When it is 'visually appealing', it not only attracts the audience, grabs their attention and engages them but also commands more 'brain time' as the audience appreciates 'beauty'.

Colour Scheme

The choice of colour plays a critical role in enhancing the visual appeal of the data visualization. If the colour soothes the eye, we spend more time on it; if the colour hurts the eye, we tend to move on to the next. Sequential shading of blue and green is most commonly used in business charts. These can be mixed with a touch of matte reds and oranges to make it attractive or to make a certain data series stand out. While most organizations have a standard colour scheme, which employees are expected to use, one needs to still think about how the audience is going to view this material. Are they likely to print it out in black and white or is it going to be viewed on screen in colour? Stick to using sequential colour schemes (light dark shades of same or different colours) for the ones getting printed, while for the others you can explore the categorical colour scheme (combination of any colour or shade). Refer to example in Figure 8.9.

Gridlines

Think of your chart as real estate, wherein every square foot is important and has a price associated with it. On your chart, every square millimetre is important, as its value is associated with the brain time it will use up. If something helps you tell the story better, it has a place on your chart. If it doesn't, get rid of it because it's only taking up valuable brain time. When making the decision on using gridlines, you have to ask the same question. But first, understand why we use gridlines.

Gridlines are used in situations where the audience cannot decipher the value of the data point associated with the line, bar or marker on the chart and, hence, needs a reference that leads them back to the axis. If your audience needs such help, use gridlines; if not, then don't. Unwanted use of gridlines not only takes away from valuable brain time but also adds a lot of clutter, making the charts less visually appealing. Refer to example in Figure 8.10.

Figure 8.9 Colour Rules

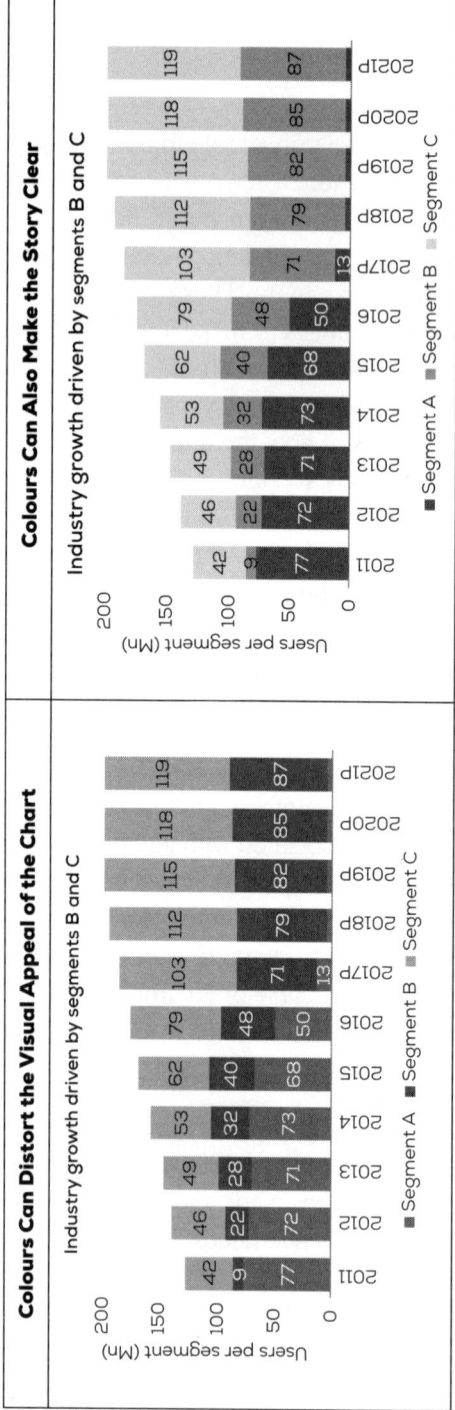

Colours Can Distort the Visual Appeal of the Chart

Industry growth driven by segments B and C

Users per segment (Mn)

Year	Values
2011	42, 9, 77
2012	46, 22, 72
2013	49, 28, 71
2014	53, 32, 73
2015	62, 40, 68
2016	79, 48, 50
2017P	103, 71, 13
2018P	112, 79
2019P	115, 82
2020P	118, 85
2021P	119, 87

■ Segment A   ■ Segment B   ■ Segment C

Colours Can Also Make the Story Clear

Industry growth driven by segments B and C

Users per segment (Mn)

Year	Values
2011	42, 9, 77
2012	46, 22, 72
2013	49, 28, 71
2014	53, 32, 73
2015	62, 40, 68
2016	79, 48, 50
2017P	103, 71, 13
2018P	112, 79
2019P	115, 82
2020P	118, 85
2021P	119, 87

■ Segment A   ■ Segment B   ■ Segment C

Explanation: Using a default Excel colour palette makes it harder to read the top left chart, while the darker shades also hurt the eye. The colour choice for the right-hand chart makes the story completely clear because with one glance, you can follow the three distinct and soothing colours to understand how one is disappearing while the other two become bigger. Even without reading the data labels or the title, the premise of the story becomes absolutely clear.

Note: The above data has been generated for explanatory purposes only. For coloured figures refer to colour plate A.

Figure 8.10 Get Rid of Clutter

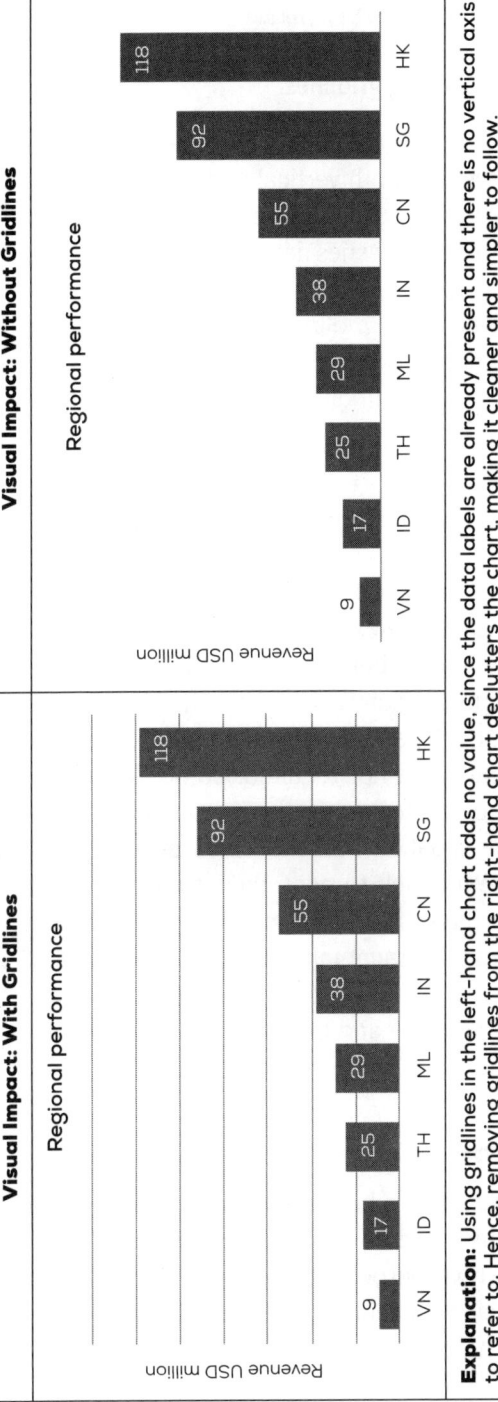

Explanation: Using gridlines in the left-hand chart adds no value, since the data labels are already present and there is no vertical axis to refer to. Hence, removing gridlines from the right-hand chart declutters the chart, making it cleaner and simpler to follow.

Note: The above data has been generated for explanatory purposes only.

Guidelines on using gridlines:

- No use of gridlines when there are data labels.
- Never use both vertical and horizontal gridlines.
- Horizontal gridlines are used more than vertical.
- Longer time series data typically demand use of horizontal gridlines.
- When using gridlines, prefer to use a light grey shade.
- Pertain to a subtle and minimal use of gridlines.
- Avoid using gridlines where not needed.

Legends

Legends are an important tool for character introduction. Their placement plays an equally important role in serving this purpose and adding to the look and feel of the visual. The standard place where the audience expects to find the legend is bottom centre, below the X–axis label. In certain situations with a single series, when the introduction is clear from the chart or axis title, there is no need for a legend. Don't take up valuable real estate (read: chart space) when not required. Some default chart-formatting options place the legend on the right-hand side of the chart area. This is one situation that should be avoided at all times! First, because we read left to right, the introduction to the characters, that is, the legend should come before we finish reading the chart. Second, this placement takes away a lot of valuable chart space, as it makes the actual chart area much smaller while leaving empty space above and below the legends. Refer to example in Figure 8.11.

Data Labels

Data Labels have to be clearly visible at all times. If you cannot decipher the value of the label or the series that it pertains to, then the whole purpose of adding these is lost and then they end up taking valuable real estate without moving your story forward. The positioning and colour choices of the data labels

Figure 8.11 The Position Matters

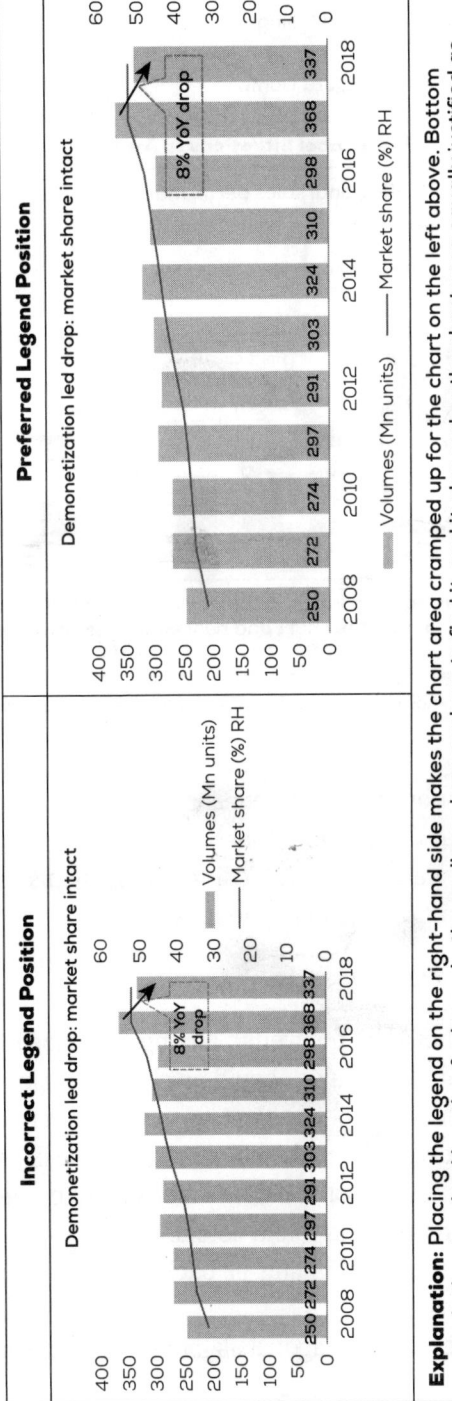

Explanation: Placing the legend on the right-hand side makes the chart area cramped up for the chart on the left above. Bottom centre is the standard location for legends; the audience knows where to find it, and it also makes the chart area equally justified as shown in the right-hand chart above.

Note: The above data has been generated for explanatory purposes only.

Figure 8.12 Don't Make It a Data Dump

Data Label Situations to Avoid

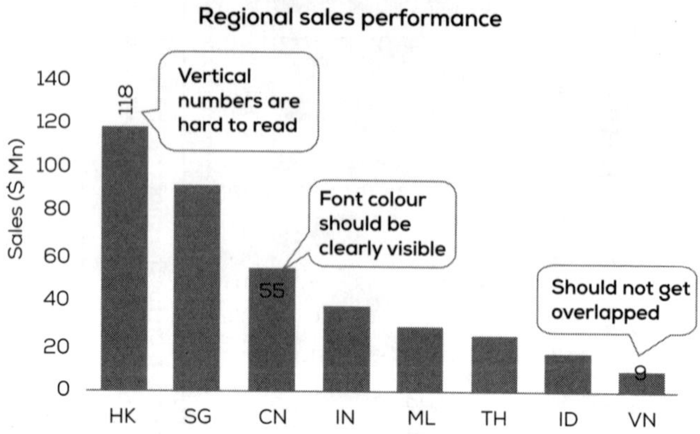

Regional sales performance

Explanation: Placing data labels in the above highlighted manner makes it difficult to read the chart and hence these situations should be avoided.

Note: The above data has been generated for explanatory purposes only.

also play an important role in enhancing the understanding of the key takeaways from the visual. Key things to watch out for are overlapping data labels, vertical text alignments and colour choices. Refer to example in Figure 8.12.

Guidelines on using data labels:

- There should be no overlap among data labels.
- Each data label value should be clearly visible.
- The series the label pertains to should be very clear.
- The label should not be cut through by the lines or bars.
- The text colour of the data label should be determined based on the background colour.
- Avoid using highlighting or background colour for data labels.
- Avoid vertical or diagonal alignment of data labels.

Bring an Order

The brain—a pattern recognition machine—understands things better when they form an order or pattern. When information on the visual is presented in a haphazard manner, without any logic or order, the mind is immediately put off because:

1. It does not like what it sees.
2. It finds it hard to decipher any meaning when there is no order or pattern.
3. It cannot take away any story when there is no order. In single series bar charts especially, I have often seen that the story becomes evident by something as simple as arranging the bars in an ascending or descending order. Refer to example in Figure 8.13.

Fill in the Gaps

When using bar charts, the width of the bar is equally important as the length of the bar. As a general rule, we want that the width of the bars should be wider than the white blank space between them. We don't want the bars to be too wide as it will cause the audience to start comparing bar widths rather than bar lengths. Under most scenarios, I find the ideal gap width to be between 60 per cent and 70 per cent. The size of the circle in the doughnut also represents a similar problem, wherein the big blank white circle in the centre causes disruptions in reading the right patterns. The ideal doughnut size is found at around 60 per cent. Refer to example in Figure 8.14.

Avoid 3D

It is often believed that 3D charts bring in the much-needed creativity to visuals. This creativity should emanate from the story you create on your visual; using a 3D chart is not the solution. The 3D charts are slightly more complex to understand, and they

Figure 8.13 Order, Order, Where Art Thou?

When there is an order in the visual, the mind can look for patterns to understand the story and its conclusions. Without an order, the audience spends undue time trying to figure out the crux of the story.

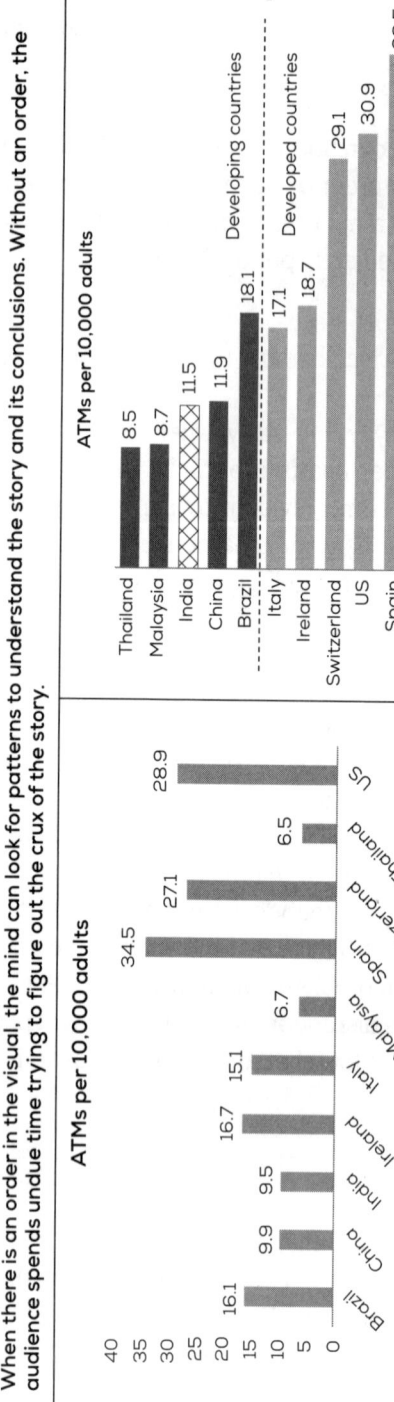

Explanation: In the left-hand chart above, when reading left to right, we start making multiple comparisons in our minds without arriving at any clear conclusion. Sorting the bars, like on the right-hand side, enables us to decipher clear patterns and, hence, arrive at concrete conclusions. The first division between developing and developed countries makes it clear that the number of ATMs is relatively higher in developed than developing regions. We can further decipher the pattern within the developing countries to conclude that number of ATMs in India, though fairly lower than developed countries, is at an average level when compared to developing countries alone.

Note: The above data has been generated for explanatory purposes only. For coloured figures refer to colour plate B.

Figure 8.14 Mind the Gap

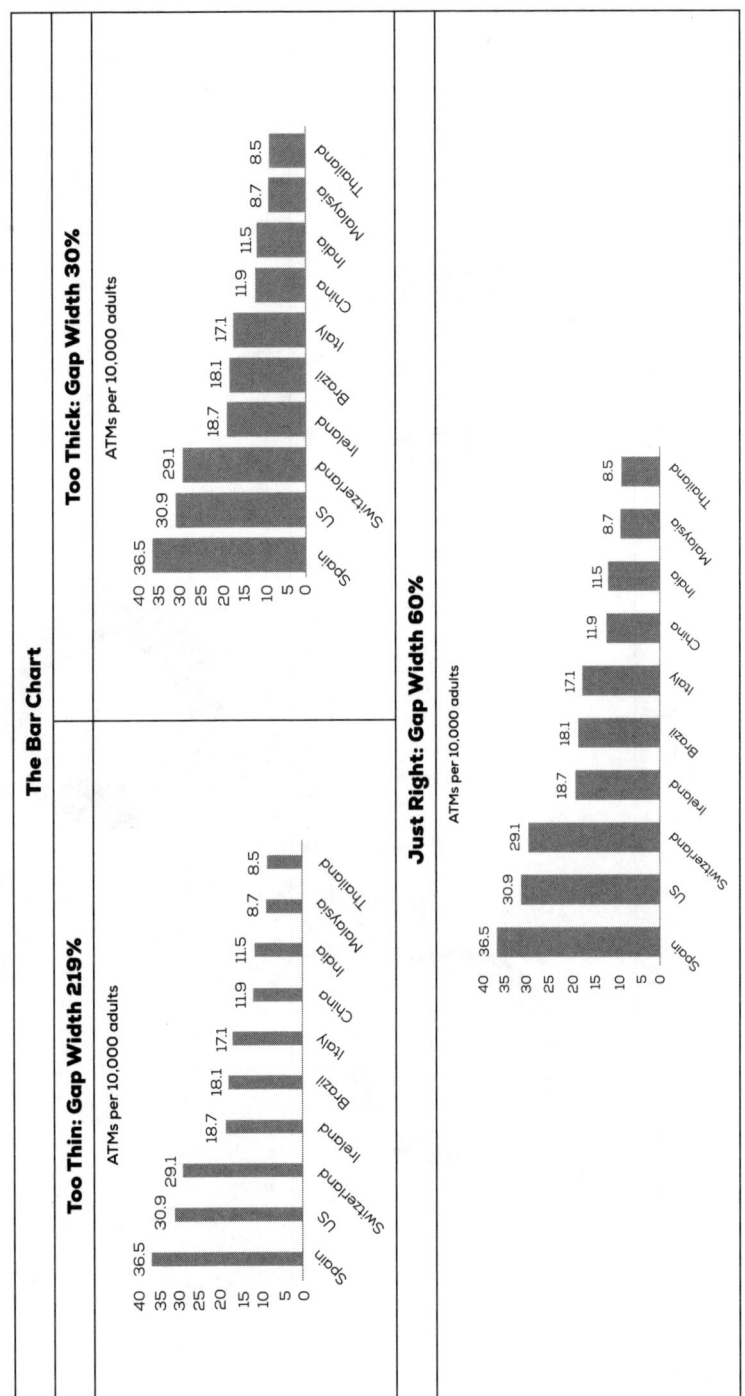

(Figure 8.14 continued)

(Figure 8.14 continued)

The Doughnut Chart

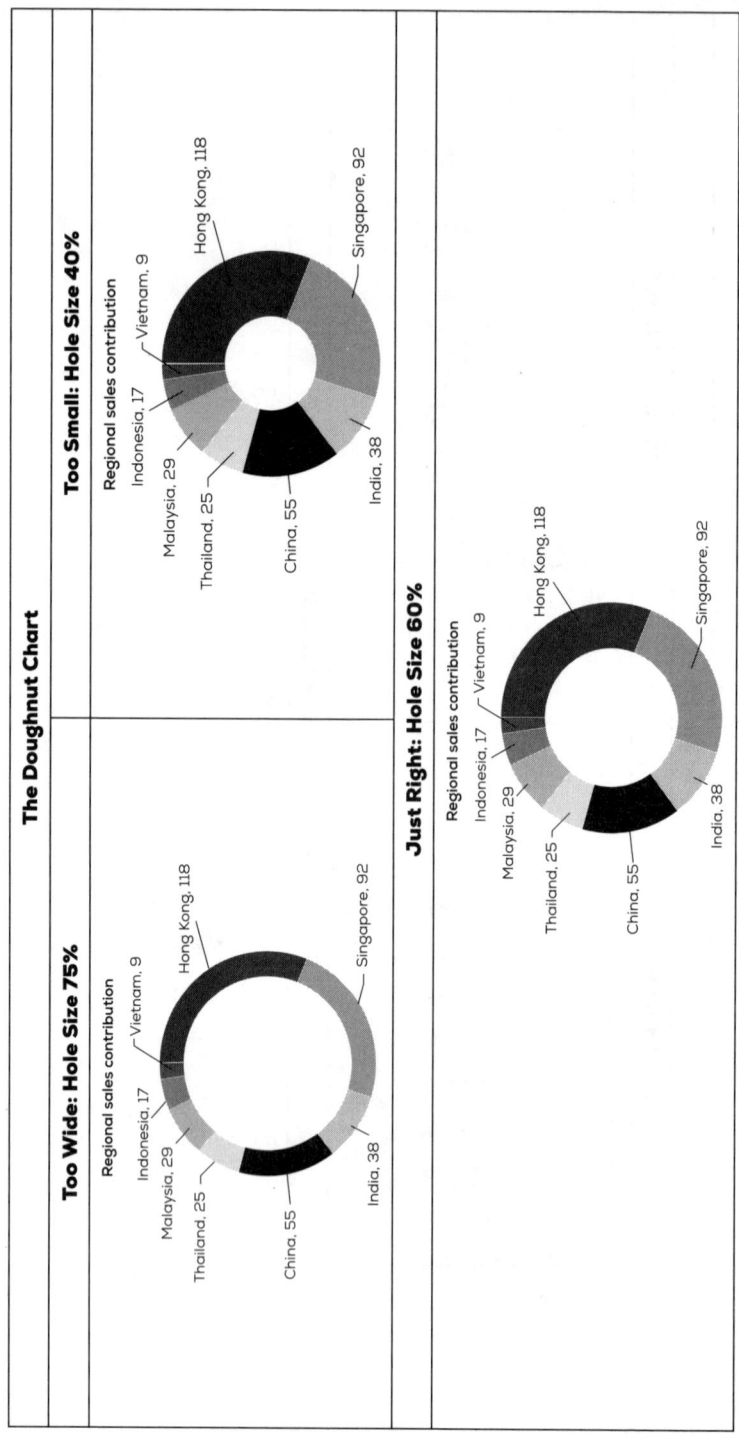

Too Wide: Hole Size 75%

Too Small: Hole Size 40%

Just Right: Hole Size 60%

Note: The above data has been generated for explanatory purposes only. For coloured figures refer to colour plate B.

demand a lot of finer formatting to make them visually appealing and easily understandable, which tends to take up a lot more time. I recommend against using 3D, unless you are adapt with all the finer formatting requirements with the time available to incorporate the same. Refer to example in Figure 8.15.

Maintain Consistency

There should be a consistency in the font styles and sizes, orders of magnitude used to define numbers, denominations, alignment for axis titles and labels, colour schemes, and title and legend positions. We should also adhere to a standard usage of all these finer chart aspects. It is common to miss these basics because you are more focused on the analysis and the story, but the audience is likely to catch these first. Any non-standard usage is a change that causes a disruption in the audience's mind. First, they catch an 'error' you have missed. Second and more important, it takes away from 'brain time' because they will first have to process this 'change' before they can go on to processing the story.

CHEAT SHEET FOR EFFECTIVE VISUAL STORYTELLING

Time and practice will ensure that all the learnings developed in this chapter register permanently in your minds and you will start applying these subconsciously without even realizing that you are doing it. But just like with an exam that you have prepared for throughout the year, it is always better to have that little cheat sheet you can refer to just before you enter the examination hall. To help you in your data-visualization journey going forward, I have devised this cheat sheet offering tips on some of the most important factors to consider when creating impactful visual stories.

Figure 8.15 Beauty Lies in Simplicity

3D Only Makes Charts Difficult to Understand

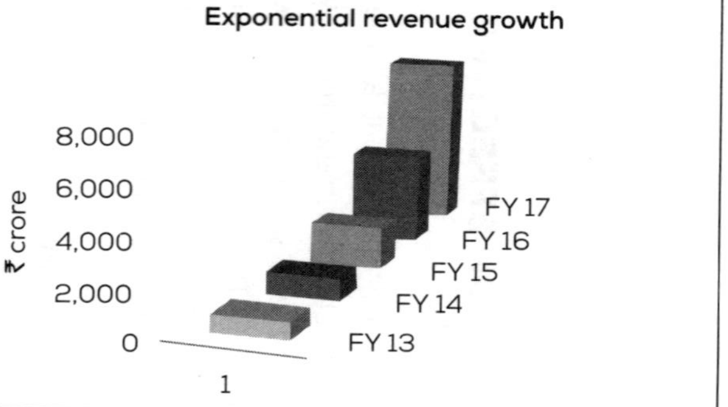

Exponential revenue growth
₹ crore
8,000
6,000
4,000
2,000
0
1
FY 13
FY 14
FY 15
FY 16
FY 17

Stories Are Better Understood When They Are Presented in Simple Formats

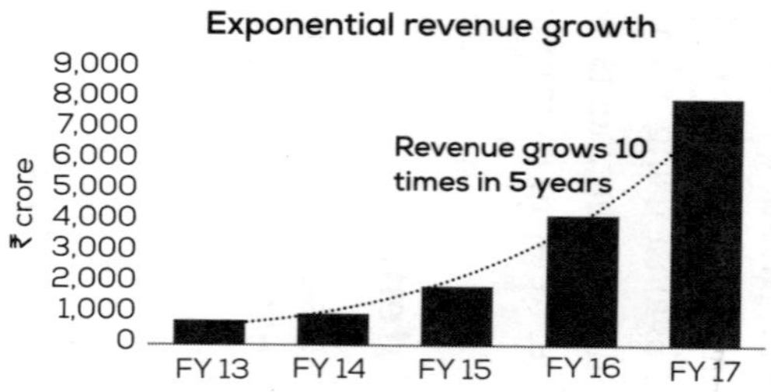

Exponential revenue growth
₹ crore
9,000
8,000
7,000
6,000
5,000
4,000
3,000
2,000
1,000
0
Revenue grows 10 times in 5 years
FY 13
FY 14
FY 15
FY 16
FY 17

Note: The above data has been generated for explanatory purposes only. For coloured figures refer to colour plate C.

Table 8.1 Titles Matter

Incorrect Usage of Title	Preferred Usage of Title
Mutual fund performance comparison	ABC fund outperforms peers
Indian banks' NPA	Indian banks' NPA: PSUs most stressed
Price and volume comparison	Price sensitivity hurts sales volume

Use Titles and Headings

Chart titles and headings are the most powerful but unfortunately most underutilized tools in visual storytelling. Chart titles are commonly used to describe the data, a job that should be done by legends and axis titles. The power of the chart title is unleashed when they are used not to describe data but to conclude the data. In situations where multiple charts come together to form a story, chart titles play an important role in not only concluding the visual at hand but also linking all visuals together to form one story. Refer to examples in Table 8.1.

Use Pictures

The addition of pictures on your charts or smart diagrams can sometimes bring the much-needed 'visual appeal' (Figure 8.16). In business visualizations, pictures are most commonly used for brand logos and country flags. You can also use pictures of products and objects that describe a product-based data series. In charts, pictures are best used in place of axis labels or markers. On any other type of visuals, pictures could be positioned on empty spaces and aligned in with the rest of the visual.

Avoid Unnecessary Visuals

Don't overuse pictures within visuals just to make them more picturesque. Over-usage of visuals within a report or presentation

Figure 8.16 Get Creative

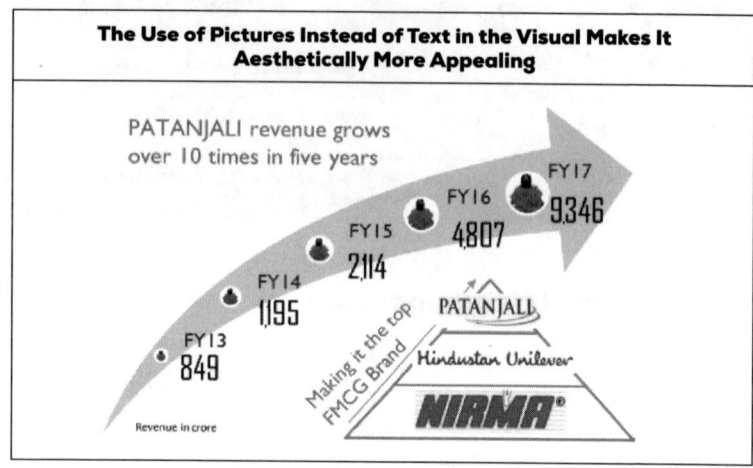

Note: For coloured figures refer to colour plate C.
Source: https://www.thenewsminute.com/article/baba-ramdev%E2%80%99s-yoga-guide-solving-biggest-problems-our-time-40186; https://www.patanjaliayurved.net/; https://www.unilever.com/; http://www.nirma.co.in/

will make it appear as lengthy and complex as the data itself. Use them only when the story demands it and align them next to the text/bullet/paragraph, discussing the particular insight or conclusion.

Avoid Excessive Information

When we come across a couple of rows or columns of data, our first instinct is to make one chart containing all the information. Such chart is a data dump which in no way communicates the story, making the chart as complex as the data. Dumping excessive information onto one chart is a fatal mistake that a lot of people continue making. In order to avoid this, focus on the story triangle and check if the event and outcome depicted in the visual lead you to answer the question raised in the purpose. Refer to example in Figure 8.17.

Figure 8.17 Break Down the Complexity

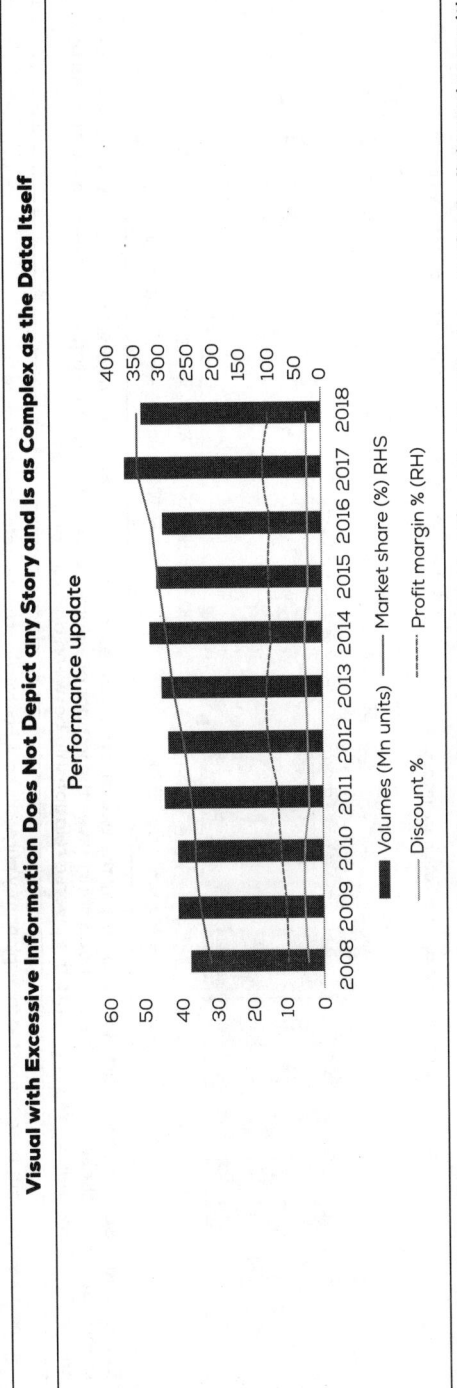

Visual with Excessive Information Does Not Depict any Story and Is as Complex as the Data Itself

Performance update

Volumes (Mn units) ——— Market share (%) RHS
——— Discount % ——— Profit margin % (RH)

Explanation: The audience will take some time to reach the right corner of the chart and decipher the impact of a declining volume with an intact market share. They cannot even get even a vague understanding of the inverse relationship between discount and profit.

(Figure 8.17 continued)

(Figure 8.17 continued)

When Data Is Bucketed into Events and Themes and Presented on Visuals Accordingly, It Allows for the Story to Stand Out

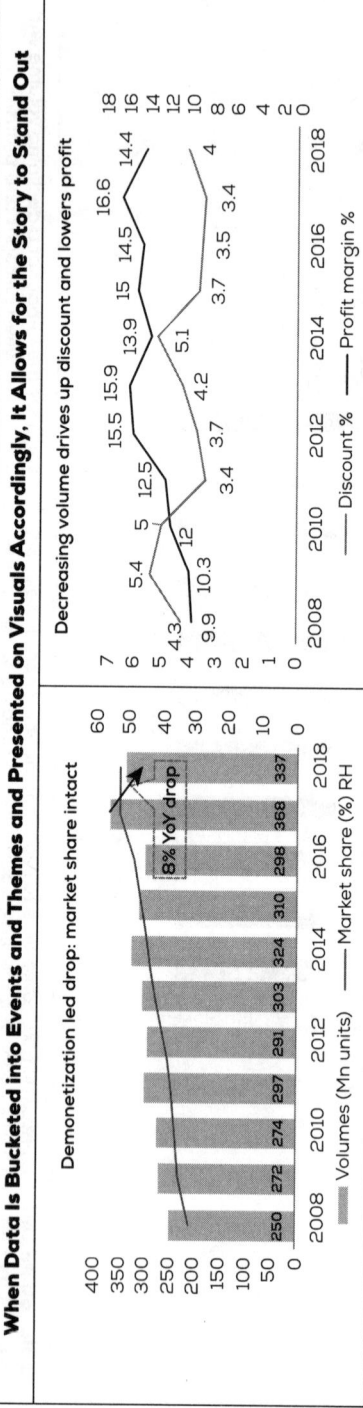

Demonetization led drop: market share intact

	2008	2010	2012	2014	2016	2018
Volumes (Mn units)	250 272 274	297 291	303 324	310 298	368 337

8% YoY drop

Decreasing volume drives up discount and lowers profit

Discount %: 5.4 5 12.5 15.5 15.9 13.9 15 14.5 16.6 14.4

Profit margin %: 4.3 12 10.3 9.9 3.4 3.7 4.2 5.1 3.7 3.5 3.4 4

Explanation: Splitting the charts into two, as per the two distinct themes identified for the story, makes the key events and conclusions stand out in both these charts. The left-hand chart gives the impact of volume reduction versus a stagnant market share and the one on the right hand side gives a peak into the inverse relationship between discount and profit.

Note: The above data has been generated for explanatory purposes only. For coloured figures refer to colour plate D.

Final Touch-up Is Important

In my data-visualization workshops, I check every chart made by each participant across all exercises, and by the last exercise of the workshop, I have often found that when the chart comes to me, it is 90 per cent–95 per cent complete. All it needs is a little clean-up and touch-up to convert the chart into a visual story. Typically, the things I end up changing or adding—in the order of frequency—are: chart titles, shapes to highlight the events, legend position, axis titles, gap width, hole size in doughnut and colour schemes. If we give importance to the theory, and the fundamentals and basics discussed in this chapter, the end result will be a 100 per cent complete data visual.

Don't Get Discouraged by the Retakes

You will never get the visual right in the first time and chances are that even after the report/presentation has been sent, you will keep thinking of ways you could have done it better. You will typically begin with a basic chart or visual, run it through a couple of iterations until you don't get the story, that is, the characters, events and conclusions, right. Thereafter, some time will be spent on getting the formatting and visual aesthetics right. And if you are someone like me, you will constantly keep thinking of how to make it better! And that's just the whole beauty of visualization— since there cannot be a right or a wrong way to do it. My suggestion to you is that do not get discouraged by the number of iterations. More number of iterations does not mean that you are doing something wrong; it just means that you are trying to build a great story. With practice and experience, the number of iterations will decrease.

SHOWTIME!

The strategy team of an automobile company is making a recommendation to its management to change its discount strategy since higher discounts are negatively impacting profitability. For this purpose, it is imperative to show the inverse relationship between discounts and profits.

Figure 8.18 shows how even a simple chart can be converted into an effective visual story if we have clarity on the message we want to convey and are armed with the right charting tools, which help us achieve the same.

Most people are used to making decent-looking charts as shown in 'The First Draft' in Figure 8.18, often not realizing that such charts require the audience to put in an additional effort to analyse the data themselves. Following the simple concepts discussed in this chapter can go a long way in ridding the world of charts and introducing them to data visuals, which convey the data story in an easily understandable and visually attractive format. Data visualization is also a highly creative process; the more you practice, the more your mind will open to new ideas and methods in which your data can be presented!

Figure 8.18 Journey of a Visual Story

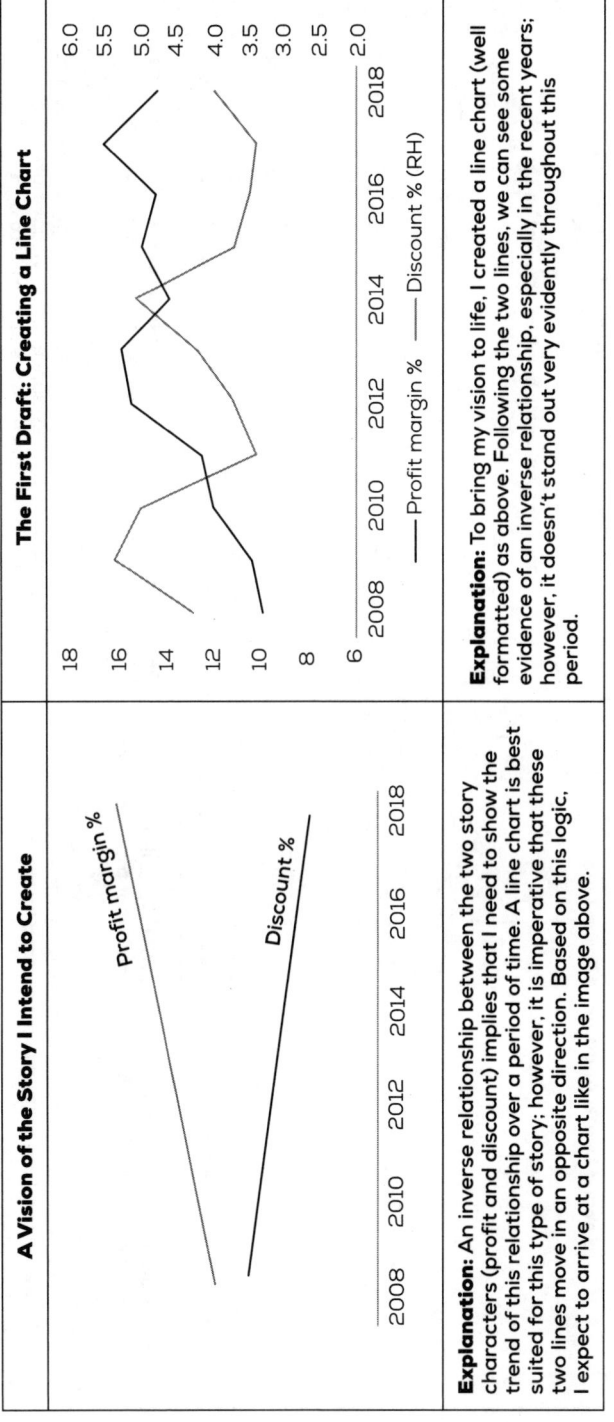

A Vision of the Story I Intend to Create	The First Draft: Creating a Line Chart

Profit margin %

Discount %

2008 2010 2012 2014 2016 2018

Explanation: An inverse relationship between the two story characters (profit and discount) implies that I need to show the trend of this relationship over a period of time. A line chart is best suited for this type of story; however, it is imperative that these two lines move in an opposite direction. Based on this logic, I expect to arrive at a chart like in the image above.

2008 2010 2012 2014 2016 2018

— Profit margin %   — Discount % (RH)

Explanation: To bring my vision to life, I created a line chart (well formatted) as above. Following the two lines, we can see some evidence of an inverse relationship, especially in the recent years; however, it doesn't stand out very evidently throughout this period.

(Figure 8.18 continued)

(Figure 8.18 continued)

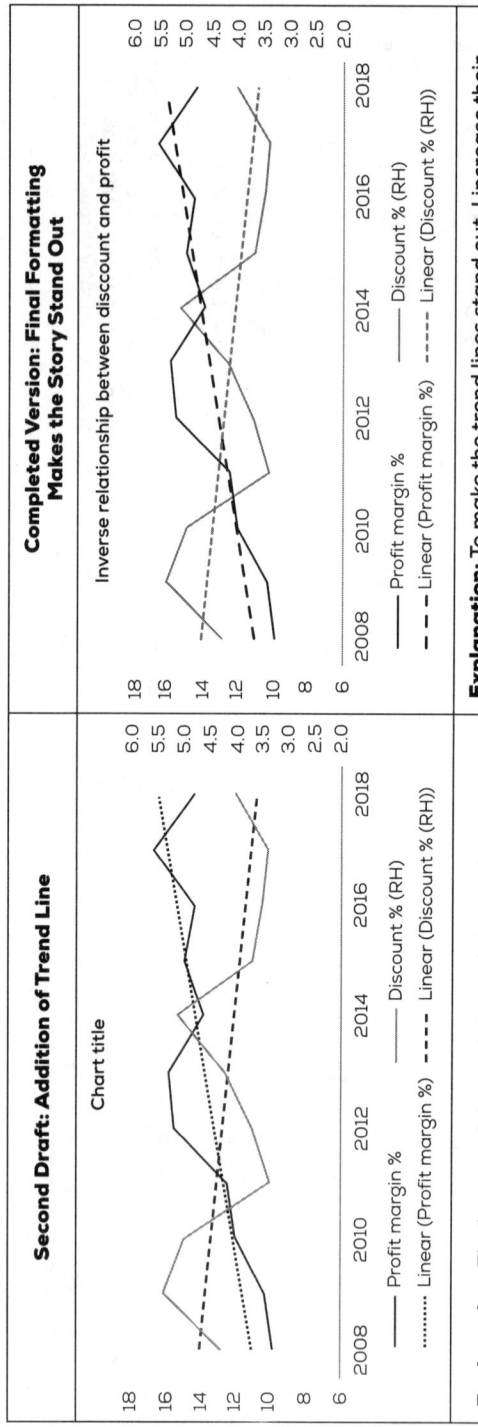

Second Draft: Addition of Trend Line

Chart title

Profit margin % — Discount % (RH) ---- Linear (Profit margin %) ········ Linear (Discount % (RH))

Explanation: The impact of discount on profit typically has a lagged and long-term effect. With this logic, I plot trend lines for both these series and that is when we can see a clear inverse relationship throughout the period. Now the trend lines become the important characters as they help me depict the desired story. However, they are getting overpowered by the actual discount and profit lines.

Completed Version: Final Formatting Makes the Story Stand Out

Inverse relationship between disccount and profit

Profit margin % — Discount % (RH) ---- Linear (Profit margin %) ----- Linear (Discount % (RH))

Explanation: To make the trend lines stand out, I increase their line weight and reduce the weight of the actual discount and profit lines, and now your eye will first catch the dotted trend lines. I change the colour for the discount lines to red to show its negative side and change the profit lines to green to depict its positive requirement. One glance at this visual makes the entire story clear to an audience who is also likely to agree with the conclusions made therein.

Note: The above data is for explanatory purposes only. For coloured figures refer to colour plate D.

Figure 8.7 Spotlight Techniques

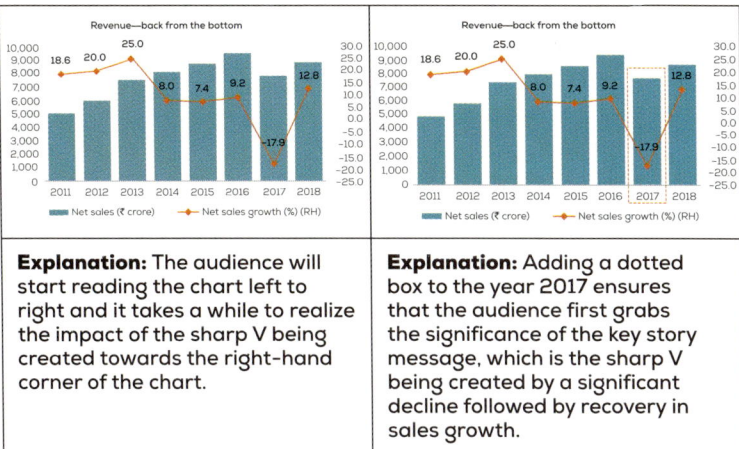

Explanation: The audience will start reading the chart left to right and it takes a while to realize the impact of the sharp V being created towards the right-hand corner of the chart.	**Explanation:** Adding a dotted box to the year 2017 ensures that the audience first grabs the significance of the key story message, which is the sharp V being created by a significant decline followed by recovery in sales growth.

Figure 8.9 Colour Rules

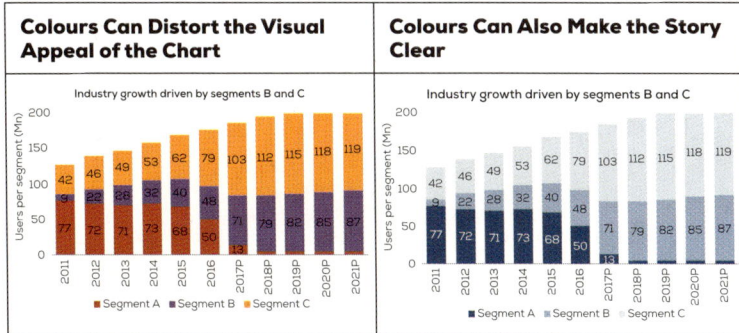

Explanation: Using a default Excel colour palette makes it harder to read the top left chart, while the darker shades also hurt the eye. The colour choice for the right-hand chart makes the story completely clear because with one glance, you can follow the three distinct and soothing colours to understand how one is disappearing while the other two become bigger. Even without reading the data labels or the title, the premise of the story becomes absolutely clear.

Plate A

Figure 8.13 Order, Order, Where Art Thou?

When there is an order in the visual, the mind can look for patterns to understand the story and its conclusions. Without an order, the audience spends undue time trying to figure out the crux of the story.

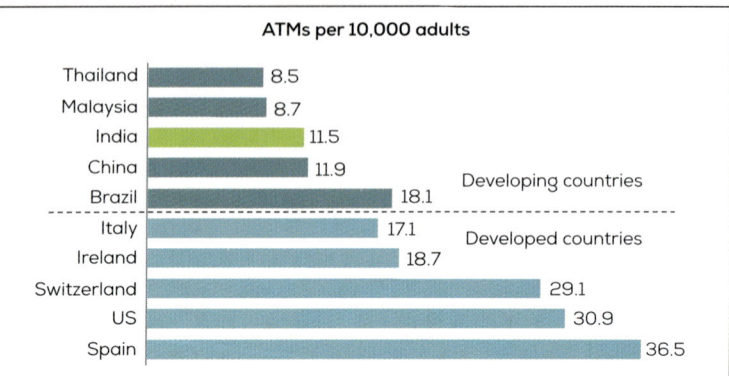

ATMs per 10,000 adults

Thailand	8.5
Malaysia	8.7
India	11.5
China	11.9
Brazil	18.1

Developing countries

Italy	17.1
Ireland	18.7
Switzerland	29.1
US	30.9
Spain	36.5

Developed countries

Explanation: Sorting the bars in this table enables us to decipher clear patterns and, hence, arrive at concrete conclusions. The first division between developing and developed countries makes it clear that the number of ATMs is relatively higher in developed than developing regions. We can further decipher the pattern within the developing countries to conclude that number of ATMs in India, though fairly lower than developed countries, is at an average level when compared to developing countries alone.

Figure 8.14 Mind the Gap

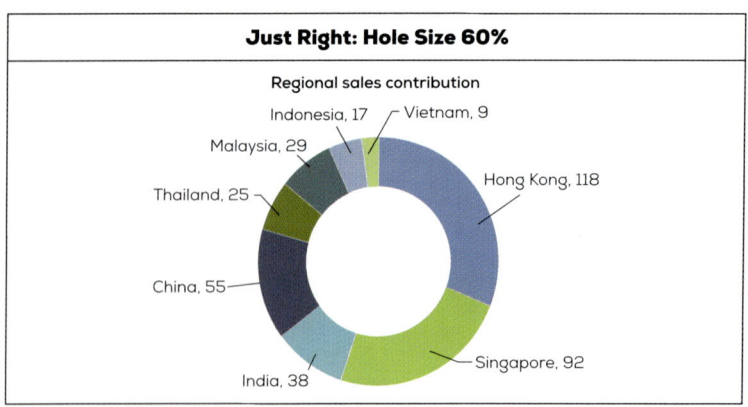

Just Right: Hole Size 60%

Regional sales contribution

Indonesia, 17 — Vietnam, 9
Malaysia, 29
Thailand, 25
Hong Kong, 118
China, 55
India, 38
Singapore, 92

Plate B

Figure 8.15 Beauty Lies in Simplicity

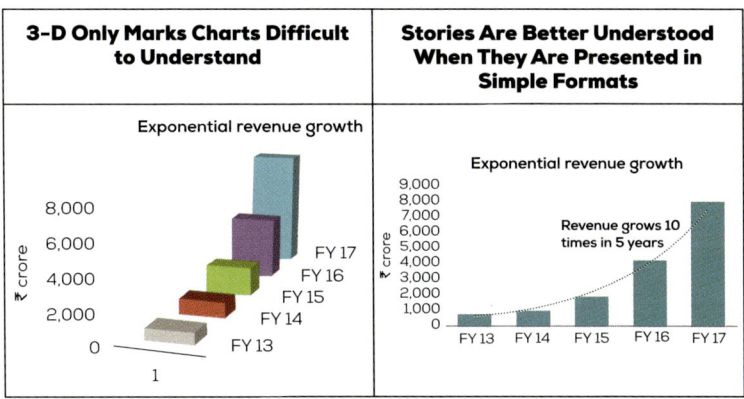

3-D Only Marks Charts Difficult to Understand	**Stories Are Better Understood When They Are Presented in Simple Formats**

Figure 8.16 Get Creative

The Use of Pictures Instead of Text in the Visual Make It Aesthetically More Appealing

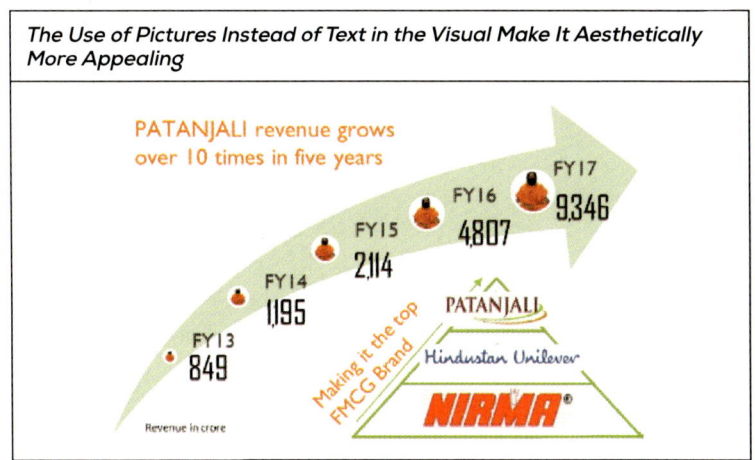

Plate C

Figure 8.17 Breakdown the Complexity

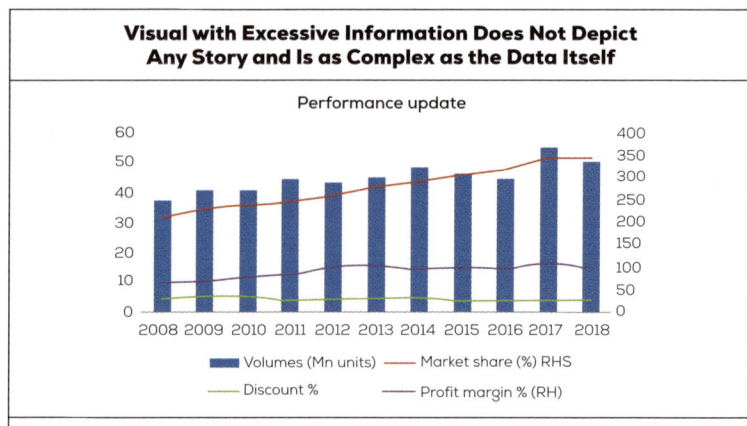

Visual with Excessive Information Does Not Depict Any Story and Is as Complex as the Data Itself

Performance update

Volumes (Mn units) — Market share (%) RHS — Discount % — Profit margin % (RH)

Explanation: The audience will take some time to reach the right corner of the chart and decipher the impact of a declining volume with an intact market share. They cannot get even a vague understanding of the inverse relationship between discount and profit.

Figure 8.18 Journey of a Visual Story

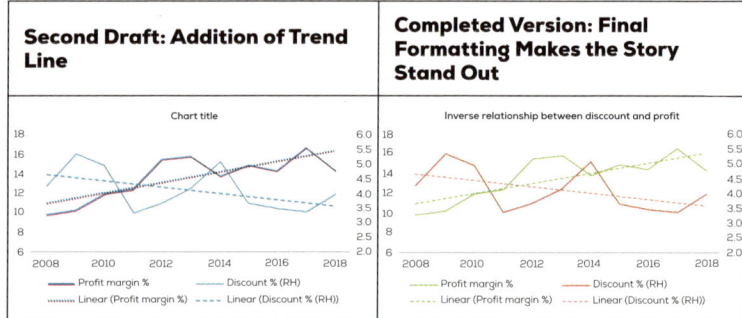

Second Draft: Addition of Trend Line	Completed Version: Final Formatting Makes the Story Stand Out
Chart title	Inverse relationship between disccount and profit
Explanation: The impact of discount on profit typically has a lagged and long-term effect. With this logic, I plot trend lines for both these series and that is when we can see a clear inverse relationship throughout the period. Now the trend lines become the important characters as they help me depict the desired story. However, they are getting overpowered by the actual discount and profit lines.	**Explanation:** To make the trend lines stand out, I increase their line weight and reduce the weight of the actual discount and profit lines and now your eye will first catch the dotted trend lines. I change the colour for the discount lines to red to show its negative side and change the profit lines to green to depict its positive requirement. One glance at this visual makes the entire story clear to an audience who is also likely to agree with the conclusions made therein.

Plate D

Figure 9.1 Data Story Created for FY2018 Business Performance Analysis

Robust Sales Growth Overshadows Slight Profit Dip

FY 2018 proves to be another healthy performance year with a 16% y/y revenue growth to 780 crore. In the last 10 years, the company's revenue has grown four times at a CAGR of 14.4%. Net profit margin is at a comfortable 9.9%, notably higher than its 5-year (8.9%) and 10-year (7.5%) averages although it came in lower than the 11% achieved in FY 2017. Sales volume recorded a steep 17% growth during the year, dominated by domestic volumes, which with ~90% of total sales contribution throughout this period continue to be the company's growth engine.

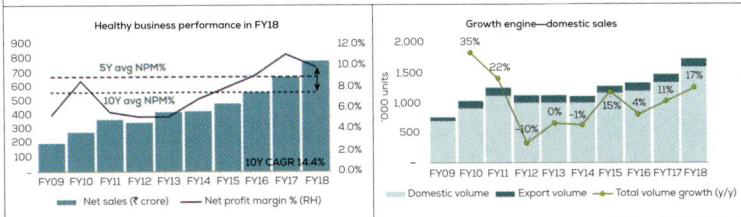

Plate E

Figure 9.3 The Production Stages: Step-by-Step Creation of the Visual

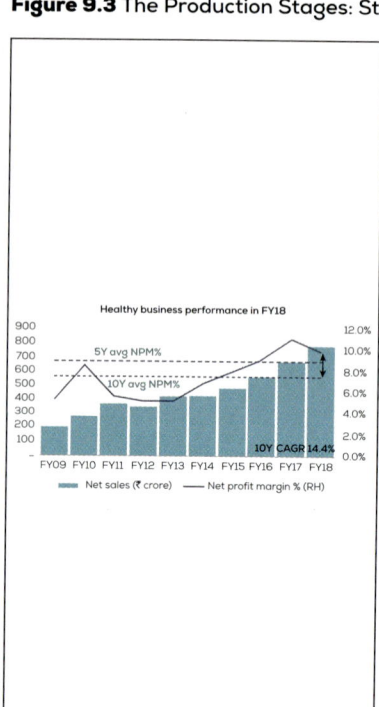

Healthy business performance in FY18

Net sales (₹ crore) — Net profit margin % (RH)

Visual Aesthetics:

- Reduce gap width to 10%. Although ideal is 60%, in this case the bars are used to represent a trend and not a relationship; hence, a lower gap is recommended.

- Bars changed to a lighter blue shade and the line to a darker blue shade with thickness 1.5 points.

- The average lines become dotted to reduce their significance on the chart and represent the same dark blue shade as the NPM line.

- 5-year and 10-year average removed from the legend and added as text boxes adjacent to lines.

- Gridlines deleted.

Conclusion:

- Add a text box stating CAGR sales growth.

- Addition of a conclusive title.

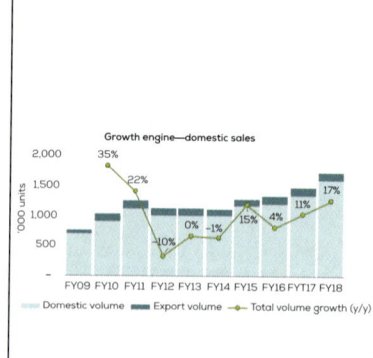

Growth engine—domestic sales

Domestic volume ▬ Export volume ─●─ Total volume growth (y/y)

Draw the Spotlight and Visual Aesthetics:

- Adjusting the bar gap width (to 10%) and changing the colours make the sales mix proportions and the dominance of domestic volume throughout this period clearly evident (the priority event).

- Adding data labels highlight the steep total volume growth in FY 2018.

- Remove gridlines.

- Remove secondary vertical axis since the total volume growth line contains all data labels.

Conclusion:

- Addition of a conclusive title.

Plate F

Figure 9.4 Data Story created for the Hotel Industry

Macro Tailwinds Support the Future of Hotel Industry

The structural demand–supply shift underway in the hotel industry bodes well for its future performance. Hotel industry supply growth consistently outpaced demand growth (with the exception of FY 2012) putting a pressure on industry occupancy rate (OR) and average room rate (ARR). However, as demand started recovering and supply slowed down, this gap has closed consistently over the years and for the first time, in FY 2016, demand growth outpaced supply growth. This gap had widened further in FY 2017 with demand growth at 10.3% and supply growth at 7.7%, resulting in peak levels of OR (68%) and ARR (5,500) which have steadily grown with the improving demand situation. Growing number of foreign tourists (CAGR 5.9%) and improving GDP per capita (6.6%) are likely to support further demand generation, in turn leading to improved OR and ARR for the industry.

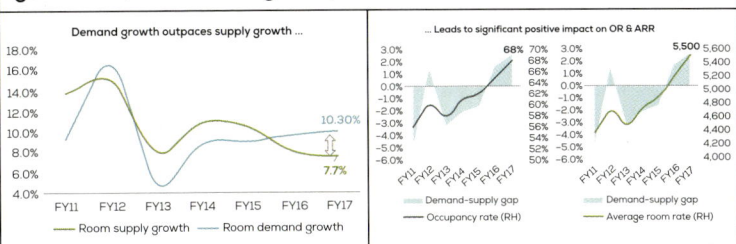

Plate G

Figure 9.6 The Production Stages: Step-by-Step Creation of the Visual

First Visual: Demand–Supply Gap	
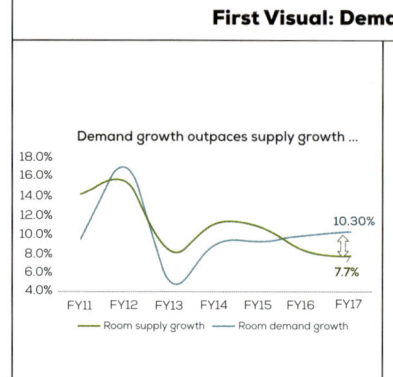	**Visual Aesthetics:** • Remove gridlines. • Convert the lines to 'smoothed lines' as this looks better in a short data series. • Add colour and data labels in the same colour as the respective lines. **Conclusion:** A conclusive title along with the spotlight makes the overall chart conclusion very clear.
Second Visual: Demand–Supply Gap Impact on OR & ARR	
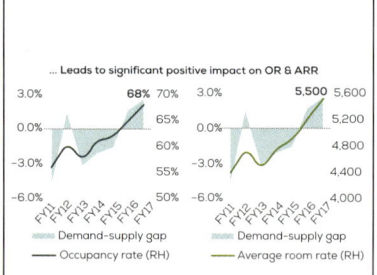	**Visual Aesthetics:** • Remove gridlines, Bring X axis labels 'low' and make the line smooth. • Change primary vertical axis number format to 'percentage with one decimal point'. • Since these are two simple charts which essentially give a similar message, I resize them and group together to form a single picture. • Since the demand–supply gap is common to both these charts, it gets the same light blue colour. • Data labels represent same font colour as their respective lines. **Conclusion:** Add a common conclusive title to this visual. The dots used in the titles ensure that the conclusions from visual one and two are linked together.

Plate H

⑨ The Final Act

Two case studies discussed in this chapter deconstruct how the given stories were built from scratch while applying the data storytelling principles discussed in this book. The pre-production discusses the planning stages of the story, which includes the story wheel, the story arc and the story map. The logical thought process for this is discussed in the screenplay at the end, whereas the production stage discusses every step that goes into crafting the visual story.

The cases discussed in this chapter are built using small and simple data sets to facilitate easy understanding of all concepts. For explanatory purposes, I have included both the planning tools, that is, story arc and story map. However, in a practical situation for smaller data sets, one can skip either or both these tools.

* * * *

CASE STUDY ONE

The finance department of a consumer goods manufacturer is presenting preliminary FY 2018 business performance analysis to its internal management.

* * * *

Behind the Scenes!

Figures 9.2 and 9.3 deconstruct the data story presented in Figure 9.1 and show how the story was built right from the planning stages to the step-by-step completion of the visuals.

Figure 9.1 Data Story Created for FY 2018 Business Performance Analysis

Robust Sales Growth Overshadows Slight Profit Dip

FY 2018 proves to be another healthy performance year with a 16% y/y revenue growth to 780 crore. In the last 10 years, the company's revenue has grown four times at a CAGR of 14.4%. Net profit margin (NPM) is at a comfortable 9.9%, notably higher than its 5-year (8.9%) and 10-year (7.5%) averages, although it came in lower than the 11% achieved in FY 2017. Sales volume recorded a steep 17% growth during the year, dominated by domestic volumes, which with ~90% of total sales contribution throughout this period continue to be the company's growth engine.

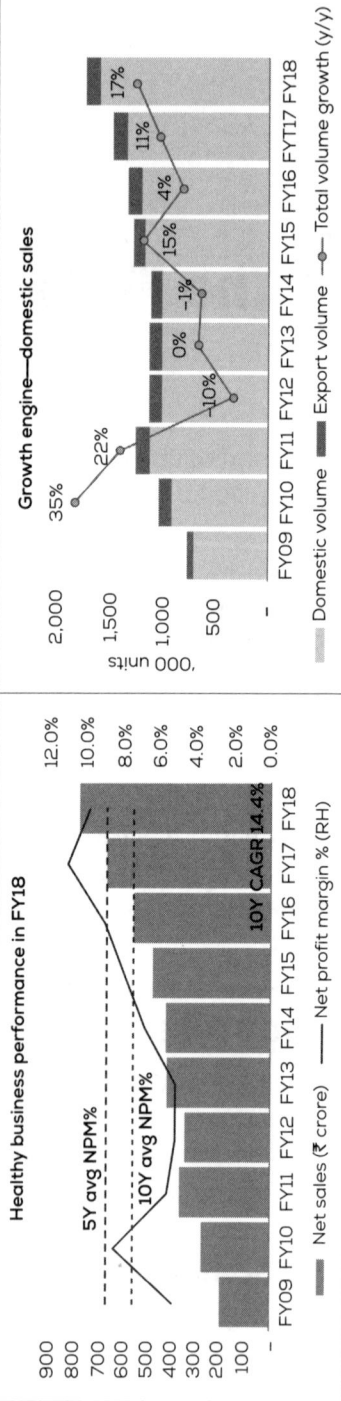

Note: The above data has been generated for explanatory purposes only. For coloured figures refer to colour plate E.

Figure 9.2 The Pre-Production Stages—Showcasing the Story Plan

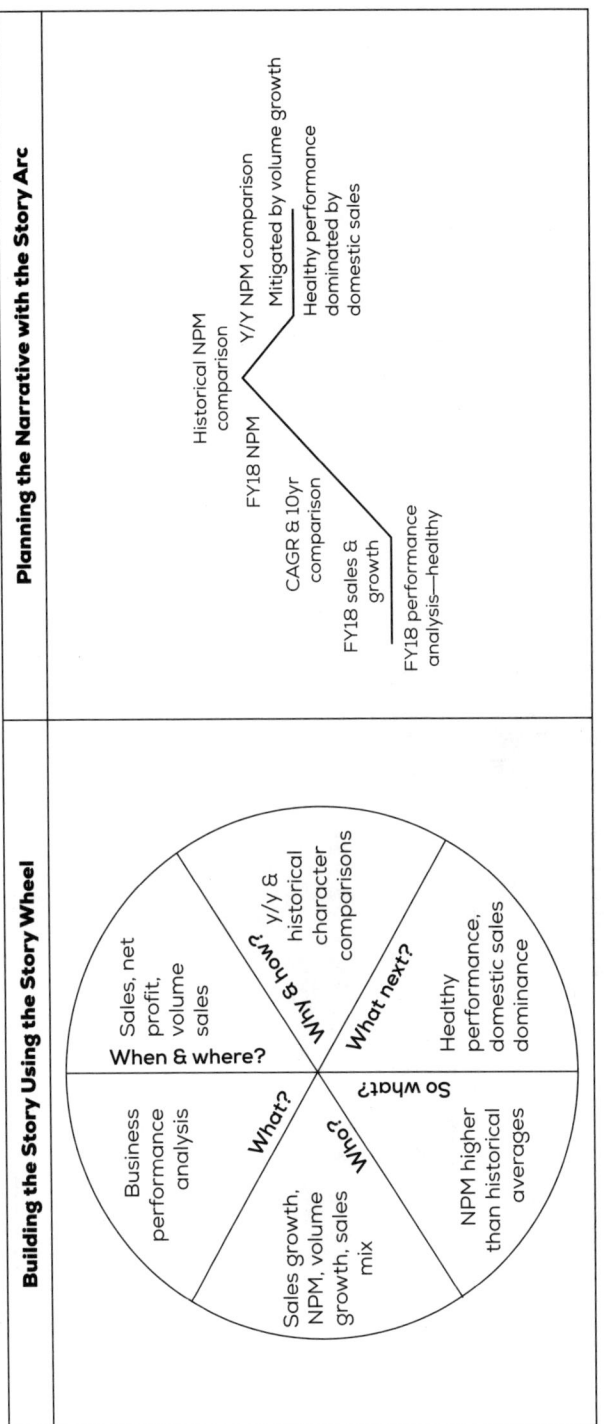

Building the Story Using the Story Wheel	Planning the Narrative with the Story Arc

(Figure 9.2 continued)

(Figure 9.2 continued)

Planning a Detailed Narrative with the Story Map

Note: A detailed explanation of the thought process behind building these planning tools is included in the screenplay, later in this chapter.

Figure 9.3 The Production Stages: Step-by-Step Creation of the Visual

First Visual: Sales and NPM

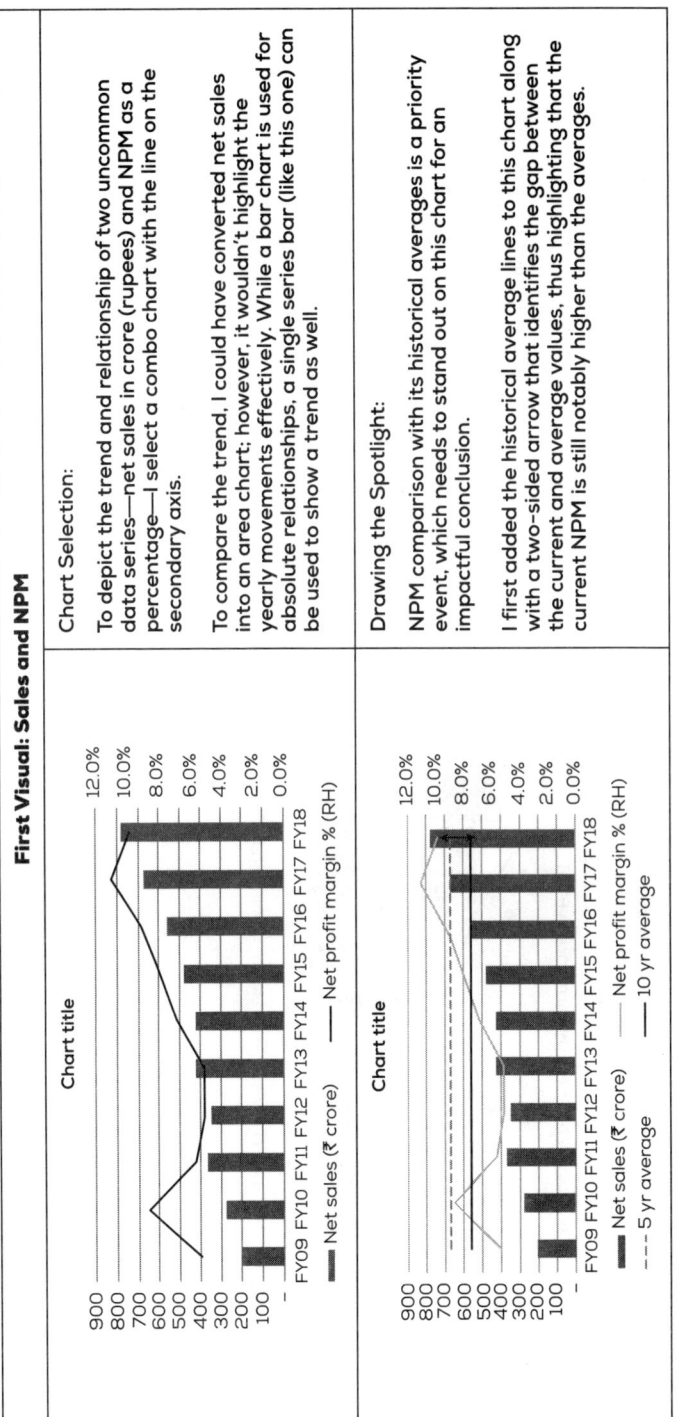

Chart Selection:

To depict the trend and relationship of two uncommon data series—net sales in crore (rupees) and NPM as a percentage—I select a combo chart with the line on the secondary axis.

To compare the trend, I could have converted net sales into an area chart; however, it wouldn't highlight the yearly movements effectively. While a bar chart is used for absolute relationships, a single series bar (like this one) can be used to show a trend as well.

Drawing the Spotlight:

NPM comparison with its historical averages is a priority event, which needs to stand out on this chart for an impactful conclusion.

I first added the historical average lines to this chart along with a two-sided arrow that identifies the gap between the current and average values, thus highlighting that the current NPM is still notably higher than the averages.

(Figure 9.3 continued)

(Figure 9.3 continued)

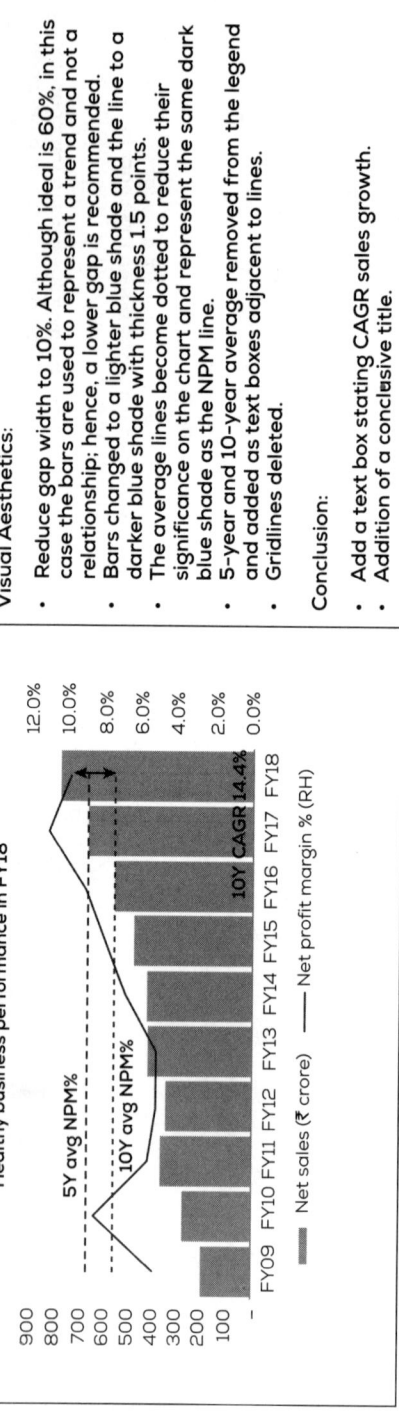

Healthy business performance in FY18

Net sales (₹ crore) —— Net profit margin % (RH)

10Y CAGR 14.4%

5Y avg NPM%

10Y avg NPM%

FY09 FY10 FY11 FY12 FY13 FY14 FY15 FY16 FY17 FY18

Visual Aesthetics:

- Reduce gap width to 10%. Although ideal is 60%, in this case the bars are used to represent a trend and not a relationship; hence, a lower gap is recommended.
- Bars changed to a lighter blue shade and the line to a darker blue shade with thickness 1.5 points.
- The average lines become dotted to reduce their significance on the chart and represent the same dark blue shade as the NPM line.
- 5-year and 10-year average removed from the legend and added as text boxes adjacent to lines.
- Gridlines deleted.

Conclusion:

- Add a text box stating CAGR sales growth.
- Addition of a conclusive title.

Second Visual: Sales Mix and Total Volume Growth

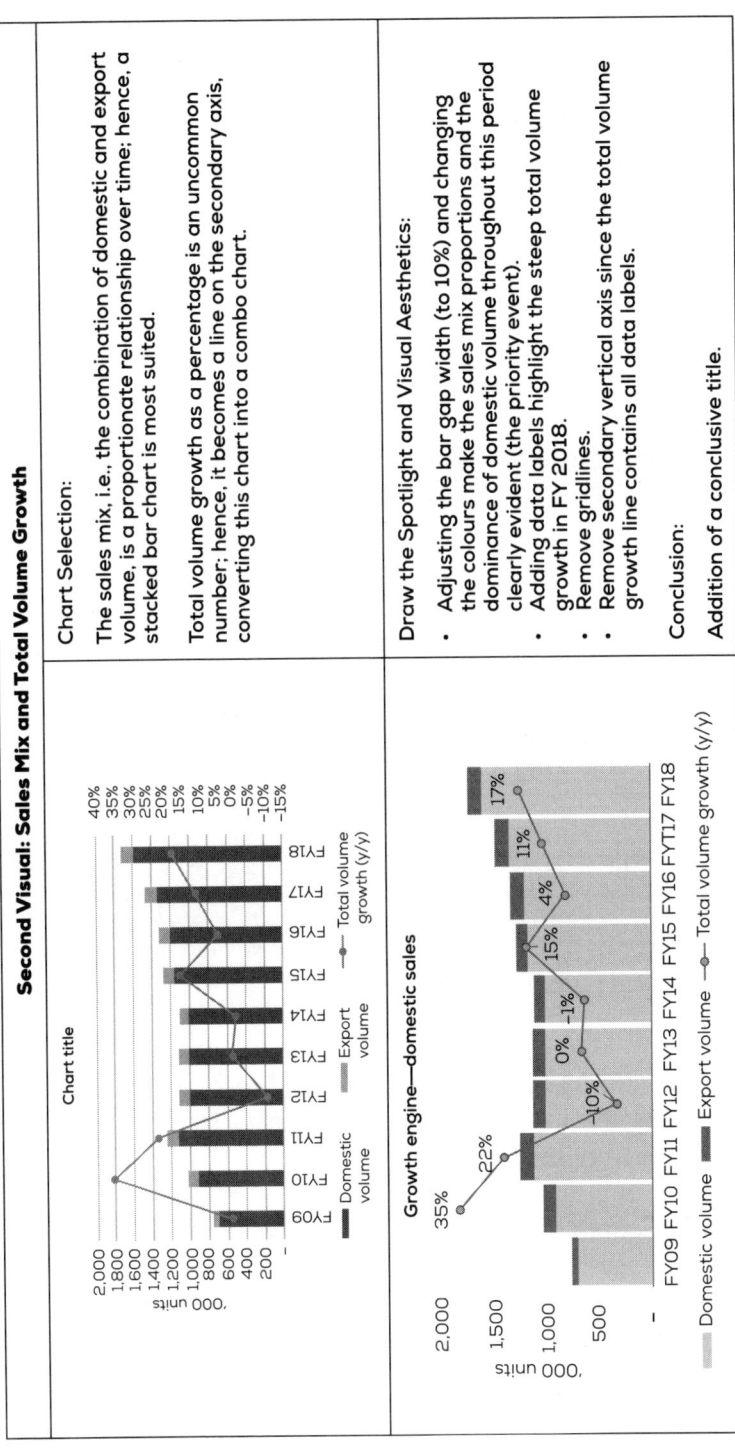

Chart Selection:

The sales mix, i.e., the combination of domestic and export volume, is a proportionate relationship over time; hence, a stacked bar chart is most suited.

Total volume growth as a percentage is an uncommon number; hence, it becomes a line on the secondary axis, converting this chart into a combo chart.

Draw the Spotlight and Visual Aesthetics:

- Adjusting the bar gap width (to 10%) and changing the colours make the sales mix proportions and the dominance of domestic volume throughout this period clearly evident (the priority event).
- Adding data labels highlight the steep total volume growth in FY 2018.
- Remove gridlines.
- Remove secondary vertical axis since the total volume growth line contains all data labels.

Conclusion:

Addition of a conclusive title.

The Screenplay

Below is a discussion on the logical thought processes that formed a part of the pre-production planning stages for this data story.

The Story Wheel

Purpose: FY 2018 business performance analysis—present preliminary insights into this topic.

Year	Net Sales	Net Profit	Domestic Volume	Export Volume
FY 2009	205	11	700	60
FY 2010	280	24	910	115
FY 2011	370	21	1,125	125
FY 2012	350	18	1,000	122
FY 2013	425	22	1,005	115
FY 2014	426	29	1,010	98
FY 2015	480	38	1,160	119
FY 2016	560	51	1,205	125
FY 2017	670	74	1,344	127
FY 2018	780	77	1,600	128

Data: The raw data extract ahead includes key elements required for the given purpose and audience.

Characters: The raw data by itself does not provide meaningful insights into the story; hence, they need to be converted into characters that can add value to the data story. To get the important story characters:

- Convert net sales into annual growth rate and CAGR
- Convert net profit into NPM
- Calculate total sales volume and its growth rate
- Calculate proportionate contribution of domestic and export sales

The following table adds some important characters derived from the above raw data.

Year	Y/Y Sales Growth (%)	Y/Y Total Volume Growth (%)	NPM (%)	Domestic Volume (% of Total)	Export Volume (% of Total)
FY 2009	–	–	5.4	92	8
FY 2010	37	35	8.6	89	11
FY 2011	32	22	5.7	90	10
FY 2012	–5	–10	5.1	89	11
FY 2013	21	0	5.2	90	10
FY 2014	0	–1	6.8	91	9
FY 2015	13	15	7.9	91	9
FY 2016	17	4	9.1	91	9
FY 2017	20	11	11.0	91	9
FY 2018	16	17	9.9	93	7

In addition to these, I calculate the historical 5-year and 10-year average NPM, as in FY 2018 as 8.9 per cent and 7.5 per cent, respectively.

Events: The events are trends and/or relationships between these important characters. The following are identified as the important events which will form the base of this story:

1. Sales growth—FY 2018 y/y growth and 10 years CAGR
2. NPM—comparison of FY 2018 NPM with FY 2017
3. Total volume growth—steep y/y growth rate in FY 2018 compared to FY 2017
4. Sales mix—dominant contribution by domestic sales throughout the years

Aha moment: The data analysis leads to an overall conclusion—'healthy business performance'. However, NPM has deteriorated since last year and this piece of information if not presented correctly can go against the conclusion. The quest for an 'aha moment' thus led me deeper into the data to retrieve an intriguing piece of analytical insight that can overshadow this negativity while also have a strong impact on audience perception with respect to this story:

- I started comparing FY 2018 NPM, not only with FY 2017 but also with previous periods.
- To enable a historical comparison, I calculated 5-year and 10-year average NPM.
- The comparison revealed that FY 2018 NPM is notably higher than previous periods on an average and can thus be considered as a healthy profit margin, making it the story's 'aha moment'.

What next: Along with providing a clear conclusion of a 'healthy business performance', I also want to provide a meaningful insight into the future. With an intention to present a simple analysis, while sticking to the above data only, I find my answer in the volume sales mix. With domestic sales at ~90% of total sales volume throughout this period, I could add a simple insight, which suggests that they are likely to continue being the future sales driver as well.

The Story Arc

An upward sloping arc is the right story arc for this data since we lead to a positive conclusion, that is, healthy business performance in spite of a negative data, that is, lower y/y NPM.

Context: The introduction needs to provide a clear context to a preliminary FY 2018 performance analysis.

Rising action: The revenue and profit events become part of the rising action for this story since they are the core parameters for assessing business performance and will be presented in the following order to generate audience interest and engagement:

- Current sales and growth
- CAGR comparison
- Ten-year sales growth
- Current NPM

Climax: Higher FY 2018 NPM comparison with historical averages is the climax, since it has significant impact on the overall conclusion.

Falling action: Lower FY 2018 NPM vis-à-vis FY 2017 becomes the falling action as it goes against the overall 'healthy performance' conclusion. Preceding this with the climax and following it up with an insight into steep volume growth ensure quick recovery from this falling action.

Conclusion: Sales growth discussed in rising action coupled with NPM comparisons highlighted in the climax leads to a conclusion of healthy business performance. Additional insight into sales mix suggesting domestic volume as being the growth engine also makes the conclusion more insightful.

Story Map

Beginning with a 'healthy business performance' conclusion in FY 2018, the story map is divided into three clear sections: revenue analysis, profit analysis, and volume and sales mix. The events as identified in the story wheel are listed down ahead along with the underlying data points in the chronological order of appearance in the story. This story map became the blueprint of the written story as the stated events and data got weaved into sentences to complete the written story.

CASE STUDY TWO

The management of a branded hotel chain wants to understand the impact of macro factors on the hotel industry.

Behind the Scenes!

Figures 9.5 and 9.6 deconstruct the data story presented in Figure 9.4 and show how the story was built right from the planning stages to the step-by-step completion of the visuals.

Figure 9.4 Data Story Created for the Hotel Industry

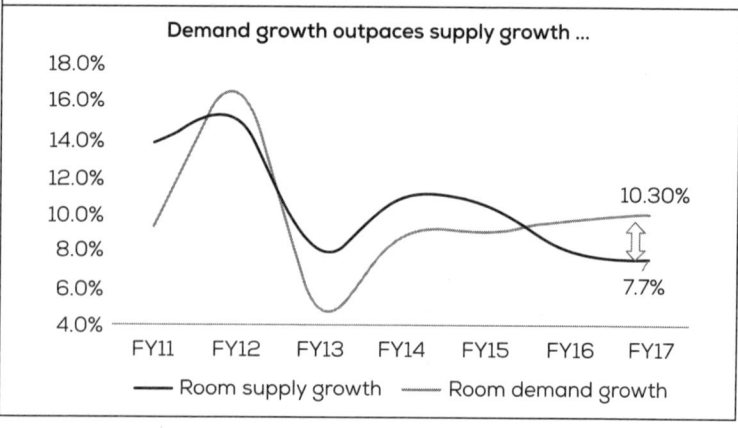

Macro Tailwinds Support the Future of the Hotel Industry

The structural demand–supply shift underway in the hotel industry bodes well for its future performance. Hotel industry supply growth consistently outpaced demand growth (with the exception of FY 2012), putting a pressure on industry occupancy rate (OR) and average room rate (ARR). However, as demand started recovering and supply slowed down, this gap had closed consistently over the years and for the first time, in FY 2016, demand growth outpaced supply growth. This gap had widened further in FY 2017 with demand growth at 10.3% and supply growth at 7.7%, resulting in peak levels of OR (68%) and ARR (5,500), which have steadily grown with the improving demand situation. Growing number of foreign tourists (CAGR 5.9%) and improving GDP per capita (6.6%) are likely to support further demand generation, in turn leading to improved OR and ARR for the industry.

Demand growth outpaces supply growth ...

— Room supply growth   — Room demand growth

(Figure 9.4 continued)

(Figure 9.4 continued)

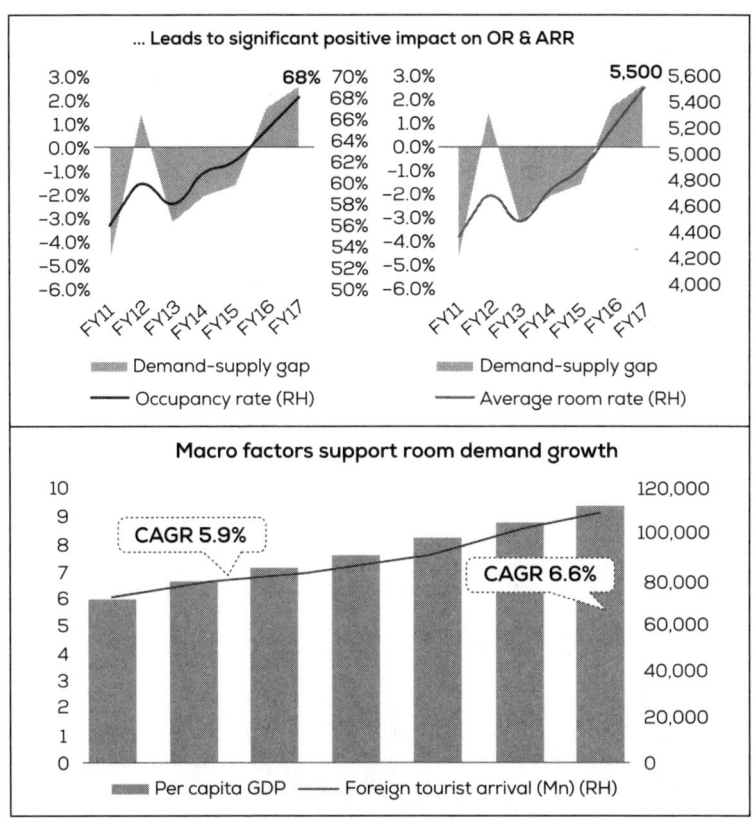

Note: For coloured figures refer to color plate G.

The Screenplay

Following is a discussion on the logical thought processes that formed a part of the pre-production for this data story.

The Story Wheel

Purpose: Impact of macro factors on the hotel's business performance.

Figure 9.5 The Pre-production Stages—Showcasing the Story Plan

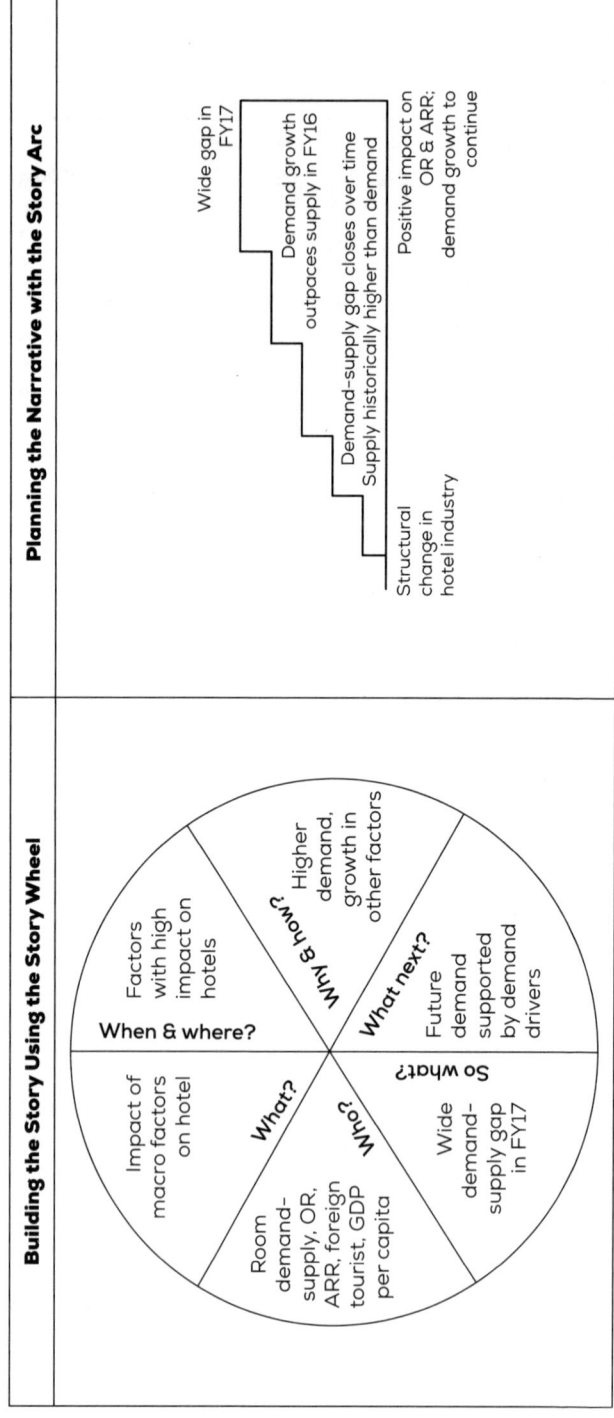

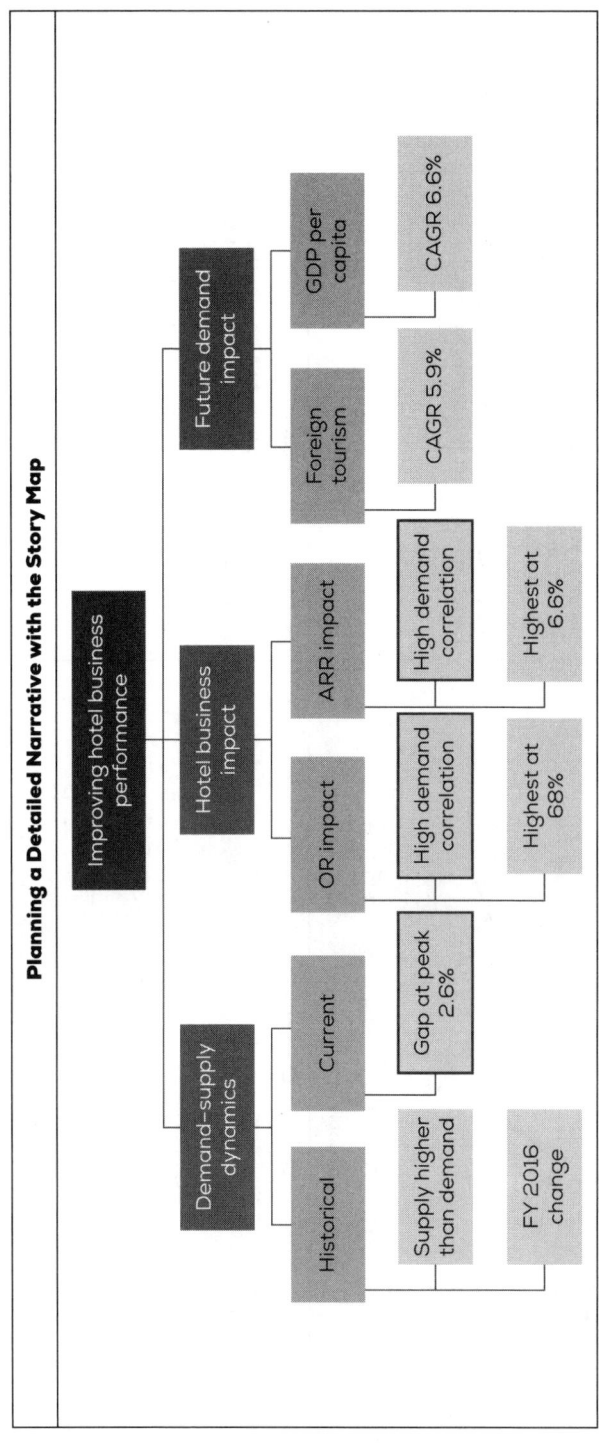

Planning a Detailed Narrative with the Story Map

Note: A detailed explanation of the thought process behind building these planning tools is included in the screenplay, later in this chapter.

Figure 9.6 The Production Stages—Step-by-Step Creation of the Visual

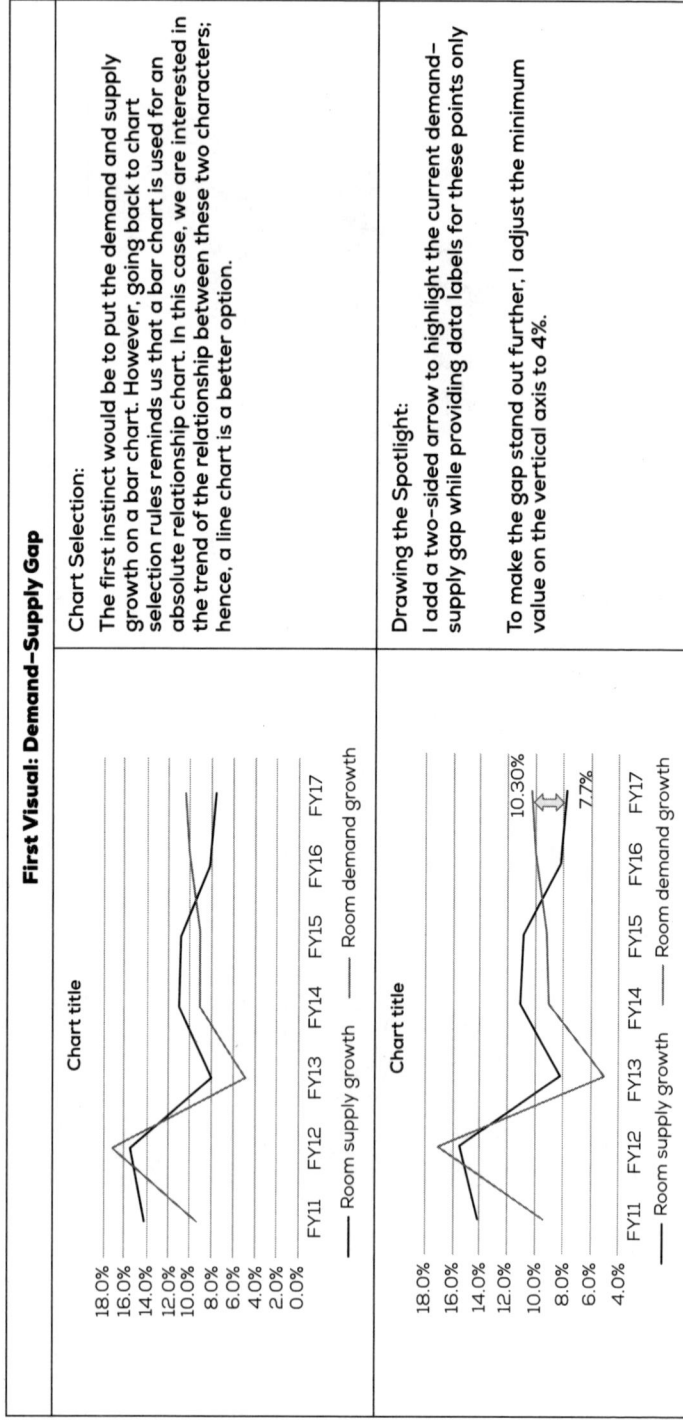

First Visual: Demand–Supply Gap

Chart title

18.0%
16.0%
14.0%
12.0%
10.0%
8.0%
6.0%
4.0%
2.0%
0.0%

FY11   FY12   FY13   FY14   FY15   FY16   FY17

—— Room supply growth   —— Room demand growth

Chart Selection:

The first instinct would be to put the demand and supply growth on a bar chart. However, going back to chart selection rules reminds us that a bar chart is used for an absolute relationship chart. In this case, we are interested in the trend of the relationship between these two characters; hence, a line chart is a better option.

Chart title

18.0%
16.0%
14.0%
12.0%   10.30%
10.0%
8.0%
6.0%   7.7%
4.0%

FY11   FY12   FY13   FY14   FY15   FY16   FY17

—— Room supply growth   —— Room demand growth

Drawing the Spotlight:

I add a two-sided arrow to highlight the current demand–supply gap while providing data labels for these points only

To make the gap stand out further, I adjust the minimum value on the vertical axis to 4%.

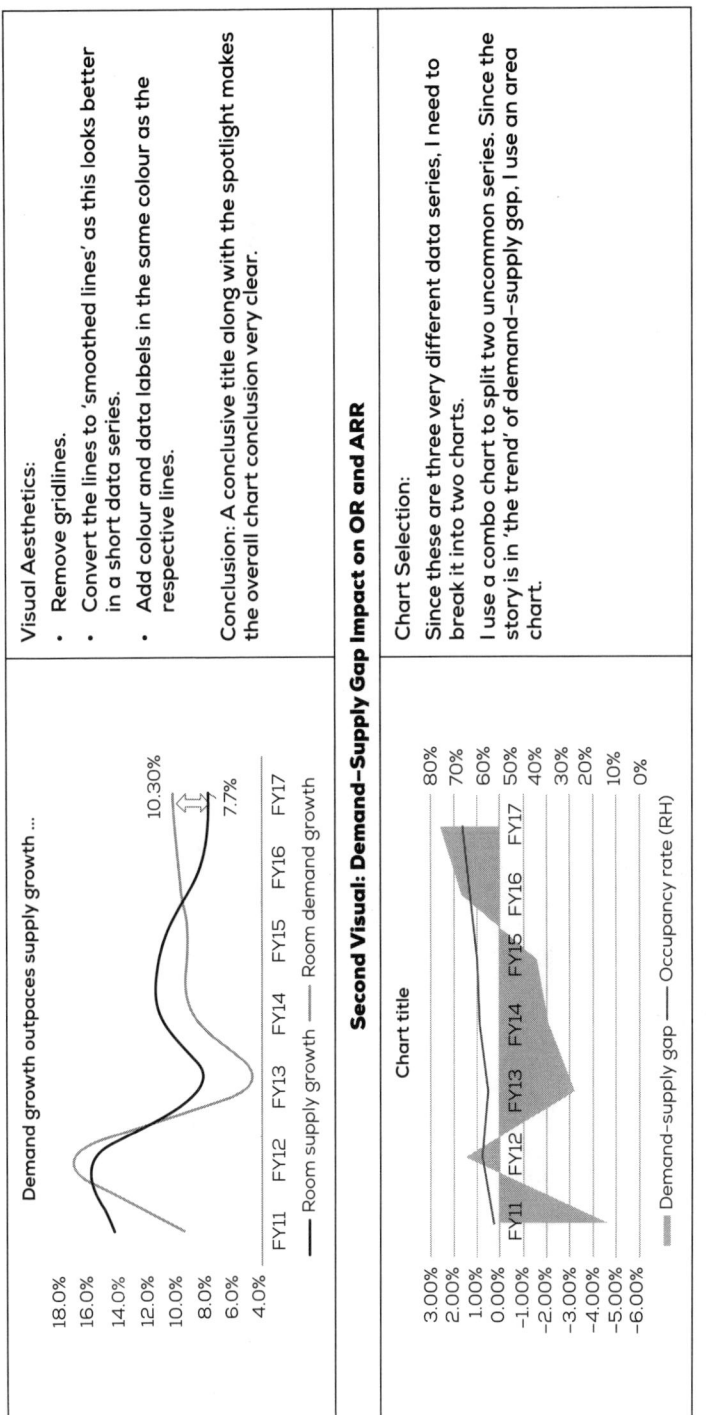

Visual Aesthetics:

- Remove gridlines.
- Convert the lines to 'smoothed lines' as this looks better in a short data series.
- Add colour and data labels in the same colour as the respective lines.

Conclusion: A conclusive title along with the spotlight makes the overall chart conclusion very clear.

Demand growth outpaces supply growth ...

10.30%

7.7%

FY11 FY12 FY13 FY14 FY15 FY16 FY17

— Room supply growth — Room demand growth

Second Visual: Demand–Supply Gap Impact on OR and ARR

Chart Selection:

Since these are three very different data series, I need to break it into two charts.

I use a combo chart to split two uncommon series. Since the story is in 'the trend' of demand–supply gap. I use an area chart.

Chart title

FY11 FY12 FY13 FY14 FY15 FY16 FY17

— Demand–supply gap — Occupancy rate (RH)

(Figure 9.6 continued)

(Figure 9.6 continued)

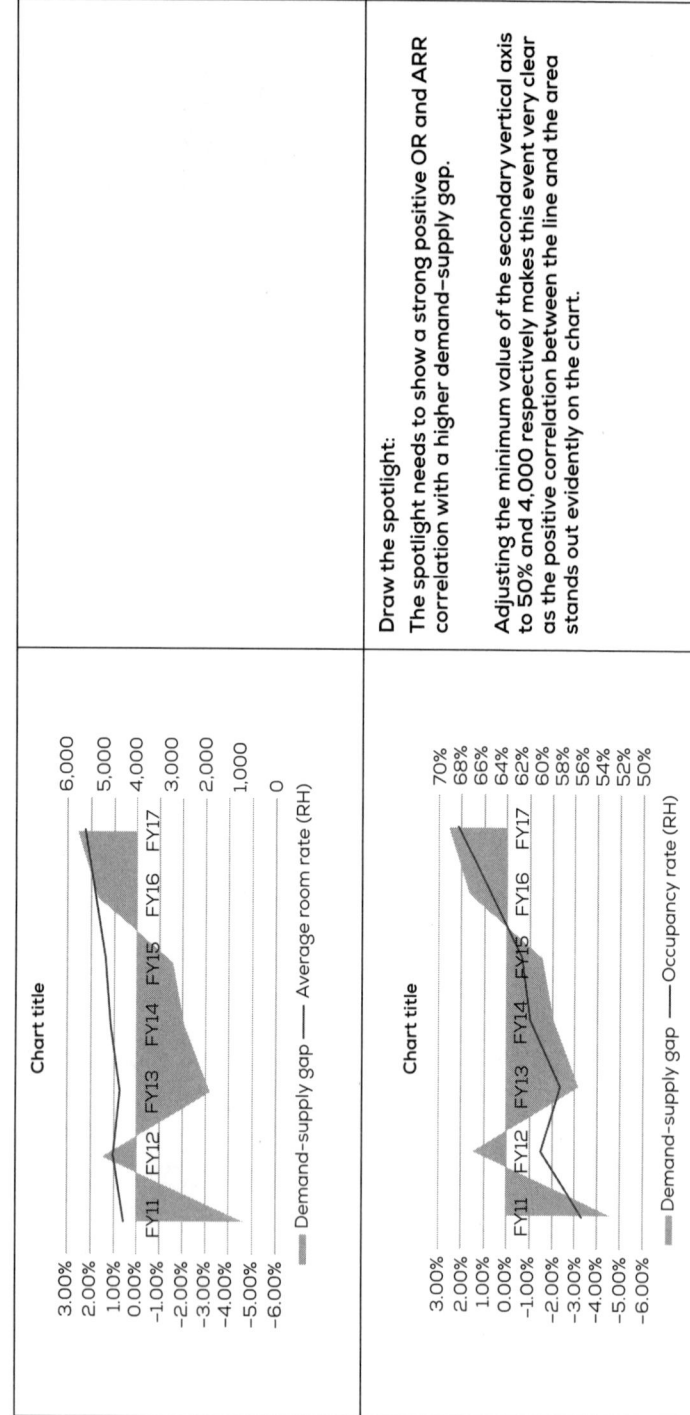

Chart title

6,000
5,000
4,000
3,000
2,000
1,000
0

3.00%
2.00%
1.00%
0.00%
-1.00%
-2.00%
-3.00%
-4.00%
-5.00%
-6.00%

FY11 FY12 FY13 FY14 FY15 FY16 FY17

■ Demand-supply gap —— Average room rate (RH)

Chart title

70%
68%
66%
64%
62%
60%
58%
56%
54%
52%
50%

3.00%
2.00%
1.00%
0.00%
-1.00%
-2.00%
-3.00%
-4.00%
-5.00%
-6.00%

FY11 FY12 FY13 FY14 FY15 FY16 FY17

■ Demand-supply gap —— Occupancy rate (RH)

Draw the spotlight:

The spotlight needs to show a strong positive OR and ARR correlation with a higher demand-supply gap.

Adjusting the minimum value of the secondary vertical axis to 50% and 4,000 respectively makes this event very clear as the positive correlation between the line and the area stands out evidently on the chart.

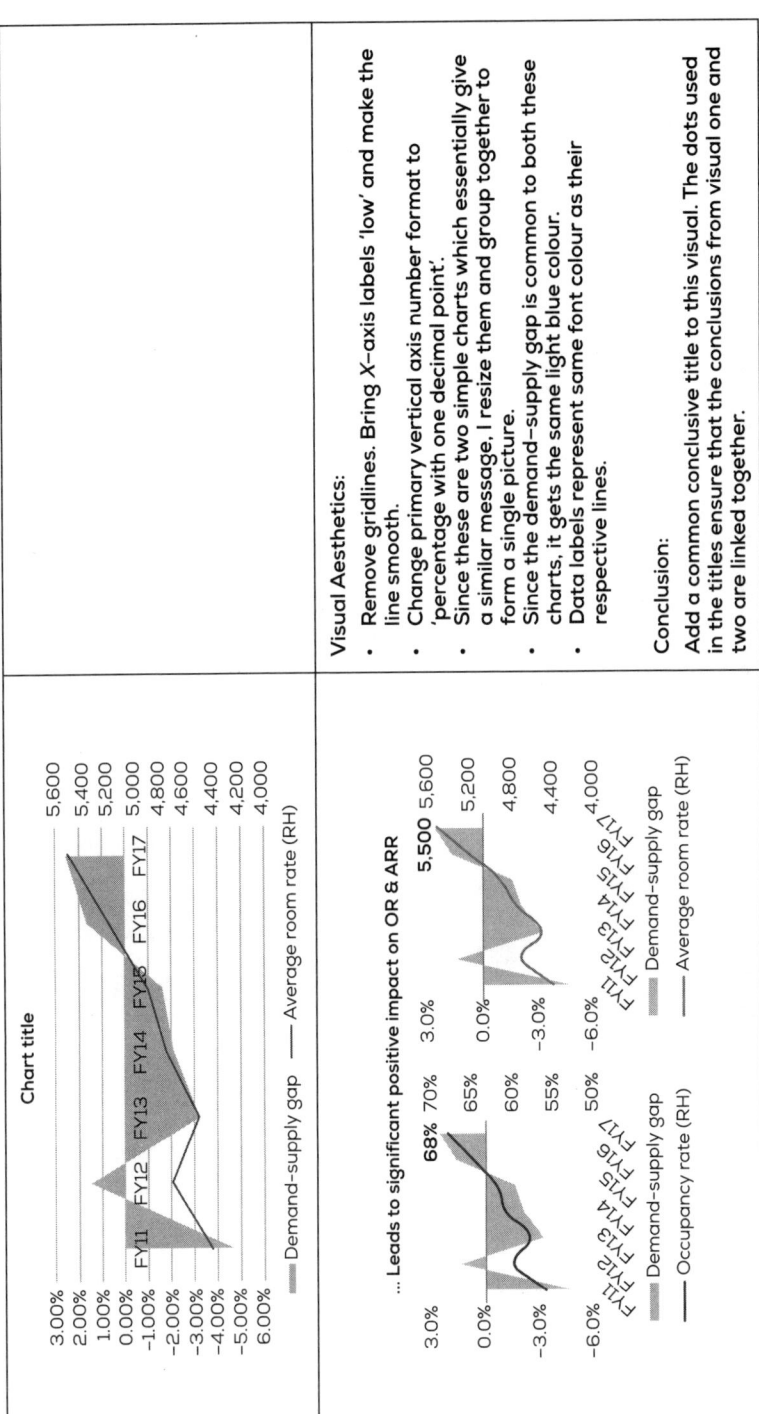

Visual Aesthetics:

- Remove gridlines. Bring X–axis labels 'low' and make the line smooth.
- Change primary vertical axis number format to 'percentage with one decimal point'.
- Since these are two simple charts which essentially give a similar message, I resize them and group together to form a single picture.
- Since the demand–supply gap is common to both these charts, it gets the same light blue colour.
- Data labels represent same font colour as their respective lines.

Conclusion:

Add a common conclusive title to this visual. The dots used in the titles ensure that the conclusions from visual one and two are linked together.

(Figure 9.6 continued)

(Figure 9.6 continued)

Third Visual—Room Demand Growth Drivers (Foreign Tourists and GDP Per Capita)

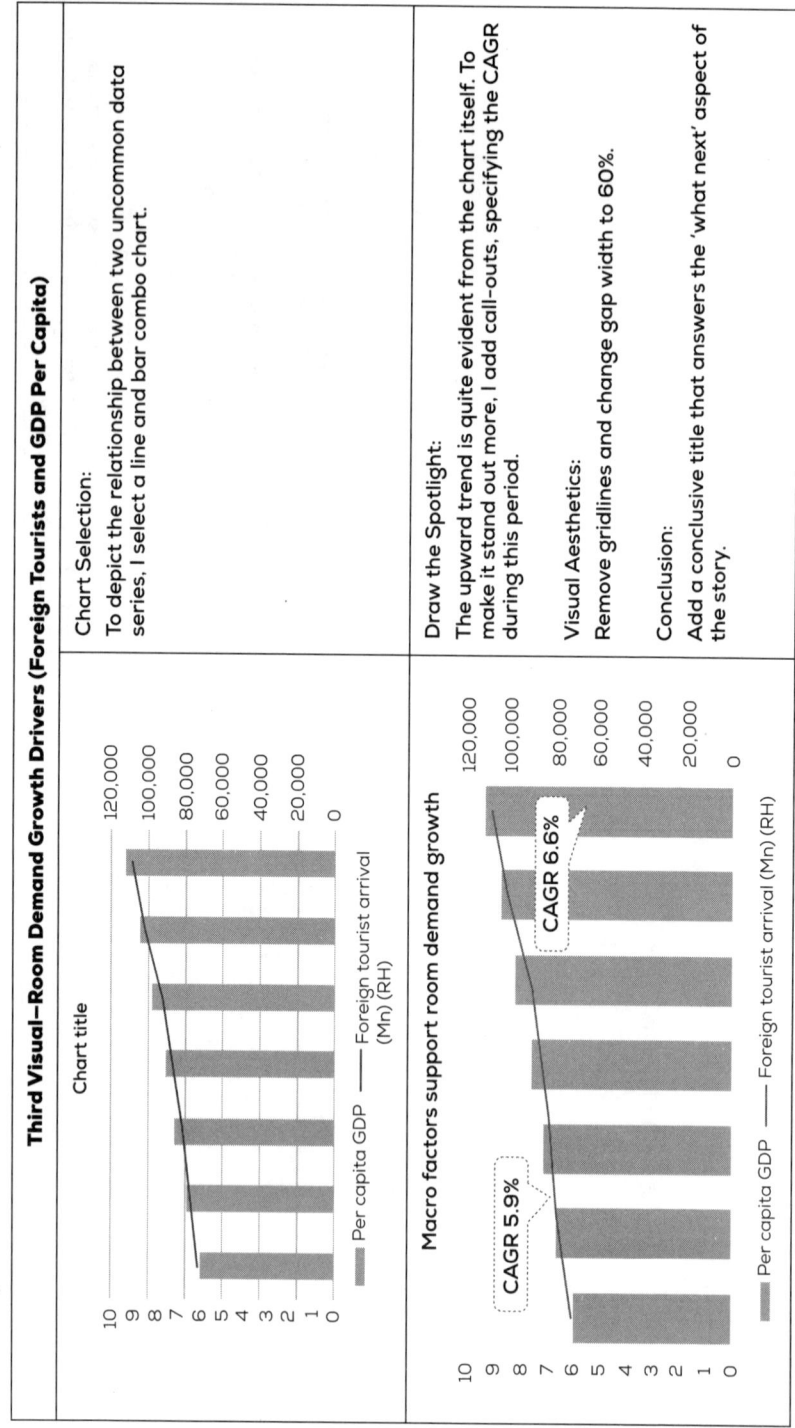

Chart Selection:

To depict the relationship between two uncommon data series, I select a line and bar combo chart.

Draw the Spotlight:

The upward trend is quite evident from the chart itself. To make it stand out more, I add call-outs, specifying the CAGR during this period.

Visual Aesthetics:

Remove gridlines and change gap width to 60%.

Conclusion:

Add a conclusive title that answers the 'what next' aspect of the story.

Note: The above data has been generated for explanatory purposes only. For coloured figures refer to color plate H.

Data: Identifying the correct data is pertinent in a probing story with a wide scope like this. The purpose has two aspects—macro factors and hotel's business performance.

- The room demand and supply are most important for a hotel industry. Along with its historical relation, future growth drivers also become important; hence, I include foreign and domestic tourism to the data as they have high impact on room demand. Finding future supply drivers can be more challenging and with higher focus on demand, they fall out of scope for this brief story.
- On the business side, OR and ARR are the key performance identifiers.

Based on this, I arrive at the following data table:

Year	Room Supply Growth (%)	Room Demand Growth (%)	Foreign Tourist Arrival (Million)	GDP Per Capita (₹)	OR (%)	ARR (₹)
FY 2011	16.1	8.30	6.1	72,000	50	5,400
FY 2012	13.2	10.00	6.5	79,500	65	5,850
FY 2013	9.1	8.40	6.8	85,500	60	5,200
FY 2014	8.7	8.60	7.2	91,000	63	5,600
FY 2015	8.2	8.70	7.7	98,300	65	6,000
FY 2016	7.5	8.90	8.5	105,200	69	6,250
FY 2017	7.1	9.50	9.1	112,500	72	6,550

Note: The above data has been generated for explanatory purposes only.

Characters

1. Room supply growth and room demand growth are the most important characters as they exert direct impact on the business performance.
2. OR and ARR become important because they determine the business performance.
3. Foreign tourist arrival and GDP per capita gain significance because of their influence on room demand growth.

Events

1. The most important event is the positive demand–supply gap in the last three years.
2. An upward trend in all other characters form the basis for strong business performance and future demand growth.

Aha moment: Wide demand–supply gap in FY 2017 is the most important and interesting factor leading to the conclusion, hence becomes the 'aha moment'.

What next

1. A positive relationship of OR and ARR with improving demand–supply gap shows that the hotel is poised for strong business performance.
2. An improvement in hotel room demand drivers, that is, foreign tourist arrival and GDP per capita, leads to a conclusion that demand will continue to rise, thus supporting OR and ARR in the future.

The Story Arc

This story builds up from a weak base to a strong positive conclusion without any evident risks; hence, the growth arc is best suited in this situation.

Context: Introducing the structural change in the hotel industry provides background information on the topic while also justifying the need for this story.

Rising action

1. Hotel room supply growth outpaced demand for bulk of the given period.
2. Demand–supply gap closes over time.
3. Hotel room demand growth starts outpacing supply growth in FY 2016.

Climax: Wide demand–supply gap in FY 2017.

Conclusion

1. High demand–supply gap to have a positive impact on OR and ARR.
2. Demand drivers suggest continued demand growth.

The Story Map

Highlighting a structural industry change, the story map is divided into three clear sections: industry demand–supply dynamics, impact of this change on hotel business and future of room demand. The events, as identified in the story wheel, are listed down along with the underlying data points in the chronological order of appearance in the story. This story map became the blueprint of the written story, as the stated events and data got weaved into sentences to complete the written story.

Applying the concepts into practice isn't that difficult after all? The step-by-step, behind-the scene activity discussed for every stage of data story production would have made the conceptual clarity of concepts and its application even stronger, and I sincerely hope that you are ready and excited to begin this new data-storytelling journey!

In Closing

D ata storytelling is a skill which does not call for strong expertise on any specific tool or data knowledge, and can hence be practised by everyone. I believe that it is a skill we all possess; in some it is active while in some it is dormant. The awareness of simple concepts learnt through this book activates this dormant skill and you are now equipped to jump-start your storytelling journey. Further, the multitude of practical nuances discussed throughout the book will shape the way you think about data going forward.

Data storytelling is a perfect blend between the science of data and the art of storytelling, and this book is only the beginning of the possibilities that can be achieved with data. The science—through the new tools discussed in this book—gives a strong foundation and the art implies that there is no dearth to imagination, and hence there is no limit to what can be achieved with data storytelling. There is never a right or wrong, or even a standard solution for a data story, a characteristic which makes it a little tricky and like any other skill, it needs time, patience and practice to develop on.

At the beginning of your data-storytelling journey, I recommend following a few steps as below, to cultivate and develop this skill.

PRACTICE, PRACTICE AND MORE PRACTICE!

Knowledge is of no value unless you put it into practice.

—Anton Checkhov

Josh Kaufman, author of *The Personal MBA*, writes that to go from knowing nothing to being pretty good takes about 20 hours of practice—that's 45 minutes every day for a month. In just four practice cases interspersed over my two-day data-storytelling training programme, I have always found a marked visible change from the first case to the last, something that trainees also experience themselves.

There is a difference between knowing and doing, and the more we do, the more we learn. The more we realize about our strengths and weaknesses, the more we can work on them. Initially, it will take time to apply these learnings and you might not receive the best result on the first attempt, but do not get disheartened and do not postpone it for another time. Even small opportunities to apply the data-storytelling principles can be great practice to help you develop this skill.

As you start getting a hang of it, the results obtained from data storytelling and the reactions received from the audience will be addictive enough to continue practising it.

START SMALL

Now that you are aware about all the data-storytelling nuances, you are likely to see data presentations differently than you did before the onset of our data-storytelling journey. In your head, you have already started thinking of all the things you are going to change and do differently and there might be a strong urge to completely overhaul your existing presentations.

And while rethinking about your data presentations is a great thing, applying drastic changes at one go might shock or overwhelm an audience, making you lose the very essence of data storytelling. Don't revamp the whole presentation at one go; start small. First begin with converting a few data-heavy slides into data stories, but do not discard the existing slides. Instead, you can push them back into the appendix, so that the audience can still find it if needed. As they get comfortable with the new format, you can get rid of older slide versions and start making bigger changes.

Think about making changes in increments while giving the audience time to absorb the new and constructive information.

KNOW YOUR TOOLS

The data-storytelling approach discussed in this book does not require anything more than the use of Microsoft Office or other similar tools or applications. However, people often have a wrong notion about their proficiency levels with regard to these tools. I have frequently seen that a lack of knowledge of such tools can be a major impediment in applying the data-storytelling concepts. In my experience, people get distraught trying to get their way around the tools, which does not leave enough time to practise and apply the storytelling concepts.

I strongly recommend taking a step back to assess your proficiency with regard to the tools you are using for the purpose of data storytelling. If you need to upskill on these, then seek help and get it done right at the onset.

GET INSPIRATION

Artists always have their antennae up, ready to take inspiration from the works of their contemporaries. The creative aspects of data storytelling and data visualization in particular can benefit from a little outside inspiration. Newspaper articles, business magazines and research reports are all different avenues to find good data visuals, which can be applied in business scenarios. You can also save snapshots, which can act as a visual library for your ready reference. When seeking outside inspiration, evaluate the visuals and think about what makes them effective and try to emulate these characteristics in the visual you are about to create.

When you come across a data visualization that you like, think about which areas of your data it can be applied to and find the best story fit from within your data to make an impactful visual story.

INCULCATE A STORYTELLING CULTURE

A skill once learnt is hard to unlearn. It is even harder to take the passenger seat and see someone else do a bad or mediocre job out of it. As a first step, educate your staff and colleagues on data storytelling while clearly showing how it can help them in doing their jobs better. Through your own or inspired data stories, set a good data-storytelling bar for your organization and help others achieve it. Provide honest and constructive feedback and help them, support them and coach them as and when needed. Seek professional guidance where needed and upskill the whole organization through training workshops.

When a skill is inculcated organization wide, it emulates desired behaviours across every level, making its adoption and impact much more effective.

LEADING A FIGHT AGAINST DATA DUMPS

Before reading this book if you believed that data and story have no relation, then you were not alone. But I hope that through this journey, you have come to appreciate the power of data storytelling. You now have a solid foundation, practical examples to seek inspiration from and a plan to embark upon your data-storytelling journey. You will never look at data the way you did before as your mind is now opened up to new possibilities. Use the knowledge gained from this book to communicate with data effectively and help drive better decision-making and motivate your audience to act. Never again will you dump data on your audience, and I hope to have added one more soldier in my fight against data dumps.

About the Author

Sejal Vora helps organizations communicate effectively with data. Her well-appreciated training workshops enable organizations to give a facelift to all forms of data communications by inculcating a data-storytelling culture. Her workshops garner strong interest from both individuals and large MNCs across financial and non-financial sectors.

Her data-storytelling talent displays a unique combination of skill sets, including analytical thinking, storytelling, visualization and writing, developed over the last 15 years through her strong education and experience.

An analyst at heart, Sejal has been telling 'data stories' through her research reports even before the terms 'data storytelling' and 'data visualization' were coined. A CFA and MS Finance (ICFAI), Sejal spent a decade in her investment research career with top financial services MNCs, including Morgan Stanley and RBS, offering extensive international exposure.

Through years of rigorous on-the-job training in the financial services sector, Sejal has developed a unique ability to find and communicate simple yet effective data stories from any type of data—quantitative or qualitative—from all types of businesses. You say 'data' and she pictures 'stories'.

Sejal's current passion is to rid the world of data dumps!

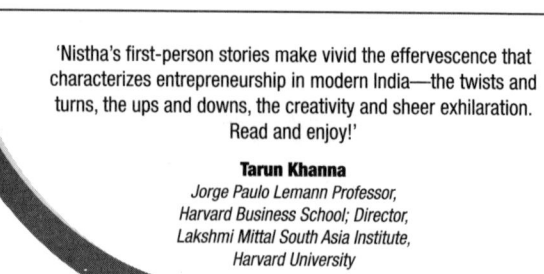